T0195311

Mad-Doctors in the Dock

Mad-Doctors in the Dock

Defending the Diagnosis, 1760–1913

JOEL PETER EIGEN

Johns Hopkins University Press
Baltimore

Johns Hopkins University Press
2715 North Charles Street
Baltimore, Maryland 21218-4363
www.press.jhu.edu

Library of Congress Cataloging-in-Publication Data

Names: Eigen, Joel Peter, 1947– , author.
Title: Mad-doctors in the dock : defending the diagnosis, 1760–1913 /
Joel Peter Eigen.
Description: Baltimore : Johns Hopkins University Press, [2016] | This is the
third of three volumes surveying a century and a half of insanity trials
between 1760 and 1913; it follows Witnessing insanity and Unconscious
crime. | Includes bibliographical references and index.
Identifiers: LCCN 2015043855| ISBN 9781421420486 (hardcover : alk. paper) |
ISBN 1421420481 (hardcover : alk. paper) | ISBN 9781421420493 (electronic)
| ISBN 142142049X (electronic)
Subjects: | MESH: Insanity Defense—history—London. | Criminal
Law—legislation & jurisprudence—London. | Expert Testimony—legislation
& jurisprudence—London. | History, 18th Century—London. | History, 19th
Century—London. | Mental Disorders—diagnosis—London.
Classification: LCC RC451.4.P79 | NLM W 740 | DDC 616.890092/2421—dc23
LC record available at http://lccn.loc.gov/2015043855

A catalog record for this book is available from the British Library.

Special discounts are available for bulk purchases of this book. For more information, please contact Special Sales at 410-516-6936 or specialsales@press.jhu.edu.

To the memory of Nigel Walker,
esteemed mentor and treasured friend

CONTENTS

One often hears the tale of a scholar who, at the end of a long and consuming research project, is asked, "So, do you *finally* know the answer?" And the scholar is said to smile a knowing smile and respond, "No, but now I know the question." Although this answer might seem a discomforting acknowledgement of failure or a reluctant admission that the solution remains unknowable despite dogged efforts, to anyone who has spent the greater part of a research career pursuing one elusive riddle, the scholar's response is instantly intelligible. Framing the right question is surely the key to finding out anything worth pursuing. In my case, the true research question did not take shape until I was in the process of completing a grant proposal for this volume. After several decades of examining, tabulating, and comparing medical diagnoses offered in a century and a half of historical insanity trials, I eventually recognized the question that had animated this research so many years ago: Where did these diagnoses come from in the first place?

Consider, for example, the diagnosis offered by a mad-doctor in the case of a seemingly heartless mother, on trial for murdering her newborn daughter. Shortly before she forced the infant headfirst into a bucket of water and fastened the lid, Annie Cherry warmed the pail because, as she later explained to a police officer, "It would have been cruel to put her in cold water." On realizing the horror of her deed, the mother might have called for help, fled the scene, or—as often occurred in cases of child murder—attempted suicide. Instead, Annie Cherry sat down peaceably and poured herself a cup of afternoon tea. Appearing at her trial, physician to the National Hospital for the Paralysed and Epileptic Dr. Henry Charlton Bastian focused his remarks on the mother's preternatural calm following the drowning. Like other late-Victorian medical men—many of whom were called to the crime scene and subsequently summoned to appear in court—Bastian saw in the mother's act and her subsequent behavior the presence of homicidal mania, a novel species of madness that profoundly challenged the law's criterion for ascribing criminal culpability: purposeful, *intentional* behavior.

How did Dr. Bastian and his cohort of London's physicians, surgeons, and apothecaries arrive at this innovative diagnosis and how did they defend it in court? What were homicidal mania's symptoms and what assumptions concerning the overpowering force of impulses did it rest upon? Further, how are we to trace the origins of a crime-driven insanity in an era beset with fears of tainted heredity that drew together insanity, criminality, and epilepsy into the haunting specter of evolutionary *degeneration*? Earlier in the century, when medical witnesses had tried to broaden the law's conception of insanity to include not just cognitive delirium but also diseased emotions and moral insanity, their efforts faced contemptuous opposition in court and in print. How did homicidal mania escape being discarded along with other too-expansive forensic-psychiatric diagnoses?

When expert witnesses in the London courtroom claimed to have uncovered a new and frightening form of insanity, they revealed how a profession asserts the possession of expert knowledge. Victorian medical men in court invoked unique experience and read aloud from specialist texts in mental medicine to explain and then defend their novel forms of madness. Of course, specialized knowledge and uncommon clinical experience could also be enlisted to argue the existence of a new disease at medical meetings; nineteenth-century alienists enjoyed an active professional association and an au courant professional journal in which to announce the discovery of a new species of derangement. But Dr. Bastian was describing the features of a novel disease in a court of law, not a royal college of medicine. Although both the Old Bailey jury and medical brethren gathered at an after-dinner lecture were likely to include doubtful and closely questioning listeners, the courtroom was only in part concerned with *whether* such a disease existed. The more pressing matter was how its acceptance would threaten the law's foundational belief that responsibility was a matter of *knowing* right from wrong. By its name, homicidal mania bridged law and medicine, crime and madness. Other medico-psychological diagnoses—delusional melancholia, puerperal mania, epileptic vertigo—compelled the jury to reason *from* the disease *to* the crime: only a direct connection between the two carried exculpatory significance. In trials that turned on homicidal mania however, the crime *was* the disease. To accept the diagnosis was to find the actions of the accused without criminal intention.

This volume is the third of three, surveying a century and a half of insanity trials between 1760 and 1913. The research began in 1982, when I was on a sabbatical leave at the University of Cambridge. There, Nigel Walker gave me the original cases he used to write *Crime and Insanity in England,* the foundational text in the history of the common law's accommodation to a defense based on mental derangement. During that year I also met Roger Smith, Roy Porter, German Berrios, and Martin Wiener, who over the next decades generously lent their enthusiasm and expertise to this project. Successive sabbatical years spent in Cambridge and at the University of Durham introduced me to a host of insightful historians and social scientists, particularly at the Wellcome Institute for the History of Medicine. Michael Neve, Michael Clarke, Tom Green, Robin Williams, Erica Haimes, Rose Melikan, Caroline Mason, Yvonne Garrod, Arlie Loughnan, and Bruce Kinsey have been patient listeners as I've spun out the narrative of these trials over decades of cups of tea and cakes.

A further note of gratitude goes to Andy Scull, whom I met when I was in graduate school and from whom I have benefited enormously in thinking about the place of alienism and psychiatry in historical sociology. His scholarship has illuminated dark corners in the social history of madness and has qualitatively changed the way historians and sociologists of medicine and psychiatry go about their work. I am particularly grateful for his support and guidance over the many years we have been working in parallel research areas.

I am also indebted to Pembroke College at Cambridge, which offered the very welcome position of visiting scholar in 2001–2, enabling me to finish my second book in this series, *Unconscious Crime.* I remain grateful to the fellows of Pembroke for providing intellectual stimulation and warm hospitality over the years. My host at Pembroke, Loraine Gelsthorpe of the Institute of Criminology has been an invaluable friend and colleague in matters of inquiry into the basis for professional and lay knowledge and the overriding theme of social justice and the law. Over the years at Cambridge, I benefited enormously by auditing courses offered by John Forrester; while attending his "Thinking in Cases" course of lectures, I met fellow non-undergraduate Michael Salzburg, who arranged my appointment to the University of Melbourne, where in 2008 I was able to immerse myself in courtroom testimony given in the trials between the years 1876 to 1913, which constitute the last third of the cases discussed in this book. Courtroom testimony offered in these cases revealed the emergence of the diagnosis of homicidal mania and the frequency with which insanity trials featured it. Also in Melbourne, I was aided by Jeremy Taylor, Director of the Medical Library at St. Vincent's Hospital, who assisted in the identification of nineteenth-century medical tracts on *médicine mentale*. In addition to Mike Salzburg at St. Vincent's, fellow psychiatrists Edwin Harari and Brian Stogall listened patiently as I explained the nature of medico-legal relations in the courtroom. Most important of all, I wish to thank Arrigo Dorissa for his loving friendship and a generous shoulder to lean upon whenever the writing spirits flagged.

At my home college, Franklin and Marshall, stalwart friend and writing buddy Scott Lerner provided, as always, a critical sounding board and much-needed encouragement over the years. Colleagues Mary Glazier, Ann Steiner, Howard Kaye, Giovanna Faleschini Lerner, and Kathleen Spencer have supplied the best sort of intellectual friendship and camaraderie. Annette Aronowicz deserves a major acknowledgement for inspiring me to dig deeply into questions of biological reductionism and the cultural setting that encourages the too-ready ascription of social behavior to natural science. Thanks are also due Robert Friedrich, who graciously helped with the preparation of the quantitative displays. These data were assembled by Matt Heller, a talented undergraduate at Franklin and Marshall, who, over the course of his Hackman Fellowship, helped me finally put the one thousand cases on a spreadsheet in the twenty-ninth year of the research. Also invaluable was the work I completed with the help of former student Sauleh Saddiqui, now launched on his own academic career. As always, Mikki Eigen Rocker deserves a major note of thanks for helping to keep the spirit of our parents' love of learning alive in both of us.

Nicole Hoover at Franklin and Marshall carefully transcribed my handwriting to help produce this manuscript. Arlene Mimm, Kathy Clark, and Meg Massey also offered welcome assistance with the preparation of the book. The college's Office of Grants provided invaluable assistance in preparing various fellowship applications, and I'm happy to thank Amy Cuhel-Shuckers and Ryan Sauder for their help. Meg Massey in the college library and Teb Locke in computing services also lent generously of their expertise. As with my second volume, Jacqueline Wehmueller of Johns Hopkins University Press supplied enduring encouragement and invaluable guidance in matters of taste and precision. I remain grateful to Jackie and the able staff at the press for their wise counsel and support.

Each of the three volumes that comprise this history of forensic psychiatry at the Old Bailey was written with the generous support of the National Endowment for the Humanities. Scholars in the social sciences that engage historical and theoretical topics have come to rely on the critical support offered by the Endowment, not only in terms of financial resources but for inestimable guidance in framing research questions and selecting the most promising sources. Under the wise stewardship of Leon Bramson, the NEH division overseeing work in sociology and psychology has brought to fruition the work of a generation of researchers, and it is a pleasure to acknowledge the support I have been fortunate to receive.

Finally, I have had the singular privilege of learning from and working with three of the major figures in twentieth-century criminology and law. The late Marvin E. Wolfgang gave me my first exposure to historical criminology and experience with large-scale quantitative work. Much of my graduate career at the University of Pennsylvania was spent learning how to conceptualize the malleability of delinquency through working on his pioneering project, *Delinquency in a Birth Cohort,* but it was his *Crime in Renaissance Florence* that turned me finally to the mysteries that Clio could deliver up to the persistent archival researcher. While at Penn, I also had the opportunity to work with Franklin Zimring, who encouraged me to mine courtroom verdicts for the unspoken policy strategy that informed and shaped judicial and prosecutorial discretion. Looking back over the present volume and the two that preceded it, I am reminded how fortunate I was to cross paths with these scholars, whose tutelage would shape my thirty-year research career.

Ultimately, it was Nigel Walker, former director of the Institute of Criminology at Cambridge, whose work with the *Old Bailey Sessions Papers* inspired me to ask my own questions and to search through hundreds of trials that he had first uncovered. It is both an honor and a sadness to dedicate this volume to Nigel's memory. From 1982 to shortly before his death in 2014, he remained the enduring influence guiding, suggesting, and expanding my inquiries into the evolution of jurisprudence regarding insanity and the authority of common law precedent. Singular scholar, teacher, and mentor, he gave this three-volume work its beginning the day he listened patiently to my 1982 sabbatical plans, invited me to his office, and removed from his closet shoeboxes full of never-before-seen records of historical insanity trials. He placed them in my newly tenured hands, saying, "See what you can do with these, Joel."

Mad-Doctors in the Dock

Disease and Diagnosis

Elements of the Medical Gaze

Medical diagnosis—whether made by psychiatrists or general practitioners—is a matter of inference. The process of interpreting symptoms and gaining insight into the body's mysteries is the stuff of conjecture because physical signs and subjectively experienced symptoms can be maddeningly ambiguous. The physician thus looks for certain patterns, assembling a clinical picture by using a battery of diagnostic tests, and yet considerable judgment remains. Arriving at an accurate diagnosis is difficult enough in matters of physical disease, when tangible body markers, blood work, and the patient's reports of pain can provide vital clues. But how much more challenging is it to identify the type of mental distress a psychiatric patient may be suffering? How does one take a case history of mental infirmity when the sufferer may be suspicious or sullen, wildly distracted, or patently uncommunicative?

Consider further the prospect of formulating a diagnosis that may carry life or death consequences in a court of law. In 1760, when the first asylum doctor offered testimony that implicitly claimed insanity as a medical condition, London's felons were regularly sentenced to hang for any of two hundred crimes, a list so expansive and lethal it became known as the *Bloody Code*. Defendants deemed by the jury to be mentally deranged, however, walked free after the trial: insanity merited a complete acquittal requiring no detention of any kind. Over the course of the next century and a half, the medical man's proffering ever more innovative species of madness took on mortal significance as the Victorian courtroom questioned the criminal consequences associated with each new diagnosis. Mental states were of obvious importance to a determination of criminal culpability but only to the extent that witnesses introducing various aberrant forms could speak to the law's definition of insanity: a failure to know right from wrong.

This restrictive conception would undergo qualitative change over the course of the nineteenth century and would coincide with the participation rate of medical men in insanity trials reaching a high of 90 percent. How much the change in the law's position relative to insanity was due to the growing presence of medical witnesses is open to debate, however; the courtroom division of labor was shifting even as the mad-doctors were becoming ever more numerous. Most prominent among the changes was the emergence of defense attorneys in a form hitherto unknown to the common law. Authorized for the first time to mount an activist defense for their clients, enterprising legal practitioners enlisted any and all witnesses who could advance their case, advocating most noticeably for testimony delivered viva voce rather than in depositions filed before trial.

One might be tempted to think that medical men, appearing as expert witnesses, enjoyed some degree of professional authority, given their unique training and sustained experience with madness, but like all witnesses, they were subject to pointed questioning by judge and prosecuting attorney alike. Did a diagnosis of delusion necessarily mean the defendant was incapable of knowing it was wrong to shoot the sovereign? Were women diagnosed with puerperal melancholia incapable of resisting an impulse to destroy their own infant? The relationship between the disease and the crime was thus the focus of the testimony: diagnosis itself only began the inquiry. The medical witness and newly empowered defense attorney rose to prominence as refinements in standards of criminal evidence, and the criterion of guilt beyond a reasonable doubt also received renewed attention. The effort to articulate recognized standards of evidence and proof would contribute their own impetus for precision in diagnosis and declarative pronouncements regarding the behavioral implications of any diagnosis.

Structural changes in the administration of criminal justice beyond the courtroom were also likely to affect medical inference. If one considers medical diagnosis as the outcome of structured social interaction between the practitioner and the defendant, any alteration in how the two met one another would likely influence the classifier's perception and interpretation of the accused's conversation and behavior. Innovations in police and court administration throughout the nineteenth century modified the venues that brought medical men and defendants together. Physicians and surgeons encountered the alleged offenders much closer to the time of the crime, affording a strategic opportunity to gauge a defendant's mood, affect, and understanding—all elements the medical man would be asked to stipulate as grounds for his inference. Not all medical-defendant meetings began at the scene of the crime, of course; London's practitioners also encountered the accused in asylums, in general hospitals and workhouse infirmaries, or in their private examining rooms. But even in settings far removed from criminal justice, medical men were likely to import categories of derangement that were themselves strongly shaped by the state's having taken a more instrumental role in the treatment of lunacy. By removing outdoor relief—money, food, and clothing—and housing vagrants instead in institutions, in mandating civil commitment after 1800 for defendants acquitted on the grounds of insanity, and by increasing daily medical supervision of all capital defendants awaiting trial, the state had not only played a critical role in the development of administrative psychiatry but provided the settings that witnessed the first conceptual innovation in descriptive psychopathology since the Middle Ages.

Nineteenth-century forensic psychiatry found itself entangled with the powerful institutions of law and the state, as well as engaged in an effort to claim scientific respectability, both in medical and in legal circles.[1] Proffering diagnoses in the courtroom would be key to forensic psychiatry's arrival as a profession; doing so was critical to establishing practitioners' bona fides as expert witnesses. Two foundational texts in the history of crime and madness have illuminated the origins of medical testimony in insanity trials and variations in the court's perception of its worth. In 1968, Nigel Walker published *Crime and Insanity in England*, vol. 1, which remains the most comprehensive survey of the common law's approach to mental derangement from the thirteenth up to the twenty-first centuries; he complemented the case review with the first quantitative study of the incidence and success of the plea over hundreds of years. Rich in historical detail and subtle in its analysis of the evolving legal reasoning relative to madness and crime, Walker's work appeared before the growth industry in the social history of crime and madness came into its own in the latter decades of the twentieth century. Walker's study was followed by Roger Smith's equally pioneering text, *Trial by Medicine* (1981), which examined the broad canvas of nineteenth-century science from neurology to psychiatry, from ideas that framed insanity in medical texts to disease categories featured in selected Victorian trials.

The erudition and insight of these two singular scholars inspired a generation of graduate students to investigate asylum registers, parliamentary debates, and contemporary medico-legal texts in order to chart the emergence of mental medicine. Walker's own source—continuous courtroom accounts of testimony given in insanity trials—made occasional reference to medical witnesses appearing at the Old Bailey, but the evolution of medical diagnosis was not his major interest. Because his study sampled selectively across several centuries, I decided to augment his survey by examining medical testimony given in all insanity trials heard between 1760 and 1843. This period witnessed the first appearance of a mad-doctor in a criminal proceeding up to the trial of Daniel McNaughtan, widely recognized as the case that introduced the formal insanity plea. His eventual acquittal led to the formation of the eponymous *Rules*, meant to instruct future juries in considering a verdict of "not guilty on the grounds of insanity." Using as a conceptual guide Roger Smith's capacious work on the history of medical concepts employed by the new expert witnesses, I was able to complete *Witnessing Insanity* (1995), a survey of 331 trials featuring medical testimony and courtroom interaction into the early Victorian era.

The *Rules* that followed the *McNaughtan* acquittal conspicuously omitted any mention of a host of insanity diagnoses (moral insanity, lesion of the will, irresistible impulse) that medical witnesses had introduced into courtroom testimony shortly before the 1843 acquittal and that jurists had dismissed contemptuously. By repositioning insanity to be a matter of cognitive defect alone—not knowing the nature and quality (consequences) of one's action—jurists had hoped to preclude courtroom consideration of diagnoses that left the defendants' intellects intact even as they were swept away by deranged emotion or volition. But it seemed to me that medical witnesses, having attained a berth in the courtroom, were not likely to permit the courts to dictate the content of their testimony. I returned to the trial narratives and examined courtroom testimony from *McNaughtan* to 1876, when an Old Bailey jury returned an unexpected and novel verdict: "not guilty on the grounds of unconsciousness." It was a construction of the jury's own devising. Announced in open court with no prompting by the judge, this anomalous verdict reveals the enduring voice of juries, discernible in an occasional idiosyncratic verdict, as well as in their questioning of witnesses . . . and sometimes of the defendant. The jury's verdict in 1876 had been delivered after a medical witness had introduced an enigmatic diagnosis of his own: *vertige épileptique*. Similar to sleepwalkers or automatons, persons in a period of absence (*vertige*) between two epileptic seizures might commit outrageous acts unconsciously. The survey of trials from 1843 to 1876 yielded an additional 199 new cases and served as the basis for my second book in this survey, *Unconscious Crime* (2003).

As with the first volume, I was left with questions regarding how other disease states engaged the unconscious directly; these questions could only be answered by returning to the remaining *Old Bailey Sessions Papers,* which ceased publication in 1913. The last third of the case retrieval contained the largest number of cases (464 in all) and featured the testimony of London's most prominent asylum superintendents, hospital lecturers, and medical authors, who at the time were well known to the general public through public speaking and their contributions to popular periodicals. Also appearing in the late Victorian insanity trial were less socially prominent—indeed, culturally anonymous—medical men employed in jails, prisons, and police stations. Prison doctors had long testified at the Old Bailey; their occupational link to the Crown usually resulted in a denial of the defendant's insanity plea. Over time, however, state-employed surgeons and physicians displayed an adventurousness in testimony that yielded new diagnoses containing innovative renderings of minds subjected to various types of derangement.

Medical diagnosis was of obvious interest to the court, but today's students of the history and sociology of the professions also recognize the critical role that diagnosis played in the medical specialists' efforts to claim unique and abstract knowledge beyond the ken of the layperson. Being able to identify a hidden, recondite state of derangement and give it a clinical name transforms a medical practitioner into a professional. Revealed in the courtroom narratives, however, is not the emergence of *a* novel diagnosis but a host of new species of madness, each with its proponents and defenders. The expanding array of diagnoses reflected widely differing types of medical education and training, opportunities for sustained interaction afforded by increasing numbers of inmates in asylums and prisons, and—especially for the diagnosis of criminal lunacy—novel employment opportunities for medical men in police divisions, jails, and workhouses.

Wherever the face-to-face interactions between medical men and defendants took place, they did not occur in a cultural vacuum. Victorian London was awash with the specter of biological degeneracy, the idea that failed evolution would result in a class of the insane and the criminal. Coupled with anxiety over cultural regression were fears of the baleful costs that mad and deviant people would exact upon their descendants. Beliefs in doomed heredity and biological degeneracy not only shared an obvious affinity but likely influenced the medical gaze of specialists in mental medicine employed in prisons, asylums, and workhouses. By the late nineteenth century, a particular form of mental derangement that revealed arrested social and moral development— seen most graphically in the diagnosis of homicidal mania—made its way into courtroom testimony, carrying the indelible influence of criminal impulses and emotional regression. The focus of this book is the origin and changing fortunes of that one particular diagnosis against the backdrop of nineteenth-century London society.

In considering the larger social world in which an unusual cultural phenomenon surfaced, there is always the danger that its emergence will seem overdetermined—in this case, that the articulation of a particular form of derangement reveals the unexceptionable diffusion of contemporary preoccupations into the courtroom, obscuring the dynamics unique to that particular forum and its participants' own work-related experiences and conceptual curiosity. Certainly, notions of mind, behavior, and, increasingly in the Victorian era, *character*, reflected the tensions and anxieties of cultural obsessions, and yet there was nothing inevitable about the form these fears took in medical theorizing. Medical history, like all history, is a matter of contingency, not inevitability. Diagnoses, especially psychiatric diagnoses, emerge out of particular social settings that bring medical personnel and the distracted together at certain historical moments.

Ways of seeing and categorizing were further informed by the interaction among an array of professionals, each group with its own career trajectory: enterprising attorneys, professionally ambitious and clinically curious medical men, asylum superintendents eager to solidify their place in the medical hierarchy of a newly created *Medical Register*. The history of forensic psychiatry reveals a web of ideas, practitioners, and governmental strategies to arrest, prosecute, and treat. The interplay of these historical actors—sometimes complementary, sometimes oppositional—might have resulted in any number of distinctive insanities. As it turned out, medical diagnosis combined elements that reflected the unique social setting and the occupational/professional devices and desires of its participants. Cultural ideas of biological and social depravity doubtless influenced the medical gaze, but the diagnoses that emerged did more than embody the anxieties of the age.

The reason for this was crime itself. London jurors were increasingly confronted with the specter of atrocious, barbaric, purposeless murder. When medical witnesses earlier in the century tried to put forward *moral insanity* or *irresistible impulse* to account for a senseless killing, they were criticized both in court and in print for trying to explain (away) the crime *by* the crime. Far from being an excuse for crime, however, the offense was in fact fundamental to the diagnosis. Forensic psychiatry was not just the application of general psychiatry to the courtroom; in many cases, the diagnosis began with the crime—with its inexplicability, with its utter lack of reason. That the accused had killed her children minutes after feeding and playing joyfully with them or that a devoted husband suddenly with no provocation destroyed a loving spouse "with whom he had lived on the best of terms" suggested the presence of something that stretched beyond standard medical nosology. Criminal behavior and the accused's recollection of his mental state before, during, and after the assault carried important implications for medical psychology's understanding of mental aberrancy. And the diagnoses that emerged—employed in case testimony in trial after trial—played a critical role in the negotiations between law and medicine that produced the professional career of the forensic-psychiatric expert in court.

Source of the Material

What the defendant said to the medical man and how his conversation, demeanor, and behavior were interpreted and translated into a disease entity attracted interest beyond the medical community. No theatrical spectacle on offer in London's West End could rival the rapt attention of the multitudes that crammed into the gallery of London's central criminal court to witness the daily morality play that was the Old Bailey trial. Those not fortunate enough to secure a seat could read about the proceedings the day after. Dating from 1673 and published continually until 1913, *The Old Bailey Sessions Papers* (hereafter *OBSP*), provided verbatim testimony of courtroom participants, occasional judicial instructions to the jury, and the phrasing of witness examination and cross-examination. Before the rise of defense attorneys, prisoners articulated their own defense after all other testimony had been given. Originally published privately, the trial narratives were eventually subsidized by the city government, which by the nineteenth century absorbed the cost of the printing.

So promising a primary source is not without limitations; these were astutely identified by legal historian John Langbein when he brought the riches of the *OBSP* to light in the 1970s.[2] They were not intended as official documents, and although they are sometimes quoted to provide precedent rulings, the level of detail historians of law would hope to find is often lamentably lost to considerable compression, at least until the mid-nineteenth century. Printed by enterprising commercial publishers, the courtroom and testimony narratives were clearly intended to engage readers sufficiently so that they would purchase them, thus more comprehensive coverage was given to sensational crimes and unusual witnesses who discussed extreme states of behavior. Fortunately, this was often the case with insanity trials, which received extensive space, especially from the mid-1800s. Coverage of medical testimony in the second half of the nineteenth century was particularly expansive. Still, today's reader does not know how much was deleted at the whim of the shorthand writer or the publisher. Langbein, whose work with the *OBSP* has established them as the single most important source for reconstructing the criminal trial in early modern England, has confirmed their trustworthiness by comparing the testimony narratives with the private notes taken by Judge Dudley Ryder in the 1750s. The comparison reveals the narratives' reliability, which is suggested also by their being quoted in subsequent trials. Langbein concluded that if the testimony appears in the *OBSP*, one can be confident that the jury and gallery heard it as well. On the other hand, one does not know what might have been said that does not appear in the narratives.

This book completes my three-volume survey of all trials heard at the Old Bailey between 1760 and 1913. Identifying an "insanity trial" is not a matter of simply checking the verdict; many defendants entered evidence alleging some form of mental impairment but were not persuasive and received a "guilty" verdict. Similarly, a simple "not guilty" verdict could hide the evidence about derangement that was offered in cases so pathetic that the jury responded with a simple acquittal on their own or were prescriptively directed to do so by the judge. In short, verdicts are an unreliable and often misleading metric of courtroom history; to capture the voice of any witness—and certainly the manner in which his evidence was probed and responded to—it is necessary to scan the entire narrative of a trial. With practice, one can do this rather rapidly. Still, there are only four to eight such insanity trials in a thousand: cases in which some form of mental impairment is put forward to defend the accused. Were it not for Nigel Walker's generosity of spirit in sharing his original case retrieval with me, I might still be reading trial narratives before *McNaughtan*. As it is, capturing the universe of insanity trials required three sabbatical leaves and ten summer research trips to Cambridge and London over a twenty-year period to complete the retrieval of the 994 trials.

This last of three volumes contains the largest number of cases and the highest participation rate of medical witnesses. London's medical practitioners appeared more frequently and they were expansive in their diagnoses; they represented the broadest spectrum of medical men engaged with the mentally distracted and introduced diseases that met new-found curiosity rather than a more familiar derision by the court. The historical emergence of new disease entities in court challenges the legal historian and sociologist to delve deeply into the relationship between language and observation, between social setting and medical gaze, and ultimately between diagnosis and claims to professional knowledge. The current volume is laid out as follows.

Chapter 1 examines the legal and criminological elements that characterized the courtroom, the novel appearance of the activist defense attorney, and the renewed attention paid to rules of evidence and standards of proof. The chapter also includes the quantitative dimensions of the sample: the incidence of the plea, rates of participation of medical witnesses, and rates of insanity acquittal. Chapter 2 offers a survey of medical terms inherited by the medical men who were soon to appear in court and the transformation over time of the meanings associated with the most familiar and enduring terms: melancholia, mania, and delusion. Chapter 3 takes up the variegated universe of medical practitioners in the eighteenth and nineteenth centuries, particularly the range in training and education, and considers the effects this variability had on diagnostic patterns. Chapters 4 and 5 examine the diagnoses offered in court, the changes over time, and noticeable patterns in how the forensic psychiatric witness was examined. Chapter 6 examines the diagnosis of *homicidal mania* in detail, particularly its grounding in the forensic-friendly concept of delusion and also in a variant of epilepsy that resulted in a convulsion of ideas, not limbs. The last chapter steps back from the medical witness and the increasingly assertive defense (and prosecuting) attorney to consider the judge's role in the rapidly evolving criminal procedures. Conventional wisdom might argue that as the defense attorney rose to prominence and with him greater attention to the trustworthiness of evidence and a tightening of the standard of proof, the bench would experience a corresponding receding of its authority and discretion. This chapter uses the trial narrative to probe this assumption. The role of the remaining courtroom participant— the juror—is taken up in the conclusion. Among the many treasures yielded up by the courtroom narratives is an important corrective to the notion that Victorian juries were passive participants in the judicial process.

Given that the focus of this book is the emerging diagnosis of homicidal mania and its reception in court, it might strike the reader as somewhat singular that it requires five chapters to arrive at this evocative species of madness. As mentioned earlier, even the most innovative of diagnoses given by the most remarkable of witnesses is part of an ongoing historical process, carried on by intersecting actors in the Old Bailey drama. The judge, the two attorneys, the on-scene witnesses, and the medical expert are each in front of the jury, each with a distinct voice and a prescribed moment when they normally speak. Certainly, the medical witness occupies a unique position: alone among witnesses he interprets the mental world of the accused and the evidence of other witnesses, and then offers an opinion.

Like all witnesses, however, his opinion is scrutinized, and not just by the judge and attorney. Although medical testimony is grounded in the claim to expert knowledge, jurors are not without their own cultural understandings, a folk knowledge they import into the court when they're sworn. The *Old Bailey Sessions Papers* reveal that juries listened, attorneys questioned, and judges commented on the diagnoses given in court, and despite medicine's supposed professional dominance and a medicalization of deviance, the Old Bailey remained resolutely a legal forum. Whether he appeared by subpoena, at the request of the defendant's family, or because he took it upon himself to mount a formal legal defense, the Victorian alienist became a regular cast member in the Old Bailey drama, but he would have to earn his hour upon the stage.

CHAPTER ONE

Nasty, Brutish, and Short

Criminal Trials before the Lawyer

Sir James Fitzjames Stephen, the Victorian era's most respected authority on the common law and author of the nineteenth-century's definitive history of criminal jurisprudence, was not given to hyperbole. His volumes on the evolution and reasoning behind the practice of criminal law remain an exemplar of judicious, temperate, restrained analysis. And yet when he turned his attention to the subject of defense attorneys, he permitted himself an uncharacteristically bold declaration: the affording of legal counsel for the ordinary felon was, according to Stephen, "the most remarkable change" in English criminal procedure that had taken place down to his day.[1]

A criminal defendant without legal representation is unfathomable to us today, and yet courtroom advocates for the accused traditionally had been barred from the Old Bailey, London's central criminal court, for a persuasive reason: no one could speak more effectively in his or her own defense than the accused. The judge, who questioned witnesses and reviewed the evidence for the jury, theoretically safeguarded the defendants' interests. Legal historian John Langbein aptly named this type of trial, "The Accused Speaks": also speaking were the victim (the "prosecutor"), the judge, and not infrequently, members of the jury, requesting clarification and sometimes posing their own questions to the defendant.[2] With no advocate to probe the prosecutor's allegation, with no skilled legal advisor to inquire into the standards for proof, defendants in central London faced a hearing, usually lasting twenty to thirty minutes and designed more to select a punishment than to attend to the vagaries of guilt fastening. Caught red-handed with stolen goods or apprehended soon after a fatal assault, eighteenth-century convicts were more likely to find themselves headed to the gallows than any other destination. Nasty in its willingness to entertain hearsay evidence, brutish in its sentencing, and short in duration, the criminal trial down to the late 1600s really does put one in mind of Thomas Hobbes's view of the social order.

This "most remarkable" of reforms—extending the right to legal representation in the ordinary felony trial—came about in piecemeal fashion: no parliamentary act or decision rendered by the twelve judges authorized so seismic a change in the courtroom division of labor.[3] By affording legal assistance in trials for treason in the wake of highly publicized scandals surrounding political and religious scapegoating, Parliament had indeed opened the door to what would eventually lead to trials in which the accused did not, in fact, speak at all. Shoddy evidence, whispered accusations, and guilt by association had brought these hearings into severe disrepute; after 1696, defendants in trials for treason were entitled to enlist the services of attorneys to ensure the probity of evidence brought against them.[4] By the 1730s, trial narratives at the Old Bailey reveal a relaxation of the ban proscribing the appearance of defense attorneys in felony cases, a change again prompted by Parliament (though inadvertently) and, one thinks, by issues surrounding the nature of evidence brought against the defendant.

In an effort to encourage the apprehension and successful prosecution of London's criminal population, Parliament had undertaken two wide-ranging initiatives: "Thief taker statutes" and a scheme to convince criminal accomplices to turn states evidence and become Crown witnesses. Both led predictably to an increase in the caseload at the Old Bailey and, just as predictably, to a zealous effort to exploit the courts for personal vendetta and financial profit.[5] This classic example of "over-incentivizing" prosecutorial fervor resulted in eighteenth-century alleged felons finding themselves in the same position as seventeenth-century accused traitors. The salient issue remained the nature of evidence; in the place of political and religious persecution stood blackmail and bribery. The extortionist threat to turn in an acquaintance, a rival, or a business competitor unless he paid protection money was very real, and reports of gang extortion regularly came to light. Recognizing how Parliament's actions had generated a different sort of crime motivation, Old Bailey judges on their own initiative extended the provision of a defense advocate to suspects in felonies. The scope of the attorney's role was markedly circumscribed, however; he could not address a jury or "present" a case as such. Attorneys for the defense were limited to questioning the prosecutor's evidence by way of examining witnesses brought forward to substantiate the charge.[6]

Although a full legal defense would not be available until the Prisoner's Counsel Act of 1836, already by the 1730s one sees signs that defense attorneys were developing skills of examination and cross-examination that would fundamentally alter felony trials from that time until our own. The testimony of on-scene witnesses or neighbors of the accused had grown in importance as the jury evolved from self-informing locals to persons selected because they possessed no prior familiarity with the accused or the offense. The exclusion of persons with pretrial knowledge catapulted witnesses into a new critical role. As the only persons with direct acquaintance with the issue the jury was to decide, witnesses were pivotal to supplying the jury with knowledge of the events surrounding the act. Admittedly, *fact* is a disputed term in academic circles, but for matters of law, the definition is blissfully straightforward: witnesses testify to what they have seen, heard, or in any other *sensory* way, perceived. Fact was distinguished from opinion—an inference drawn from these reports—which was thought to be the sole province of the jury.[7] This distinction between fact and opinion made the credibility and trustworthiness of the witnesses' "facts" of paramount concern. When defense attorneys were restricted to *only* questioning witnesses, this limitation was not a severe one. The opportunity to cast doubt upon a witness's on-scene identification of the defendant or any other detail germane to the prosecution was seized and effectively exercised.

The common law's reliance on facts as grounded on direct personal experience reveals the enduring influence of John Locke's conception of sensory perception as the foundation of knowledge.[8] Without disputing the centrality of perceptual evidence as pivotal to the court's business, however, jurists differed regarding the wisdom of relying upon witness memory as a credible source of details for the jury to employ in arriving at a verdict. Lord Chief Baron Gilbert's preference for written over oral testimony was widely held: "The Testimony of an honest man, however fortified with the solemnities of an Oath, is yet liable to the imperfections of Memory; and as the Remembrances of Things fail and go off, Men are apt to entertain opinions in their stead . . . contracts reduced to writing are the most certain and deliberate Acts of Man, and are more advantageously secured from all corruption by the forms and solemnities of the Law than they possibly could have been if retained in memory only."[9] Gilbert's preference was easily understood in matters of civil disputes that hinged on the integrity of a contract or a deed, or to trials under the sole authority of a judge. The caseload at the Old Bailey, however, featured opportunistic, spontaneous criminal acts—thefts or sexual assaults—in which written evidence was likely to have played no role at all. As doubtful as memory might be, it was the witness's recollection of what was heard or seen at the time of the crime that provided jurors with the fullest picture of what had transpired. Still, the accuracy of such memories, the likelihood that the witness might "entertain opinions" was ripe for the probing of a zealous defense advocate.

The increasing focus on how best to present evidence to the jury rendered written documents problematic: how does one cross-examine a contract? William Evans, representing a generation of jurists including Thomas Peake and Henry Wigmore, had taken issue in print with courtroom evidence, written as well as oral, that had been secured by a magistrate's pretrial examination of witnesses. The defendant, in such cases, "has not those assistances for analyzing the proofs which are adduced against him which exist upon a solemn trial, where he can call in aid the exertions of judicious advocates, and is sure of the protection of a learned and impartial judge."[10] Whether trial judges were reading legal texts is anyone's guess, but it seems clear that the shift from written evidence to testimony given viva voce had been endorsed, perhaps even initiated, by individual trial judges, much as they had instituted qualitative changes in courtroom dynamics by permitting activist advocates for the defense. Whatever its provenance and however broad may have been the initial intent, the rethinking of the guilt-fastening process during the early eighteenth century was the most qualitative change the common law had yet to witness. The role played by the defense attorney cannot be overstated: Fitzjames Stephen's observation was no exaggeration.

A Renewed Focus on Evidence and Proof

The emphasis now placed on evidence presented in real time meant that the scrutiny of courtroom testimony would move to the forefront of the defense attorney's activity. Hearsay evidence was clearly in the defense advocate's sights; not only was the author of such "facts" unable to be sworn, spirited cross-examination designed to test the accuracy of the supposed observation was impossible since he or she was not in court.[11] The same reservation extended to published texts and commentaries; regardless of their totemic authority in a particular field, the author was not present in court, which rendered even the most revered texts (works of medical jurisprudence, for example) liable to objection on the principle of rejecting hearsay evidence.[12] Beyond a tighter focus on criminal evidence, the introduction of defense attorneys also brought about efforts to enhance the integrity of the verdict by establishing the criterion of "guilt beyond a reasonable doubt."[13] Although maddeningly ambiguous regarding its precise meaning—about what significant life decisions does one *not* entertain substantial doubt—the new standard set a conceptual benchmark for which juries ought to strive, compelling them to be as convinced as possible before voting to convict.

Whether these reforms were spearheaded by newly arrived defense attorneys or by trial judges, it is clear that members of the advocacy bar were invested in the courts' newfound appreciation for oral testimony, its careful scrutiny, and a standard of proof they could make increasingly exacting through spirited, and often withering, cross-examination. Each development would prove to have direct bearing on the testimony that sits at the heart of this study. The witnesses who would offer expert testimony had also undergone a change in job description. Before, they had been advisors who helped the judge or jury decipher information or ambiguities—for instance, explaining the nuances of the wording in a contract for ship building, the meaning of Latin terms in a document, or the likelihood that wounds responsible for the victim's death were suicidal or homicidal.[14] These advisors appeared in court in an anomalous capacity. They were clearly delivering opinions—thought to be the jury's responsibility—yet they remained specialist witnesses whose experientially based inferences the jury and judge were free to be guided by or to ignore.[15] They had no firsthand knowledge of the crime or the accused, and their testimony was based on the facts of others. Therefore, they were not exactly witnesses in any commonly accepted sense, although their testimony could likely be critical to the jury's deliberation. They might be questioned by the judge and jury, but before the eighteenth century, this scrutiny did not rise to the level of cross-examination. After all, the court was seeking their advice, not trying to identify faulty assumptions or unsupported inferences, let alone suspected partisan bias.

The advent of medical testimony bearing on two criminal matters particularly—insanity and suspected poisoning—is inextricably bound up with the qualitative changes in the eighteenth-century felony trial.[16] Medical men were no longer advising the judge but testifying in trials, and they were subject to the same protocols as all witnesses: examination and cross-examination. Their participation was now framed by their appearing for either the prosecution or defense, and questions about how they came to their inferences and how their loyalty to one party or another might have compromised their professional objectivity were fair game. The more doubt opposing counsel could cast upon the grounds for the specialist's conclusion, their extent of familiarity with this particular defendant's condition, and the depth of their training and knowledge in the subject area, the more difficult the attorney could make the opposing side's ability to enlist the specialist's testimony to inform (or undermine) a finding of guilt beyond a reasonable doubt. Without the evolving courtroom preference for testimony given orally and the arrival of defense and prosecutorial attorneys, the career of the mad-doctor would likely have taken a very different trajectory in the nineteenth century.[17]

A Defense of Its Time

When medical witnesses participated in trials that turned on the mental state of the defendant, they found themselves part of a larger courtroom inquiry concerned with possible exculpatory conditions or states of being that might stay the hand of an executioner. Between 1688 and 1820, Parliament passed legislation fixing a penalty of death for some two hundred crimes, most concerning theft or other property violations. Lacking a metropolitan police force, successive political figures had put their faith in the power of deterrence to encourage would-be malefactors to think again before reaching for a bauble or a weapon.[18] Although the ultimate sanction of death remained a potent threat in eighteenth-century London, juries were reluctant to couple conviction with the noose. Into the early 1820s, juries balked at the draconian penal code by adopting creative approaches to guilt fastening. They might, for example, lower the value of goods stolen to fall conspicuously below the thirty-shilling threshold mandating death, or they might convict the accused of "lesser included" crimes.[19] This effort to arrive at lighter sentences by convicting the accused of lesser crimes obviously frustrated the Georgian government's efforts, but juries were not alone in seeking to keep undeserving felons from the gallows. Judges routinely sought a Royal Pardon to scale back from execution to life imprisonment.

These efforts to soften Parliament's harsh decrees were not undertaken in an arbitrary or random fashion. Thomas Green's illuminating study of how "twelve good men and true" arrived at partial verdicts reveals jurors' consideration of the social constraints ordinary Londoners faced in their daily lives. Although it has become commonplace today to speak of offenders as "products of their environment," there seems to have been a parallel eighteenth-century concern for antecedent influences acting upon a person's actions. Jury leniency and requests for royal pardons were often associated with offenders' youth or general economic stress upon the destitute.[20] Recognition of the effect of real-world pressures, one should note, did not yield an acquittal but rather mitigation of the degree of culpability, as reflected in a finding noticeably less severe than the True Bill, the indictment.

Might the evolving standard to establish guilt beyond a reasonable doubt serve to throw social and economic constraints into relief, leading jurors to question how *anyone* in such straightened circumstances could exercise choice? Were jurors perhaps anticipating the next century's infatuation with positivism—conceiving of human behavior as reducible to scientific laws of environmental determinism? Something beyond simple empathy is suggested: If juries were simply experiencing compassion or a revulsion for meting out the ultimate sanction, why do historians of law find predictable patterns in the partial verdicts and the consistent down-valuing of goods only for certain subsets of the defendant population? And further, why do the actions of trial judges in requesting pardons reveal the intrusion of thoughts regarding "necessity" dictated by economic need?

What is significant here is that social and, by extension, psychological forces are clearly at work in sentencing, as well as guilt fastening. Peter King's insightful analysis of judicial requests for pardon in Essex mirrors Green's results. The consideration of factors eliciting pardons had shifted earlier in the trial process, a point significant for English jurisprudence. A host of factors thought to constrain human will were entering into the deliberations of various courtroom actors, and their leniency in the face of an unyielding punishment code suggests that they were thinking about how hunger, fear, and desperation had likely drained the defendant's customary resolve.

One of the innovations introduced by defense attorneys was the calling of the defendant's acquaintances to contrast the neighbor they knew with the unrecognizable felon in the dock. With the defendant's customary propriety and moral compass at issue, character witnesses could play an influential role in the jury's conviction that the act was so out of character as to have been committed by someone quite different.[21] Again, it is noteworthy that these witnesses appeared not at a (post-conviction) sentencing hearing but during the trial itself. The defendant was not alleging that he did not commit the action; his attorney was instead presenting evidence that would allow the jury to construct a narrative that described how a social circumstance like starving children or searing economic want had left the accused bereft of his habitual self-possession and morally upright bearing.

There was, of course, only one defendant on trial. The jury's challenge was to make sense of the testimony of the neighbor who knew him or her best and to consider it against the evidence of seemingly purposeful villainy that had targeted either property or the victim's person. It is little wonder, then, that a courtroom newly disposed to the proffering of oral testimony and willing to consider the distance that separated a devoted mother from the merciless parent who had methodically dispatched her children to a better world was prepared to listen to testimony regarding stress of an entirely different sort. The defendant's neighbors could attest to her maternal devotion and countless displays of affection, but it would require another type of witness to explain how a pitiable mother could have suckled and comforted her infants minutes before chucking them into the Thames.

The Oral Courtroom and the Novel Expert

Judges and juries at the Old Bailey in the latter decades of the eighteenth century were introduced not only to the newly emerging defense attorney but also to the London mad-doctor, who described a host of mental ailments for the court to consider. Although medicine had been associated with madness since Hippocrates, the medical healer was not the only specialized practitioner concerned with mental derangement. Religious leaders and astrologers also claimed mental derangement as falling within their spheres of knowledge and could just as easily have appeared in an expert capacity had madness remained an extra-medical concern.[22] The courtroom, however, had long grown familiar with medicine in its capacity as an advisor to the criminal tribunal, especially in areas of expertise that traveled far beyond the understanding and experience of the layperson sitting in the jury box.

The beginning of medical witnesses appearing at an insanity trial is conventionally dated to 1760, with the appearance of John Monro, Physician Superintendent of Bethlem.[23] That he had never treated nor indeed met the defendant underscored the significance of Monro's testimony, which professed a degree of knowledge that enabled him to speak of the symptoms and effect of lunacy on a *class* of mentally deranged persons. The defendant was eventually convicted and summarily hanged—albeit with a noose made of silk, as he was, after all, a member of the House of Lords—did not augur well for future defendants who looked to medical specialists to support their plea of derangement. The verdict was not unexpected, however; lunacy was by nature a labile condition and stood conspicuously outside the law's insistence that only complete insanity—a total want of understanding and reason—satisfied the criterion for an acquittal.[24]

The early decades of the nineteenth century witnessed the introduction of partial states of insanity as a defense and not only by medical witnesses. One can already surmise that there was more than a little commonality of purpose between the new advocacy bar and the emerging specialty of mental medicine. Criminal trials that featured mental derangement as a possible exculpatory condition offer today's historian of forensic psychiatry an extensive scope for inspecting the incidence of the insanity plea over time, its success in securing an acquittal, and the fluctuations in the participation of medical witnesses against the backdrop of changes in criminal prosecution and sentencing.

The evolution of the insanity trial and, with it, the creation of a new professional specialty of proffered expertise did not, therefore, take place in a vacuum. Few periods in English legal practice have seen such dramatic changes in courtroom dynamics and disposition of offenders as the late eighteenth and early-to-mid nineteenth centuries. These years also fostered the creation of a new specialist witness in the criminal courts, inviting historians to consider how the evolution of this singular expert witness illustrates the subtle and not-so-subtle ways that practitioners of law and medicine shaped each other's career trajectories.

Rates of Criminality and Insanity, 1760–1913

Literary characters often endure in the reading public's imagination long after the last page of the novel is finished. Mr. Darcy, Anna Karenina, and Hedda Gabler have thus attained an immortality in Western thought, and to this pantheon one can add the Artful Dodger, Charles Dickens's most memorable rogue and the embodiment of opportunistic street crime.[25] Larceny in all its forms—lifting a wallet from a gent, a watch from a pocket, or a purse from a lodging—occupies Fagin's youthful apprentices in the novel, just as in Victorian London, it provided work for a sustained population of prostitutes, pickpockets, and light-fingered servants. Grand or petty, planned or random, committed in Surrey, Essex, or Westminster, shoplifting and robbery constituted the majority of the Old Bailey caseload through the middle of the nineteenth century. Most offenses were listed on indictment simply as theft, although notation was also made of breaking and entering, stealing, and fraud or forgery. A good number of cases of arson were also recorded.

In the years surveyed in the present study, little distinguished the crimes of the alleged insane offender from those committed by defendants whose mental state played no role in their defense.[26] Figure 1.1 reveals that fully three-quarters of late eighteenth-century insanity trials were precipitated by a property offense.[27] Although this is much to be expected, given the overall caseload in the London courtroom, today it strikes us as odd because the insanity plea has come to be associated with lurid tales of violent personal attack. Placed in historical perspective, however, the situation becomes more

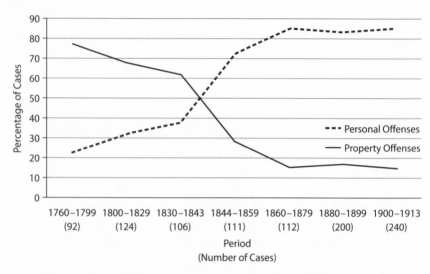

Figure 1.1. Type of Offense as a Percentage of Total Cases Alleging Insanity

comprehensible when one considers the punishment that could attend conviction in such an "ordinary" crime as larceny: death by hanging. There was
every reason, therefore, to raise a plea of mental derangement, just as there
was ample reason to mention necessity, or poverty, or the starvation of one's
family, and to provide character witnesses to attest to how out of character the
theft was. Seen in this context, a plea of mental distress was yet another factor
to consider in limiting the accused's capacity to withstand forces compelling
him or her to crime.

Although historians have found property crimes to predominate in com-
mittals to trial through the midpoint of the nineteenth century, the same is
not true in the trials of the mentally deranged. By 1800, the difference between
property and personal crimes had narrowed appreciably, and it remained almost static for forty years. By the middle of the century, however, the two
types of offenses had begun to reverse in proportion.[28] And by 1860, the two
had completely shifted, and they remained stable for the next fifty years. This
stability is not only remarkable in terms of the number of years, but over
the course of a rapidly changing number of trials, the proportion stays exactly the same. One very likely reason for the fall in property offenses was
the dramatic decrease in capital punishment for such offenses. Between 1808
and 1841, more than two hundred capital offenses were removed from the
statute books, restricting the death-eligible offenses to eleven.[29] After 1841,
executions were usually only carried out in cases of murder. Robert Peel,

who along with other political figures and jurists could see that the draconian Bloody Code had actually produced leniency, had spearheaded this remarkably comprehensive consolidation of capital statutes; jurors had routinely resorted to "pious perjury," circumventing the prescribed sentence by finding the accused guilty of lesser offenses.

The shift in offenses seen in insanity trials early in the nineteenth century thus reveals a change in defense strategy among this particular population of defendants. As the punishment for stealing or breaking and entering became a prison sentence rather than the gallows, the desirability of a prisoner serving a fixed term of punishment obviously increased, resulting in fewer property offenders entering an insanity plea.[30] And as the death sentence was retained for murder, one would expect to find a noticeable growth in the proportion of personal offenses. Within this category—which includes assault, rape, attempted murder, and abandoning children—murder clearly predominates. Of all the allegedly insane defendants on trial for personal offenses at the Old Bailey in the years following the restriction of execution for murder (and it must be said, forgery as well—at Peel's insistence), more than half were tried for murder.

A further reason for the drop in property offenders tried in insanity cases from the start of the nineteenth century was the special verdict that followed an insanity acquittal, beginning in 1800. The trial of James Hadfield, discussed in chapter 2, resulted in a number of significant changes in the manner of prosecuting insanity defendants. Prior to 1800, anyone found not guilty by the jury was released into the community, even those who'd been judged insane. After the passage of the Criminal Lunatics Act of 1800, however, defendants acquitted and given the new verdict of "not guilty on the grounds of insanity" were kept in custody for an indefinite length of time.[31] Facing fixed jail time rather than an elastic confinement, the prisoner awaiting trial could hardly be blamed for choosing the more limited option. Furthermore, by not acknowledging his role in the offense, which he was by definition divulging in order to set up an insanity plea, the accused could hope for an outright acquittal.

One feature of the insanity trial that did not change over time was the gender distribution of defendants. As male defendants predominated in court throughout the eighteenth and early nineteenth centuries—George Rudé found eight in ten defendants to be male in the late 1700s and early 1800s—the proportion of insanity defendants right through Victoria's reign identically mirrored the gender distribution among the allegedly mad defendants: two in five were women.[32] In the early years of the present study, when property crimes predominated, women were well represented among the purportedly mad thieves; their rates of participation in larceny exactly mirrored their proportion in the population of insane defendants. When they found themselves in the dock at the Old Bailey in the latter years of this period, they were also much more likely to be on trial for murderous personal assaults, often against a family member. Men were much more likely to kill business associates, social acquaintances, or spouses, and murder of a spouse was likely to invite severe punishment due to a hardening of attitudes regarding domestic violence.[33] Women appearing at the Old Bailey were much more likely to have targeted family members, typically their children, either in infancy or in the child's very early years.

What chances of acquittal would a defendant indicted for murder or theft face in the late eighteenth and early nineteenth centuries? Before considering the methodological issues surrounding determining an acquittal rate, let alone its possible interpretation, it would be well to keep in mind historian Cynthia Herrup's cautionary observation about trial outcomes: "a verdict is the clearest point of a trial's history but the weakest focus for the historian. It is a filter built from artificial materials and one that obscures as much as it clarifies, reinforcing rather than upsetting the notion of a trial as a story with an objective ending."[34] Consider, for example, how often trial outcomes today leave one dumbfounded, and this at a time when news outlets exhaustively report the physical evidence, courtroom testimony, and examination of witnesses. The demeanor of various courtroom actors is reported—indeed dissected—by self-professed body-posture experts projecting how the jury appears to be *leaning* to one side or the other. Eventually, the verdict is announced, and the grounds for the jury's opinion seem more opaque than ever.[35]

One must be cautious therefore about speculating about how juries in history listened to evidence, observed the bearing of the accused, and heard the victim's tale of assault, all while being asked to consider the possibility of impelling forces catapulting the defendant into unspeakable crime. And yet, although the elements that brought it about must remain speculative, the verdict is an unmistakable fact for the historian of law and forensic psychiatry. Twelve good men and true might have chosen to acquit because the defendant was just too pathetic to warrant censure and punishment. Fatally attacking a beloved child or a cherished friend, stealing a trifle, or attempting to stab the sovereign with a butter knife might easily warrant an acquittal and a straight-out finding of not guilty at that. Particularly after 1800, when an acquittal based on insanity meant indefinite detention, a simple finding of not guilty could end the matter and leave the hapless defendant to be watched over (one hoped) by family members. Alternatively, a jury might choose to acquit because the evidentiary standard of beyond a reasonable doubt cast the prosecutor's narrative in question. Without even considering the merits of the insanity plea, the jury might simply find the prosecutor's facts unconvincing. Finally, prosecutors could appear vindictive and petty, prompting the jury to acquit as a show of its disdain. Herrup could not be more correct: reasons for any verdict are maddeningly various.

The difficulty of reading a jury's verdict was made even more challenging when mental derangement sat at the center of the defense. After 1800, jurors could return a verdict of "not guilty on the grounds of insanity" and, after 1883, "guilty of the act but not responsible at the time." Can one infer with confidence that the acquittal was driven by the specialist's evidence of manifest madness?[36] Were other decisions—"unfit to plead," for example—the result of a claim of mental infirmity? Although the finding of unfit to stand trial was not, of course, an acquittal, it is likely that in cases where grounds for suspecting madness were sufficiently compelling to preclude a trial, there would have been an insanity acquittal had the case proceeded to trial. Figure 1.2 displays the acquittal rates over time. For the purposes of this study, an acquittal is recorded if insanity was voiced in the verdict, if the accused was found "unfit to plead," or if a finding of "not guilty" was noted following a trial in which mental derangement was the subject of the defense.[37]

In the late 1700s, acquittal rates in insanity trials did not differ appreciably according to the defendant's type of crime. Whether the accused had stolen or committed assault, the chances for acquittal differed little: both types of offense yielded an acquittal rate in the mid to high 40 percent range. The rates diverge noticeably in the early decades of the nineteenth century following the trial and verdict of James Hadfield, prosecuted for the attempted assassination of George III. As explained in the next chapter, this trial introduced the idea of *delusion* into the criminal insanity trial and, to many observers today, the first form of *partial insanity* to find success with the law's criterion of an appropriate degree of derangement. Fatal errors in belief would seem to find resonance for the defense in a personal crime; delusions of persecution, of love, of believing that Satan would steal one's children unless the mother killed them first were no doubt easier to argue than a delusory conviction that the jewelry in someone else's home really did belong to you. In the years that witnessed the increasing prominence of delusion in courtroom testimony,

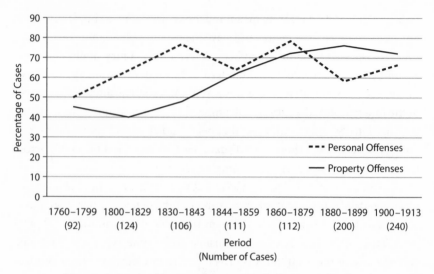

Figure 1.2. Acquittal Rates in Insanity Trials, by Type of Offense

there is a noticeable rise in acquittal rates in personal crimes, although one sees a slow rise in property crimes as well.[38]

Although the acquittal rates for the two types of offenses appear similar in the second half of the century, there is a noteworthy shift in acquittals for personal crimes directly after the McNaughtan verdict. If this occurred in both types of crime, one would be tempted to conclude that the *McNaughtan Rules,* discussed in the next chapter, resulted in a tightening of the criteria that subsequent juries were compelled to employ in insanity trials, resulting in fewer findings of "not guilty on the grounds of insanity." This would not be a difficult argument to make: the *Rules* explicitly constrained medical witnesses from introducing a host of recently catalogued species of madness that juries had heard in the 1830s and early 1840s. And slip the acquittal rate did, to the rate seen at the beginning of the century, but only for offenders tried in personal crimes. At this preliminary point, one might wonder if there was something in the offense, the substance of the courtroom testimony, or the trial proceedings that worked to the advantage of one type of offender but not another. By the last few decades considered in this study, the acquittal rates for both types of offenders returned again to resemble each other, coming closer to two-thirds rather than the two-fifths returned during the early years surveyed in this research.

The present study begins with the entrance of the first medical witness called to testify to a defendant's mental condition in 1760. The latter decades of the eighteenth century featured medical men who offered opinions on the manifest derangement of the defendant, but their participation was noticeably infrequent. No more than one in ten insanity trials featured medical practitioners, and the reason for that scarcity is not hard to fathom. Before 1800, common law views held out for a total madness, a total want of memory and understanding, as the grounds for acquittal. With such a conspicuously distracted state as the criterion, neighbors, social acquaintances, and family members were in just as privileged an observational perch—arguably better— than the medical man to testify. A specialty in mental medicine had still to be claimed by medical practitioners, who in the late 1700s hardly belonged to a "profession" at all. Physicians, surgeons, and apothecaries could each claim a sustained familiarity with the deranged of London, but such experience could not translate into a knowledge base because there was neither a recognized course of study nor a standard training that medical practitioners received in either mental or organically based abnormality. The enduring eighteenth-century belief that "madness was spectacularly on view . . . few doubted nature's legibility" put the non-medically trained in a valued position to advise juries on how to consider the defendants' aimless wanderings and incoherent conversation; medical men had little to add to such firsthand observations.[39]

As data in figure 1.3 reveal, however, the first decades of the nineteenth century witnessed an immediate doubling of the participation rate for the second half of the 1700s and a rapid rise thereafter. One would do well to keep in mind that besides the introduction of delusion—a hidden form of derangement that medical men argued required the services of a skilled clinician to detect—the early 1800s also saw a variegated group of medical practitioners who contributed to the rate of trial participation in ways that need mention (see fig. 1.2). These medical witnesses were not all, or even mostly, appearing for the defense. The most frequently participating medical man was the prison surgeon, who, in the employ of the Corporation for the City of London, visited prisoners suspected to be fashioning a plea of mental derangement.[40] In time, others were also called to serve the interests of the state; the Home Secretary summoned private practitioners, authors, and lecturers to visit and then report their observations to juries. This practice was formalized in parliamentary acts in 1865 and 1877 that mandated routine medical exams for all prisoners, resulting, according to Roger Chadwick, in an increase in insanity verdicts and commitments to Broadmoor, the first hospital for the criminally insane, opened in 1864.[41]

Although it can hardly be doubted that the population within Broadmoor

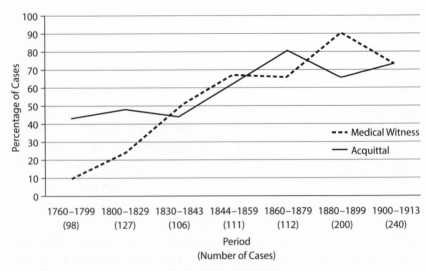

Figure 1.3. Comparison of Rates of Acquittal and Medical Participation

swelled as a result of routine medical evaluation of prisoners awaiting trial, the effect of medical testimony on a jury's proclivity to acquit is rather more challenging to argue. When rates of medical participation and acquittal are placed side by side (see fig. 1.3), there is no obvious relationship between them for half of the century, from 1844 to 1900. Indeed, one could argue for an inverse direction of influence, if indeed there is any influence at all. From 1844 to 1860, a dramatic rise in the acquittal rate occurs against a leveling off of what had been a continuous rise in medical participation since 1800. And in the last few decades of Victoria's reign, a span of years that saw the most impressive gains in medical participation witnessed the only *drop* in the acquittal rate since the mid-eighteenth century. Clearly, one can hardly make the argument that the more medical men flooding into the courtroom, the more likely the jury was to relinquish its role as the trier of fact, assuming an obeisant posture to the cultural authority of a specialist and rendering, in effect, a verdict by medicine.

Of course, the reverse inference—that medical participation somehow depressed the conviction rate—would be just as misguided. Rather, the diverging rates remind one of the complexity in interpreting any particular rate and of the complexity of inferring some necessary significance in how two rates appear to work in concert. The acquittal rate, as stated before, is composed of several jury determinations: outright acquittals, acquittals on the grounds of insanity, findings of "unfit to plead," and simple discharges of prisoners.

One has no way of knowing how a jury would have ruled absent the medical testimony or how such testimony affected jury decision making when it was present. If medical participation appeared to coincide with a jury's decision to acquit, perhaps medical witnesses had chosen to appear in only the most compelling cases of, in Arlie Loughnan's term, manifest madness. That this was clearly not the case can be seen in figure 1.3. As suggested earlier, many of the medical men testifying over the course of these one thousand trials were appearing at the behest of the government, and, to the eye of the reader of the *OBSP,* they often went to great lengths to deny the putatively insane defendant's madness: "I saw nothing of madness in the prisoner." If we were considering only the testimony of "the prosecutor's medical man," an increase in this type of testimony would, if anything, be likely to coincide with a fall in the acquittal rate. But many other practitioners, including prison surgeons, appeared to bolster the defense arguments, and it is their testimony, particularly, that sits at the heart of this study. To put it simply, medical witnesses did not seem predisposed to support any particular side based on who was paying their salary.

The Medical Witness in Context

The criminal defendant at the Old Bailey was likely to encounter an array of medical practitioners with a range of work-related experiences to impart to a jury. Individual police districts employed surgeons to attend the crime scene to see if medical treatment was required, and they often encountered a dazed and bewildered offender. Once committed to a prison and awaiting trial, the accused would encounter the prison doctor, often a surgeon, who, similar to the police doctor, could testify in court about his observations of the accused's appearance, conduct, and conversation. Criminal suspects often arrived at the courtroom with a history of asylum incarceration, so there were madhouse superintendents appearing in the dock as well. Alternatively, a private practitioner, who might have treated the defendant before the crime, could read from his case notes to account for his diagnosis.

The rise of the defense bar was critical as well over the course of the century, with the calling in of prominent medical figures to interview the prisoner and opine on the likelihood that the accused was "not in his proper intellects" at the moment of the assault. As there was no standard forum that brought the medical witness and the accused together, there was no standard body of knowledge these varied practitioners shared. That they each contributed quantitatively to the "medical witness rate" is clear; what is not so evident is *how* their testimony engaged legal conceptions of the will and responsibility, nor indeed how the medical witness formed his judgments of the accused's mental state. How did medical witnesses support their inferences? How did they explain the grounds for opinion? Did the professional experiences of various types of medical practitioners who worked with the deranged translate into noticeably different patterns in diagnosis, and how do these diagnoses differ over time as medical practitioners become medical *professionals* with the Medical Registration Act of 1858. Finally, how can one account for the striking observation that the years that saw the highest rates of medical participation also recorded the first fall in the acquittal rate in the entire period in which the evolution of the forensic-psychiatric witness reached its greatest representation in court?

The medical witness's rise to prominence in frequency of testimony in the late eighteenth and mid-nineteenth centuries occurred during a period of radical change in the courtroom division of labor. With the shift from written to oral testimony, the way was opened for courtroom evidence to be given pride of place. And with the admission of and structuring of the defense attorney's role, the court experienced a defense that could draw on specialist witnesses to present evidence through the lens of professional expertise or to question and ultimately degrade the evidence of the prosecutor. This type of evidence revealed the limits to what a lay observer could make of what previously had been thought to be the unambiguous reports of eyewitnesses or of people who had daily interactions with the offender. Furthermore, the plea of insanity itself was but one among many states of being—starvation, necessity, economic distress—that could justifiably qualify the offender's intention to contemplate evil.

Certainly, madness had its own features and its own self-described experts at decoding its mysteries, skilled practitioners able to "pierce sanity's smokescreen." And there were, to be sure, emerging rulings in the court—*Hadfield, Oxford, McNaughtan*—that would attempt to clarify the nature of madness and its necessary consequence in matters of criminal liability. Still, the medical witness was walking into a highly structured forum whose purpose was the dispensing of justice, not the negotiation of ever-more finely delineated species of mental abnormality. The proffering of expertise would have to take place in a space that reflected the shifting relations between the Home Office, the prison system, and Broadmoor.[42] It was into this fraught setting that the newly emerging specialist in mental medicine entered, armed with an expanding set of diagnostic terms supporting his claim to possess the knowledge to decipher the mind of the mad.

CHAPTER TWO

Delusion and Its Discontents

The year 1800 marks a pivotal moment in the history of the modern insanity trial, not only for the consequences that would accrue to defendants acquitted on the grounds of mental derangement but for the trajectory of forensic psychiatric evidence. As long as insanity remained a matter of conspicuous display of extravagant or dejected behavior, one hardly needed the services of a physician or a surgeon to diagnose an exotic species of derangement. As madness moved *inward*, however, as the subjective state of the madman's mind and the "contents of consciousness" served as the focal point for medical speculation, refinements in descriptive psychopathology identified discrete forms of derangement that engaged the passions and volition, having little to do with intellectual delirium. Indeed, medical men in print and in court depicted states of insanity that left the afflicted perfectly—and frighteningly—lucid while in the throes of abstract fury. In their venturing beyond intellectual incoherence as the defining element of insanity, however, medical men would find that a century that began with a remarkable concurrence between law and medicine regarding delusion as the "true" nature of madness would soon find the term acting as a wedge, separating medical from legal practitioners and mad-doctors from their own medical brethren.

Given the often fractious relations between law and psychiatry, it is well worth remembering the role that defense attorneys played not only in prompting the mad-doctor's appearance in court but in shaping his testimony as well. When attorney Thomas Erskine called physician and author Alexander Crichton to testify in the case of James Hadfield, on trial for the attempted assassination of George III, he had already laid the groundwork for the medical testimony with a bold reworking of insanity's essence for the purposes of the common law.[1] Up to 1800, the year of Hadfield's trial, English legal opinion had mandated that only a total madness—a complete want of understanding and memory—would rise to the level of a legally significant madness. The suspect in the attempted regicide had managed to procure a weapon, load the ammunition, secrete himself in the theater where the king was due to appear, and choose his moment to shoot. The attorney's work was cut out for him: few attempted murders could have appeared more methodically planned out, and further, the defendant revealed a clear understanding of the consequences of shooting the firearm. Having fallen under the sway of a millenarian cult, Hadfield intended the act to secure his own public execution—a death that would mirror Christ's—to effect the Second Coming. This was the reason he found himself in the Drury Lane Theatre, preparing to shoot the sovereign as the audience struck up a chorus of "God Save The King." Could there have been a more intentional, purposeful political murder? What possible chance for success could a defense based on a "total want of understanding and memory" hope to have?

Although the first recorded acquittal on the grounds of "unsound mind" dates to 1505, one suspects that mentally deranged persons accused of serious crime had escaped punishment since at least the Middle Ages. The justification for acquittal can be found in a thirteenth-century legal treatise compiled by Henri de Bracton, Henry II's chief justiciary. With its defining focus on intention and wicked will, the common law held that for criminal culpability to attend to any act, a requisite mental element must accompany a physical act. Thus a "will to harm"—a purposeful *resolve* to do evil—framed the thirteenth-century conception of mens rea. "Madmen have no will," wrote de Bracton: "For a crime is not committed unless the will to harm be present . . . In misdeeds we look to the will and not the outcome."[2]

Although de Bracton's principle is easily grasped, he left no instructions for how future legal minds could identify those mental states that might preclude the forming of a will to harm. Over time, the courts adopted a very exacting standard—total insanity—leaving little room for states of mind that fell short of a complete want of memory and understanding. Matthew Hale's seventeenth-century treatise attempted to distinguish partial from total insanity. Partial states of derangement, such as "melancholy distempers," left the afflicted with "ordinarily as great an understanding, as ordinarily a child of 14 hath." Since these youths could be found guilty of treason or a felony and executed, the lunatic who experienced only periodic, partial derangement faced a similar fate. Though mad, he was not mad *enough*.

Still, *partial* could take on another meaning: derangement with regard to particular subjects. Such persons, according to Hale, were "yet under a particular *dementia* in respect of some particular discourses." The nature of "particular discourses" and the possibility of derangement circumscribed by an idea or a fear would become the subject of increasing medical interest immediately following the publication of Hale's treatise. To some, his singling out melancholy persons left the impression that this familiar state of mental distraction failed to satisfy the law's stricture for an acquittal.[3] Melancholia may have been familiar in name, but it shared with other centuries-old terms associated with mental affliction (mania, delirium, insensibility) a tendency to evolve and adapt to changing attitudes and meanings in contemporary culture. Over the course of the nineteenth century particularly, it would take on a host of characteristics that would make it ideally suited for the enterprising defense attorney. James Hadfield's attorney, Thomas Erskine, eventually named solicitor general of England, was nothing if not enterprising.

Melancholia in Text and Delusion in Testimony

According to historian of medicine Stanley Jackson, few mental states have been described with such "remarkable consistency" as melancholia.[4] Paired since Hippocrates with sorrow and dejection, sometimes attended by a preoccupying fear of death or some impending physical calamity, melancholia figures prominently in medical texts and artistic imagery in early modern Europe. The melancholic's presence has been recognizable to the medical man by the downcast expression, the lower jaw gaping away, the tear-filled eyes, and the face buried in hands. Artists have captured the melancholic's aspect, showing a person with geometric tools at the ready and books in abundance, signifying a mind too engaged in an esoteric search for truth that has tragically come off the rails.

The association of dejected mood with preoccupying fear intrigued medical writers in the nineteenth century. Whether they referred to it as delusion or illusion, authors of various medical tracts isolated a state known as "simple melancholia," describing a depression of feeling that need not involve delusion. This state could also be described as *melancholia simplex,* in which the imagination appeared to work overtime. Even when appearing in its simpler states, though, some medical writers considered melancholia to be but an initial stage on a continuum, advancing eventually to a more serious condition in which delusion predominated in the mind of the distracted. In the end, it was the presence of delusion—an insistent fear or suspicion about a conspiracy or some vague physical ailment auguring impending demise—that distinguished melancholy from melancholia, the former reserved for states of sorrow or grief that could usually be connected to a real life loss or tragedy. For Hippocrates, Galen, and the centuries of medical men who followed, melancholia signified grief that went on "too long" or a state of lassitude and torpor that appeared disconnected from any identifiable cause.

Identifying the cause of melancholia was rather formulaic. Medical theorizing since antiquity blamed an imbalance in the humors for a variety of discernable temperaments; a surfeit of black bile was responsible for the dark moods and brooding sadness of the melancholic. The idea of a dark shadow thrust upon the mind is found in Aristotle and remains part of the preoccupying, compelling conception masking the afflicted's grasp of reality right up to *McNaughtan,* the most influential insanity case of Victorian England. Referring to the defendant's delusion, one medical witness testified, "I mean that black spot on his mind."[5] Humoral medicine would loosen its hold on medical theorizing in the seventeenth century, when Thomas Willis sought to identify the nervous system's role in mental processing. Some aberrant vibration in the nerves transporting stimulation to the senses was thought to preclude sober reflection and deliberation. Overcome by a flood of thoughts, confusion results; the afflicted labor under delusive constructions of external reality. Madness could thus be described a century later not as global delirium but as "deluded imagination": the deluded are "fully and unalterably persuaded of the Existence or the appearance of any thing which either does not exist or does not actually appear to him, and who behaves according to such erroneous persuasion."[6]

In 1758, Dr. William Battie's attention to deluded imagination prompted other medical authors to distinguish partial from general delirium, "ideal" from "notional insanity," the latter reserved for a derangement particular to some "subject or subjects" in which the patient is under "the most palpable and extraordinary delusions." The forensic implications of notional insanity would become clear when enlisted in court: there was not "the smallest distinguishable trait of ideal [i.e., general] delirium" in the notionally insane, who enjoyed "the sound and unimpaired use, in every other respect, of the rational faculties."[7] In the same year that witnessed the Hadfield trial, another text appeared isolating the hold of the "predominant idea" on the mind of the delusional, "inter[fering] and derang[ing] all the trains of thought with which it is intermixed."[8] In the waning years of the eighteenth century and into the early decades of the nineteenth, the conviction that insanity "may be called a delusion . . . an erroneous association of ideas on particular subjects" characterized the efforts of medical men to locate derangement in material being (Battie's "medullary substance") and to maintain insanity's meaning as a derangement of thought, of reason, of the intellects.[9] The continuing—and restrictive—focus on insanity as a derangement in reasoning attested to the enduring influence of Locke's conception of madness as distracted reasoning.[10] The first sustained challenge to a uniquely cognitive derangement surfaced with the French school of *médicine mentale* in the early 1800s. Philippe Pinel's attempt to simplify the burgeoning number of clinical species of insanity resulted in a four-fold scheme of classification in which he retained melancholia, narrowing its focus from generalized mood to delirium on one exclusive idea. Pinel departed from the uniquely cognitive frame, however, by proffering his own mental term, *manie sans délire*, which identified patients who were dominated by the force of an abstract fury, suffering no lesion of understanding.[11] For all of its revolutionary significance in describing a purely affective insanity, one that left the sufferer's intellects intact, *manie sans délire* did not engage forensic questions surrounding the blameworthiness of those afflicted with a derangement of feelings. The volatile questions that would bring mad-doctors into fierce debate with jurists were put forward by Pinel's prolific students, Jean-Étienne Dominique Esquirol and Étienne-Jean Georget.

Melancholia's long reign in medical nosology came to an abrupt halt in 1817 with Esquirol's formulation of *monomanie* and its various permutations. Removing the singular preoccupying fear or delusion from its association with melancholia's brooding anxiety and worry, Esquirol combined delusional preoccupation with a lively, expansive temperament, generously borrowed from the conception of mania. Of the various forms of *monomanie* (affective, instinctual) he devoted one to crime: *monomanie homicide*. Characterized by an impulsive urge to kill—a force beyond the restraint of those afflicted—homicidal monomania could propel a hapless mother to kill a beloved infant, a devoted husband to destroy a cherished spouse, a close friend to murder a treasured companion. No delusion had prompted the action, no long simmering resentment or enmity had precipitated the fatal assault. This was a purely affective insanity, leaving both the victim and offender helpless to intrude upon its inexorable course.[12] Pinel's other famous acolyte, Georget, penned perhaps the most conceptually (and professionally) venturous diagnosis, lesion of the will, to account for the crimes of those who, like Esquirol's tragic patients, were as mystified by their actions as the court and jury were when the diagnosis reached the witness box. "I have nothing at all to impel me to the act but a strong impulse" was all a defendant could say on her behalf.[13]

In the years in which *monomanie homicide* and lesion of the will were taking root in France and then making their way across the Channel, medical theorists in Scotland were putting forth a similar approach, looking beyond cognitive impairment to consider the passions as capable of suffering their own discrete distraction. *Moral insanity,* associated most closely with James Cowles Prichard, connoted a derangement of feelings, of sentiments. Prichard and his fellow followers of commonsense philosophy rejected the materialism of nerves, instead speaking in terms of the mind's innate, inductive faculties.[14] Instead of focusing on melancholia and delusory, preoccupying ideas, Prichard and his cohort turned their attention to the mind's inherent faculties of attention, memory, and comparison. The passions particularly worked on the faculty of imagination, resulting in a mind disturbed in its ability to separate fantasy from reality and to judge what was true.

With his sustained interest in the role that affect alone could play in generating insanity, Prichard was the first of many medical writers—and Old Bailey witnesses—to disparage the law's growing reliance on delusion as the sufficient criterion to merit a credible insanity plea in court. The morally insane were far from clear-headed, but their derangement could not be described as a disordered state of the intellectual faculties. Delusion might well describe the actions of someone who kills out of fear, vengeance, or groundless jealousy, but how can any form of distracted thinking hope to explain a purposeless assault on a beloved child or spouse? In their effort to explain how sentiments could be deranged independently from cognitive error or how the mind's faculties could be "suspended" without the individual being unconscious of his actions, theorists of moral insanity revealed a logical inconsistency in the law. If culpability was based on willfully chosen action and if understanding was key to the capacity to *choose* to do evil, how could the courts assess the criminality of actions that stemmed from no logical purpose or even an "insanely" logical purpose? Shooting a king because one's eventual execution would initiate the Second Coming may be a delusional reason, but it *is* a reason. On the other hand, shooting at the queen because, as Edward Oxford informed the court, "Oh, I might as well shoot at her as anybody else," does not even rise to the level of insane logic. How could it be conceived to be purposeful behavior?

Three years after an Old Bailey jury heard this declaration of seeming indifference at having emptied two pistols at the queen, the London court was faced with yet another assassination attempt, this one targeting a prime minister. Like the defendant whose cavalier attitude signified to his medical witnesses a lesion of the will, Daniel McNaughtan was acquitted on the ground of insanity, but this time, the House of Lords posed pointed questions to the trial judges, the better to inform future juries of the law's position on an insanity acquittal. The judges' answers, known as the *McNaughtan Rules,* sought to return insanity to a matter of cognitive defect: *knowing* right from wrong, *knowing* the nature and quality of one's acts.[15] Delusion played a pivotal role in the trial and particularly in the medical testimony of nine witnesses who were among the most famous authors and practitioners of psychological medicine at the time. Although making no mention of moral insanity or other specific forms of volitional chaos, the eminent asylum superintendents and well-known physicians and surgeons did not stop at merely articulating the defendant's persecution delusion. No one sitting in court or reading the medical opinion in the pages of the *OBSP* could have any doubt of the power of the defendant's delusion: "the commission of the act is placed beyond his moral control . . . the impulse was so strong that nothing short of a physical impossibility would prevent him from performing an act which his delusion might impel him to do."[16]

The ineluctable consequences of delusory fear or conspiratorial conviction were rarely stated with such apodictic conviction, but it did not take the McNaughtan trial at midcentury to couple cognitive defect with the loss of "moral liberty." Beginning with its introduction in *Hadfield* (1800), jurors were guided to an understanding of defendants' fears, such as that Satan would capture a mother's children unless she killed them first or that one's neighbor was the source of imminent murderous threat. These fears moved the deluded beyond mere fretfulness and worry: they were seized instead by desperate need to act. To the deluded, their actions did not amount to criminality; rather, a defendant would be described in court as "not conscious that he is doing wrong." A secret enemy, a conspiring prime minister, or an employer plotting to deprive one of his livelihood could unleash a deluded person's maniacal fury in service to saving one's own life or those of loved ones.

To an historian of forensic psychiatry, the noteworthy element is the court's apparent acceptance of how powerless the delusional were to intrude upon their thoughts, and thus their consequent actions were undertaken to preclude the supposed nemesis carrying out some nefarious plan. No judicial dismissiveness or contemptuous aside greeted such a conception of mind, and there was no hostile questioning on the part of the prosecuting attorney either. As long as a cognitive error or intellectual incoherence was at the center of the proffered derangement, the testimony was received and considered soberly. What legal—and much medical—opinion rejected soundly after

McNaughtan was the notion that derangement of feelings or volition could unleash its *own* forces, propelling the afflicted into crime or disposing them to commit criminal acts to which they were indifferent.

In the former case, critics charged *monomanie homicide* with attempting to explain the crime *by* the crime; an obvious tautology is set up when a homicide results from a homicidal impulse. Further medical as well as legal opinion resisted calling insanity anything but a delirium of the intellects, whatever mad asylum patients might report.[17] Homicidal monomania threatened to dissolve what barriers still remained between insanity and criminality. Many of these reservations were also sounded against moral insanity and its variant, lesion of the will. Legal opinion was prepared to accept criminal acts precipitated by delusional thoughts that, in the words of a medical witness, "carried [the defendant] quite away"; they were not willing to accept an *autonomous* force propelled by deranged sentiments or a will that was itself diseased. At their most indulgent, judges were willing to sit through testimony and conclude the proceedings with the question that suggested an obvious dismissal of all they had just heard: "Does he have any delusion at all?"

Melancholia at the Old Bailey

Describing his brother, on trial for felonious assault, the Right Honorable Lord Audley characterized the defendant in language that was easily recognizable to the lay juror: "sitting in a pensive manner . . . his look was downcast . . . with very great austerity of countenance, and sometimes rather the reverse . . . eyes suffused . . . dreamy expression." The two medical witnesses at the 1844 trial of William Ross Tuchet concluded that the defendant was "laboring under melancholia to such an extent to render him incapable of distinguishing right from wrong."[18] The prescribed legal language—incapable of knowing right from wrong—was part of insanity trials at the Old Bailey long before the *McNaughtan Rules* in 1843 but was rarely linked to a specific disease. Melancholia now found its mooring in the Victorian insanity trial. This "arrival" would mark a pivotal moment in the evolving role of forensic psychiatric testimony.

Certainly, there can be a hazard in seizing upon the appearance of a specific medical term at any point in legal history since, especially in psychological medicine, usage could vary among medical observers, between historical epochs, and even from one publisher of the *Old Bailey Sessions Papers* to his successor. "Melancholy moods," "pensive and melancholy," and "despairing melancholy" appear repeatedly in medical texts over the course of the seventeenth and eighteenth centuries, but it is only in mid-nineteenth century trials that melancholia appears at the Old Bailey as a disease in its own right. Again, one makes this observation with care—it might have been the preference of the editor to adopt the noun rather than the adjective—and yet one finds in mid-nineteenth-century medical testimony the effort to distinguish the disease from the mood. Medical witnesses distinguished melancholy from melancholia by the presence of delusion, and only the latter implicated cognitive defect; hence, one suspects, the easy return of melancholia to the courtroom after *McNaughtan*.

Melancholia had been discarded earlier in the century because of its association with bodily humors; to the enlightened physician, Galen's scheme situating temperament in corporeal fluids was pre-scientific. Thus Esquirol had removed melancholia's "preoccupying idea" that accompanied the dark mood and coupled it with an expansive, indeed, ebullient energy borrowed from traditional mania.[19] The sorrowful, downcast temperament traditionally associated with melancholia was renamed *lypemania*. In the 1820s and 1830s, Esquirol's terms were current in French medicine and found their adherents in England as well. By the 1840s, however, resistant voices on both sides of the Channel, though more voluble in Paris, questioned the usefulness and even the existence of Esquirol's neologism.[20] By the 1850s, asylum registers in England reveal a sharp drop-off in persons admitted with this diagnosis. At the Old Bailey, monomania made its first appearance in the 1830s, but readers of the trial narratives later in the century would learn that "monomania is not much believed in now."[21] Throughout the 1800s, monomania appears rarely in medical testimony, and its first mention is in a case of forgery, not murder.[22] It seems to have been used more to describe the single-minded pursuit of an objective rather than an autonomous disease possibly ending in homicide (as articulated by Esquirol). That it appears in court at all after the 1850s is a surprise since the medical literature and asylum registers barely mention it. In its stead, medical writers reintroduced melancholia and mania, giving them a contemporary new twist.

When William Ross Tuchet's brother described him in court as displaying "great austerity of countenance, and sometimes the reverse," his testimony anticipated the introduction of a circular insanity, advanced by two medical theorists whose claims to have discovered the condition were made apparently independently of each other.[23] The notion that mania and melancholia could rotate was not new: since antiquity, medical observers had claimed that melancholia, after its initial stages, would lapse into mania. Medical testimony at the Old Bailey does not contain an express mention of *folie circulaire* or *folie à double forme,* but medical witnesses routinely commented upon the alternating nature of the two states: "he came to me suffering from nervous excitement and melancholia, severe pains in the head and restless at night . . . the victim to that disease may go on for a long time without betraying that the brain is affected by it, and then may have an outbreak of suicidal or maniacal mania."[24] When melancholia and mania were drawn together in court, the brooding torpor of the melancholic precedes the exuberant outbreak: there is no *return* to restless despondency.

The one element that seems to unite the two states is their association with delusion. In mania, preoccupying, haunting belief accompanies exalted, wild behavior; in melancholia, subdued behavior and dejection are conjoined with the fateful error in cognition. Still, the two states' distractions do not always follow a predictable pattern—dejection could be found in mania, "grandiosity" in melancholia. But standard to both was the unshakable delusory fear or conviction the sufferer was incapable of seeing—and dispelling—for what it was. Juries learned of a host of delusions: a talking clock that egged the defendant into crime, fears of poison having been added to one's beer (or tea), and suspicions of a wife entertaining countless lovers while he lay next to her at night. Surgeon James Hicks informed an 1847 courtroom that "one of [the defendant's] delusions was wanting me to open his head and take something out of it."[25] From haunting visions to incessant voices, from adulterous spouses to hectoring household items, the delusions of defendants diagnosed with melancholia may have been vivid and perhaps intriguing to the jury, but their significance for matters relating to criminal responsibility was often left unexplored in courtroom testimony. According to medical witnesses, it was the diagnosis of delusion itself that established the insanity.

Late in the nineteenth century, melancholia and delusion were drawn together with a telling new element: a criminal compulsion. On trial for assault with intent to murder his wife, Charles Lindus was reported by a local physician to have a history of appearing "vacant," but it was the impression he made on the medical officer of Holloway Prison that revealed the fateful turn his "notelessness" (a "Sussex term for dejection," the medical witness explained) had taken: "The symptoms I spoke of certainly accompany a well-known form of insanity, melancholia, and are consistent with it—melancholia is frequently accompanied by homicidal and suicidal tendencies—delusions are a frequent accompaniment of melancholia—about the most common delusion is that there is a conspiracy . . . that a person is being poisoned by what he is given to eat and drink—I fancy he is very suspicious still with regard to his wife's fidelity—I asked him a question . . . and a wild expression came to his eyes, and evidently he had great difficulty in controlling his feelings."[26]

Traditionally associated with desperation ending in suicide, melancholia by the end of the nineteenth century was increasingly paired with "homicidal tendencies," both in the medical literature and in courtroom testimony. Delusion's role was often characterized as pivotal: the presence of an insistent, intrusive delusive idea came to distinguish the disease of melancholia from the presence of (mere) melancholy states. In the medical testimony cited above, one can spot the moment when the accused migrates from a "noteless," "vacant," inwardly afflicted melancholic state to wild-eyed, uncontrollable mania—it happens at the moment he is asked about his wife. Although it hardly required a preexisting mental ailment to explain an assault with murderous intent, for this defendant, melancholia itself carried the homicidal tendency. The fury released by the physician's question need not even be related to a delusion; the disease itself could carry the afflicted "quite away." Those diagnosed with *raptus melancholicus* were "freed from terrible overwhelming emotion: the act *and* the delusion were the mainspring of his variant of insanity."[27] Thus, a mother who kills beloved infants in a state of despair or a husband who murders an adored spouse in a "paroxysm of frenzy" could find a ready diagnosis in melancholia toward the end of the century.

Although late-nineteenth-century medical literature depicted melancholia with tendencies resulting either in homicide or suicide, defendants at the Old Bailey were diagnosed with a condition that accommodated both. Most often, the accused had killed—his or her children—and was apprehended in the act of trying to end his or her own life, trying to join their children. Many defendants faced the Old Bailey jury then as failed suicides. For female defendants, one begins to find a diagnosis of puerperal melancholia: the actions of "a woman of melancholy temper" were ascribed to reproductive upheaval—confinement, delivery, or lactation. Even when the plea of mental derangement did not succeed, punishment could be commuted. This was not, however, a consistent outcome, nor was it grounded in codified rulings.[28] The jury's receptiveness to a defense grounded in puerperal insanity was doubtless encouraged by the draconian punishment for infanticide, particularly in cases where the pregnancy and delivery had been concealed. Adding the adjective *puerperal* to melancholia in the latter 1800s therefore resulted in a condition doubly evocative: both states carried the potential for impulsive violence. When the two were coupled, the potential needed little provocation to manifest as action: "The prisoner was suffering from puerperal melancholia, a form of disease not infrequently following childbirth . . . persons suffering from that disease are fully aware of what they are doing . . . very often the woman is seen to be affectionate a short time before the act—the suppression of milk is a frequent cause."[29]

The suppression of milk, childbirth, and the incomprehensible switch from nurturing mother to child murderer had been familiar elements in infanticides in general and cases of puerperal mania in particular. Unique to puerperal melancholia, as related in court, was the afflicted's full awareness of the nature and consequences of her action. This was, of course, a far cry from moral insanity or lesion of the will, and yet the diagnoses contain hauntingly similar elements: motiveless crime, clear consciousness, and derangement of sentiments about how one ought to feel toward one's child. In the case of puerperal melancholia, however, there is a clear materialist culprit: suppression of the menses, lactation, and the sheer physical upheaval of delivery, which had apparently unsettled everything but consciousness. As if killing one's child was not horrific enough, the perpetrator committed the act while fully "awake" yet powerless to intrude upon the homicidal tendency. As they had tried to do with moral insanity earlier in the century, medical witnesses challenged the law's insistence that insanity was a matter of cognitive impairment alone, trying to expand the scope of their testimony to implicate hopelessly compromised resources of emotional control and volitional sovereignty. Although medical witnesses were unanimous that puerperal mania did indeed exist, there was no consensus on the presence of unconsciousness. As some witnesses affirmed, "It is quite possible for a woman in such circumstances to be unconscious of her doings at times," begging the question of whether the acts could be described as intentionally chosen.

Medical men who incorporated in their diagnosis of melancholia the law's traditional focus on knowing right from wrong reveal a pivotal moment in courtroom testimony. Jurors heard a physician describing the defendant as "suffering from melancholia, so as not to know the quality of his acts," or as "incapable of understanding the position which he now is in." Although obviously precluded from lodging a defense of puerperal melancholia, male defendants toward the end of the nineteenth century were repeatedly diagnosed as suffering from melancholia, especially when they had killed their own children. While allegedly insane women charged with murder had almost always killed their offspring or their husbands—since puerperal mania might target anyone at hand—men indicted for murder and pleading insanity due to melancholia targeted business associates, social acquaintances, spouses, and occasionally their own children. When the latter were killed, melancholia was frequently the basis of the plea.

In 1908, Henry Walter Popple stood trial for the murder of his two daughters. True to melancholia's suspected tendencies, he intended suicide, but the razor that he had used on his daughters had apparently lost its edge by the time he put it to his own throat. Although described at the police station as not "conscious of his position," he was sufficiently aware of the proceeding to say to the person cutting a bandage but finding the scissors too blunt, "it is only fit for the scrap heap, like my razor." At his eventual trial, the defendant's melancholia was the focus of the testimony offered by William Stoddart, a medical officer at Bethlem Hospital, a rare appearance in the early twentieth century, as asylum doctors had largely been replaced by prison doctors and divisional surgeons assigned to police stations.

> I came to the conclusion that he was suffering from melancholia . . . he had lost the natural instinct of self-preservation . . . [He] told me he had intended to commit suicide for three days and that he did not intend to kill his children until the last minute . . . when he thought he could not leave his wife with the responsibility of raising three starving children—I did not think of the fact that he had killed his own children rather than his stepchildren but it strikes me now that it is a natural instinct to preserve one's own offspring and that instinct had obviously gone—my opinion is that at the time he committed these acts he was prevented by mental disease from controlling his conduct.

Cross-examined to expand on his last point, Stoddart emphasized, "the natural instinct of self-preservation is inborn . . . I consider that a man who takes away the life of those he loves must do it from an insane point of view."[30]

Given melancholia's capacity to encompass delusion, homicidal tendency, and an inability to know right from wrong, it should probably not be surprising to discover that it was sufficiently commodious to accommodate unruly, compelling instincts as well. What was singular about Stoddart's testimony was the conjoining of melancholia with a conception of natural instincts overridden by "mental disease." Such "natural instincts" had not been a part of melancholia before: women who killed their children in states of melancholia—whether simple or puerperal—were thought to have been weakened by some physiological mechanism, implicated in their throwing the children into the Thames or mixing Battles Vermin Killer in with their rice pudding.[31] What had been left as a vague association had now found its expression as a matter of instincts overridden. The destruction of self—not just in one's own suicide but by "taking away the life of those he loves"—places the "instinct for self-preservation" and an insane state of being in curious relation to one another.

Melancholia by the end of the Victorian era now encompassed the "newer" disease states accounting for purposeless, self-destructive action, the latest effort to make sense out of inexplicable crime. It would be a decade before Freud would place instinctual energy at the center of mental torment in *Mourning and Melancholia*: introjected libidinal drives, frustrated at their nonsatisfaction, were turned back on the ego in the form of self-punishment. Aggressive impulses targeting the self and others thus became part of melancholia, overcoming the instinct for self-preservation. At the Old Bailey, jurors were asked to consider the extent to which the instinct to preserve one's being could be "overridden" by this disease.[32]

The Enduring Influence of Delusion

Of all the terms employed by lay witnesses to describe defendant Popple—erratic, passionate, eccentric—it is his wife's characterizing him as delusional that reminds the medical historian of the continuing association of melancholia with fateful error in belief, as well as delusion's diffusion into lay testimony. Earlier in the century, delusion surfaced as the one term that distinguished medical from lay testimony. Although there was little that was particular to expert testimony in delusion—it was hardly an esoteric or mysterious state of derangement—the term itself had been part of a concerted effort in the first decades of the 1800s to claim a unique role in insanity tribunals. The essence of a delusion had been its placement: hidden, recondite, and subterranean. Apothecary to Bethlem John Haslam argued in 1817 that the untrained observer was likely misguided in mistaking surface calm for a full return to sanity. If conversation was extended, however, if the topic turned to "the favorite subject . . . afloat in the mad man's brain, [the observer] will be convinced of the hastiness of his decision."[33]

Given its circumscribed nature and the defendant's misleading outward impression of calm and coherence, delusion's legal significance was somewhat disguised when the condition was referred to as a "partial insanity." There was an unfortunate comparison to lunacy, a state that also alternated delirium with lucid thinking and consequently fell short of the law's criterion of a total derangement—a complete want of memory and understanding. This was the state of affairs Thomas Erskine had confronted at the beginning of the century when he deftly circumnavigated global delirium by placing delusion at the center of Hadfield's insanity. The attorney effectively excised delusion from its long association with melancholia, perhaps hoping in the process to remove "melancholy distempers" from its association with partial insanity. Over the course of the nineteenth century, delusion as partial insanity lost whatever *partial* legal significance it might have had when first articulated in *Hadfield*; common-law judges (and juries) accepted delusion as rising to a sufficient level of debility, precluding an intention to harm because the choice to do evil had been precluded by an inability to know what one was about.

Given the emergence (and threat) of a species of insanity based solely on emotional or volitional chaos, it is not difficult to understand why delusion was the law's preferred term.[34] A profound confusion regarding the true nature of one's acts or their consequences kept the jury's focus on the cognitive capacity of the mind: understanding, intention, and choice. But the nature of this consciousness was curious. Surely the two most public insanity defendants, James Hadfield and Daniel McNaughtan, were fully conscious of their actions. Planned and executed with methodical precision, the construction of their crimes may have been framed by conspiracy or religious delusion, but they well knew there was a gun in their hand. In Hadfield's case, the defendant knew the quality of his act and understood the consequences that would follow his conviction: he *intended* to effect his own execution. No "gauzy" consciousness attended either would-be assassin's act. Their activities were purposefully chosen, although the nature of that choice was ambiguous when "laboring under a delusion." Still, they were not sleepwalking or under the control of a hypnotist. In accepting delusion as the essence of insanity, the court had opened the door to acquitting defendants who had acted when they were not themselves, when they ceased to operate with their customary self-control and discretion.

The years following *McNaughtan* brought a new twist to delusion when the Old Bailey found itself home to a novel variety of mental derangement. It was an age when music hall hypnotists and salon mesmerists brought before the public the frightening display of individuals pursuing physical ends not of their own choosing. In the courtroom, these cultural anomalies were supplied by sleepwalkers, automatons, and a new variation of an old disease: epilepsy. This particular form, *vertige épileptique,* denoted a patient who, following a convulsive seizure, appeared to "return to herself," engaging in physical activity or carrying on a conversation. This seeming return was then followed by a second seizure, after which the person regained consciousness but was completely oblivious to all that had transpired between the two seizures. The *ver-*

tige, or period of absence, strongly resembled the state of somnambulism.[35] Sleepwalking enters the Old Bailey insanity trail in 1859; epileptic vertigo is introduced in 1876.

Holding her daughter in one arm and a bread knife in the other, Elizabeth Carr entered her kitchen intending to slice bread and butter for her daughter's tea. She descended suddenly into a state of *vertige épileptique,* sliced off her daughter's hand instead, and realized with horror what she had done only after coming to, following a second seizure. At her trial, the medical witness abjured even the mention of insanity, casting her mental derangement in terms of this novel diagnosis, imported from Paris: "They are purely automatic acts: the patient is perfectly unconscious . . . the fit comes on with a perfectly quiescent condition . . . the patient may be perfectly sane and fall in that condition, there is neither homicidal or [sic] suicidal tendency, but any act which is begun before the fit may be continued . . . this is not convulsive epilepsy, we have no name for it in English, but the French call it *vertigé* [sic] *épileptique."*[36]

Carr's affliction was not melancholia, which by the 1870s definitely carried homicidal tendencies, nor was it some variant of puerperal mania, which most often figured a horrified but still lucid consciousness as murderous impulses took hold. Carr shared with a cohort of absent, sleepwalking, or otherwise "missing" defendants a self that was discontinuous from her habitual mental state. This latest variation in deranged functioning engaged the law's conception of the person as a sentient being capable of maintaining a consistent consciousness. Intrigued with how consciousness and identity were linked, Locke observed, "as far as this consciousness can be extended backwards to any past action or thought, so far reaches the identity of the person."[37] Consciousness therefore justifies God's (and man's) censure: rewards or punishments were merited because the person was conscious of having done an act. This is all perfectly applicable to consciously chosen crime, committed by a sentient—that is, a consistent—human being. But just as Locke observed that punishing a person for actions done while asleep was "no more right" than punishing a brother for what his twin had done, the Old Bailey confronted the conundrum with the idea of a second self—active and criminal—that acted while its host was unconscious and absent.

It may not seem immediately apparent how delusion featured in courtroom debate concerning missing or "second" selves, but a medical term does not attain the distinction of being the most frequently invoked diagnosis throughout a century marked by wildly different notions of insanity without being adaptable. Noted author and lecturer Thomas Mayo appeared at the Old Bailey to comment upon a defendant's delusion that he was passing urine through his anus and would eventually drown one night. Although he initially chose to refer to the defendant's condition as hypochondriasis rather than delusion, the defense attorney read from the author's own book: "In dealing with the grounds which I recently considered, for imputing insane delirium—namely the presence of inconsecutiveness of thought in cases of certain delusions . . . each of these elements throws light on the other [allowing the *medical witness* to] . . . arrange his evidence . . . to have incoherency and inconsecutiveness exist there is little difficulty—continual inconsecutiveness I believe involved the presence of morbid delusions, this is sure to produce them."[38]

Mayo's testimony is important for having introduced the concept of inconsecutiveness not only into a medical text but into medical testimony. The Old Bailey was familiar with delusion in the context of a conspiracy; it had heard from defendants who spoke of having objects inside the body (from engines to serpents) or of being frightened by the devil into killing their children before he dragged them down to hell. But in the decade following Mc-Naughtan's acquittal on the grounds of a persecution delusion, Old Bailey juries were presented with defendants whose criminal selves were distinctly discontinuous with their sane selves. This dual state had always been a part of delusion as partial insanity: an ostensibly sane person, when the "fatal string" was pulled, in Haslam's language, became "as mad as any there are in Bedlam." During the years when sleepwalkers and automatons wandered into the London courtroom, the delusional wandered in right along with them, their uncharacteristic, unknown selves attributed not to epilepsy or somnambulism but to a consuming obsessional belief. If consistency of consciousness links individuals to their acts and both to culpability, finding their actions blameworthy would prove to be a challenge.

Perhaps owing to its adaptive, staying power in the courtroom, as well as to unqualified pronouncements from the bench that it was indeed the true nature of insanity, delusion (divorced from its mooring in melancholia) enjoyed pride of place in legal circles straight through the nineteenth century. Medical writers were not willing to elide delusion with *all* insanity, however; there were too many examples of homicides committed by persons with a "vague fear or distress, dejected, sleepless, and feeling themselves overladen with the heavy burden of their miserable lives . . . they manifest no actual delusion."[39] The author of these sentiments, Henry Maudsley, continued:

> We are in much need of a term to denote insane feelings, which shall carry as distinct a meaning in the moral sphere, convey as definite a notion of mental derangement, as does the word delusion when applied to an insane idea. Delusion is a term which is understood by lawyers to mark insanity: who will help [legal] understandings by the invention of a term which, applied to the more fundamental mental conditions of insane feelings . . . [will] enable them to realize and talk of such states? The right word is always a power; it gives definiteness to conception, and makes action more clear; and it would make a mighty difference if the fit word . . . to denote insane feeling could be found and take its place in the vocabulary.[40]

Maudsley was in no way abjuring the power of delusory ideas, freely admitting that some acts are done "in consequence of a delusion"—but he forcefully reserved space in the medical conceptions and *vocabulary* for "insane feelings" short of intellectual confusion. Thus he describes an impulse to kill in which "the deed of violence is, as it were, an explosion of it, an uncontrollable convulsion energy; knowing not what he is doing, he kills someone, friend or fancied enemy, or perhaps an entire stranger."[41] Beyond the need to appreciate the autonomous role of deranged passions, a reliance on delusion as the criterion for (legal) insanity invited a host of problems, not least Erskine's conviction that a connection between the crime and the delusion had to be manifest. Maudsley was not alone to ask: What does it mean to insist that a sane relation exists between an admittedly insane state and a crime?

Growing disquiet in medical circles was prompted by the increasingly unanimous opinion among jurists in print and prosecutors in court that delusion was the "essence" of insanity.[42] In part, this opinion was prompted by the medical man's refusal to be drawn out on the question of defining insanity; medical witnesses warned each other of this tactic on the pages of their professional journals. But there was the corresponding belief that a reliance on delusion eclipsed the influence of affect in mental derangement. One did not have to subscribe to Prichard's moral insanity, Georget's lesion of the will, or the blind force of irresistible impulse to see how limiting an insanity restricted to deranged intellects would be. Pinel's work had introduced a generation of medical theorists (and witnesses) to forms of madness in which the afflicted experienced no derangement of thought, no confusion, no delirium. For all his attention to delusion in the area of partial insanity, Maudsley was not convinced that all forms of insanity "required" delusion, a sentiment shared by other medical authors of his day.

A further hesitation to enshrine delusion in medical writing, if not in court, was the law's parallel employment of consciousness in arriving at assigning levels of culpability. Someone who understood the nature of what he was doing and the likely consequences retained the capacity of choice: he could *choose* to do evil. The deluded person, fatefully confused regarding the nature and likely result of his or her act, was not held to be blameworthy because he or she lacked a capacity to choose. But this conception presupposed that human behavior was pursued, in the main, at the conscious level. How much of one's activity, medical writers questioned, operated at the unconscious level? The mind takes in countless bits of information, sorts them, and stores them all in a sequence beyond the individual's conscious awareness. And beyond his conscious will, as well. The closest the sane come to this movement of ideas and sentiments is in a dreaming state. While dreaming one is gauzily conscious of ideas but powerless to intrude upon the narrative unfolding and change it to suit our fears and desires. The life of the insane, alienists contended in the late Victorian era, is "real dreaming"; they cannot intrude upon the sequence of thoughts and are unable to recognize distorted reality.

This inability, after all, was the nature of delusion. It was not the mere existence of a fantasy or an overwhelming fear—fantasies and fears are experienced by the sane as well—but the inability to *intrude* upon the belief, to see it for what it was. The will rarely appears in medical writing, certainly not with the vulnerability to a lesion (except among the followers of Georget), but few medical theorists did not recognize the incapacity to exercise control in the throes of delusion. For the deluded, some defect in the ability to evaluate, to judge, and to dispense with conspiratorial ideas or hypochondriacal fears had taken hold. When a medical witness in 1843 referred to the delusional defendant as having "lost his moral liberty," he was drawing the jury's attention to the accused's inability to resist the act impelled by delusion; he had ceased to exist as a moral person. Even without the use of such a haunting phrase, however, other medical witnesses throughout the century had drawn attention to the power of the cognitive defect in producing the crime. Few witnesses invited the jury "in" to the defendant's failure to exercise self-control at the level of cerebration, although medical authors enthusiastically took up this theme.

From its initial home in brooding melancholia at the dawn of the nineteenth century, to its incorporation into monomania and forms of circular insanity in the middle of the 1800s, to its eventual coupling with an instinctually homicidal melancholia at the beginning of the twentieth century, delusion had been the one constant element in medical testimony and medical writing from 1800 forward. Its place in medical theory had been secured through twenty-five centuries of a remarkably consistent definition of melancholia—the dejected mood, the head in the hands—but also the preoccupying idea that accompanied the sorrow and might well have animated it. Mid-eighteenth-century authors focused increasingly on variations in mental disturbance, isolating as one form a "notional" insanity: a condition hidden from the untrained eye and partial only in that its consequent global delirium when engaged was limited to particular episodes.

In 1800, the first of many defense attorneys—themselves new arrivals in common-law courts—enlisted delusion and its medical interlocutors to argue the helplessness of the defendant. The imagery employed by the new expert witnesses was unequivocal regarding delusion's influence. Described as besieged with fears of conspiracy, or of a wife's infidelity, or of reptiles in one's stomach, medical men characterized the deluded as "under a strange, morbid impulse," or an "uncontrollable instinct to take someone's life," or "incapable of controlling [their] actions by reason." There was little need for lesion of the will in medical testimony; delusion could easily house both demented belief and an overpowering need to act.

As the nineteenth century witnessed delusion's easy elision with a host of new and sometimes returning ailments, it became clear that the common law's insistence that the mental element needed for ascribing culpability (a will to harm) grew increasingly problematic as medical theorizing became more expansive. The law was fully prepared to acquit by insanity behavior animated by conspiratorial beliefs or unwarranted and outlandish suspicions "that no sane man would accept." Jurists had tried to hold the line at moral insanity, and yet many insanity trials at the Old Bailey turned on the features if not the diagnosis of Prichard's neologism: motiveless crime, perfectly purposeless destruction of beloved family members, murders that seemed to leave the accused every bit the victim of the deranged, diseased sentiment that revealed no lapse in consciousness or delusion. Juries do not need to discern motive to find intent, but they do need to be able to connect the deed to *something*. Sentiments, feelings, and affections were very much a part of any Londoner's folk psychology; they were also increasingly a part of nineteenth-century medical psychology. Without invoking the legally toxic diagnoses of moral insanity and irresistible impulse, medical witnesses were able to incorporate the features of emotional and volitional chaos by coupling delusion with melancholia and mania, all three enjoying a pedigree in common culture and the common law, although their meanings had altered to account for the inexplicable.

CHAPTER THREE

When Practitioners Become Professionals

The Alienists' Claim to Knowledge

New York born and Edinburgh educated, Dr. Joseph Hart Meyers found employment in London as physician to the Hospital for German and Dutch Jews. Among his patients was John Glover, whom Hart Meyers described as suffering "a great delirium; he had every symptom of insanity . . . a perfect fatuity, absolute fatuity," at his 1789 trial for theft. After explaining the grounds for diagnosing "absolute fatuity," the physician was asked by the judge, "Were you able from attending him for a week after his fever left him, to form any judgment whether his disorder was of a permanent nature or not?" Given that only a total, permanent degree of insanity carried exculpatory value, Hart Myers's response was critical: "From his having been deemed incurable by other professional men, I was convinced his disorder would not yield to treatment . . . he had a ticket to St. Luke's, to which I recommended him." The other professional men the witness referred to were present at the trial. Drs. Benjamin and Daniel Jacob de Castro were also émigrés to England and had become acquainted with the defendant after his friends asked them to provide medical relief. As one of the de Castro brothers testified, "I looked back to my books . . . I saw him in a state of melancholy so late as February, I went to carry some charity to him." The jury returned a not guilty verdict and was informed by the other brother: "I shall take care of him, he shall lie in close confinement; it is out of foolish humanity to let him go at large; I shall certainly take care that he is either put into Bethlem, St. Luke's or a private madhouse."[1]

A century later, another Old Bailey jury considered an insanity plea. Both cases featured medical men advising the jury of their professional opinion, and both ended with a verdict that found the defendant not responsible for the crime. The verdict in the later trial carried more severe consequences than the (full) acquittal in the eighteenth-century case, as the offense in the later case was murder, not theft. During the hundred years between the cases, the plea of insanity had become more likely to surface in personal rather than property offenses, a significant change given the preponderance of suspected thieves raising the insanity plea before Robert Peel's reforms beginning in the 1820s. Although both trials featured medical witnesses, the diagnoses proffered in the later case reveal something beyond *delirium* for the jury to consider. The occupational backgrounds of the later medical witnesses also reflect a policy decision that placed physicians and surgeons in prisons, jails, and, most important of all, police stations.

Given these two developments—increasingly expansive diagnoses introduced into testimony and the changing professional affiliation of the witnesses—one wonders about the influence of social setting in the introduction of novel and adventurously described species of madness for the common law to consider: "[H]e suffered very much from neuralgia, giddiness and headache, they are all nervous symptoms." When asked by the judge to elaborate on the symptoms, the physician said that the defendant had been "falling down unconscious" and suffering from "a loss of memory," due to "a type of epilepsy, not by any means well marked." Medical testimony had moved beyond citing the manifest madness of "absolute fatuity" to describing unconsciousness, loss of memory, and epilepsy. Medical witnesses no longer necessarily had an informal or private prior acquaintance with the defendant but now based their knowledge of the accused on an encounter precipitated by the crime itself. As was apparent to judge, jury, and readers of the *OBSP*, expert testimony bearing on insanity was fast becoming the province of medical men in the employ of the state, whose experiences informed a mental medical *gaze* all its own, an acquaintance that encouraged innovative turns in medical diagnoses.

In the second case, for example, the surgeon to Newgate Gaol and the physician to St. Luke's Hospital reported having received a subpoena from the solicitor to the Treasury to attend the trial. Rather than recount their treatment of or social acquaintance with the individual defendant on trial as the grounds for their inferences, the surgeon and the physician referred to having made a "special study" of insanity: "I know from my own large experience of epilepsy in hospitals where patients suffer from *petit-mal* the friends and the patients themselves always speak of the attack as faintness or giddiness." Questioned by the judge to expand on the defendant's conversation in jail, the surgeon asserted, "he said that something came over him which compelled him to commit this crime . . . I had no reason to suppose he was not speaking the truth, he said it was as if it was a dream—he always expressed himself as being very fond of his family."[2] The verdict that followed resembled in some ways the earlier finding—a finding of nonresponsibility—but in the latter case, there would be no "interested parties" to ensure some sort of confinement. In 1889, defendants found insane were removed for an indefinite period of commitment to Broadmoor.

The years that separate these two trials witnessed the arrival of medicine as a profession and increasingly voluble courtroom claims to expert knowledge. A madhouse superintendent had been in evidence from the first insanity trials, as were private practitioners and medically qualified acquaintances of the accused who could report casual impressions of mood change and odd, uncharacteristic antics.[3] Their testimony differed little from the medically "unqualified" neighbors who were, after all, in a better position to report the defendant's habitual behavior.[4] What is remarkable in the eighteenth-century medical man's testimony is its unremarkable nature—his use of everyday language and thoroughly familiar imagery rather than specialized diagnostic terms. But more than language and abstruse diagnosis would define the substance and phrasing of an assertively self-confident nineteenth-century forensic-psychiatric witness. There would need to be a claim to privileged knowledge itself, and that would require the gathering together of heretofore discrete categories of medical practitioners whose jealous gate-keeping of their territorial preserves was matched only by their preference for constancy over change. From 1789 to 1889 however, there would be nothing so constant as change.

What Kind of Doctor?

Although the first medical witness to appear at an Old Bailey insanity trial to claim madness as a medical condition was indeed a physician, he might just as easily been a surgeon or an apothecary. As historians of medicine have long maintained, there was no unified medical profession in the eighteenth century. Only with the Medical Registration Act of 1858 was there a delineation of a medical profession with recognized licensing; a practitioner required specific credentials to be included in the Register. The Act, however, functioned more to exclude the unlicensed than to define the professional qualifications of the recognized medical professional.[5] It is a stretch even to use the term *community* to characterize medical men before 1858. One finds instead a fractious and competitive array of gentlemen doctors schooled in "physic" in ancient universities, surgeons learning their craft by apprenticeship, general practitioners trained in both private medical schools and public hospitals, and finally apothecaries, who did not have a royal society of their own until the early nineteenth century.

With such an expansive range in education—training gained at elite universities, on-the-job training at the table of a Mr. Saw Bones, and tricks of the trade gained by apprenticeship to herbalists—is it any wonder that parliamentary action was required to authorize the compiling of a more or less comprehensive register of credentialed practitioners? Just as the educational and experiential backgrounds of medical men could vary in mid-eighteenth to mid-nineteenth-century England, a practitioner's familiarity and sustained interaction with the mentally distracted could be just as diverse, creating a population of mad-doctors whose testimony in a criminal court asserted the possession of unique knowledge gained through sustained study of medical texts, through hospital rounds, through supervision in a jail or a prison, or through a post as health officer of a large public asylum. Given the breadth of possible backgrounds for those in both general and mental medicine, one can hardly be surprised that the proffered diagnoses, the grounds asserted for their selection, and the varied therapeutic methods were themselves maddeningly diverse.[6]

At the top of the hierarchy of practitioners were physicians, gentlemen who completed a course of study at a university but who could only ascend to fellowship in the Royal College of Physicians with a degree from Oxford or Cambridge.[7] It is worth noting that Dr. Hart Meyers, testifying in 1789, received his degree from the University of Edinburgh. As a Jew, he was excluded from attending Oxbridge because of the long-standing requirement that students take an oath affirming the sovereignty of the Church of England. Jewish physicians, along with Roman Catholics, religious dissenters, and atheists, sought medical studies therefore in continental Europe and in Edinburgh and Glasgow. Beyond religious tolerance, Edinburgh offered aspiring physicians the opportunity to attend anatomical lectures offered by Alexander Munro. As the "queen of the sciences," anatomy and its study of nerves had been of interest to medical writers since at least the publication of Thomas Willis's seventeenth-century foundational writings in "neurologie." His anatomical inquiry was greatly embellished by Charles Bell, whose own work revealed nerves to be bundles of filaments performing discrete functions with distinct connections to the spinal column.[8]

But where were aspiring neurologists—and surgeons—to learn basic science? London lacked the institutional structure of a major university, and laboratory science remained something of an avocation among Oxbridge dons whose efforts were devoted to producing medical gentlemen, schooled in classical liberal arts.[9] The dearth of practical schools for medicine in the nation's metropolis provided the impetus for enterprising practitioners, most notably surgeons, to create private medical academies. In time, large metropolitan hospitals, beginning with Westminster Hospital in 1719 and growing to include five more major establishments after 1815, supplemented private instruction in anatomy and medicine, providing students sustained exposure to patients, mostly the poor of London.[10] Through ward rounds and outpatient treatment, medical practitioners—physicians and surgeons alike—gained critical clinical experience.

These novel institutions in the urban landscape were called hospitals, but their precise medical mission was ambiguous. They were establishments designed for the care of the short-term sick; their role in curing and treatment may seem unproblematic to the modern ear, as one hears *hospital* and immediately thinks of cure. Boards of governors of metropolitan hospitals, however, were anxious that medical training did not impede the care of patients.[11] These early teaching hospitals remained, however, the one resource where medical practitioners could gain clinical experience. Throughout the nineteenth century, Oxbridge lacked any hospital or clinic sufficiently large to offer experience with patients; aspiring doctors needed to gain two years of clinical training in London and then return to the university for the qualifying exam.[12]

Although hospital boards might have been less than enthusiastic at the prospect of their charity wards being turned into clinics of medical instruction, the widespread cultural embrace of science as the path to knowledge ensured medicine's role in the public health of the city. Following the Enlightenment, advancement through scientific learning held out the promise for ordering the social—as well as the natural—world.[13] Basic advances in anatomy, physiology, and chemistry could be translated into progressive efforts to ensure the health of the body as well as the city. Keenly disposed to esteem the pursuit of scientific knowledge, Victorians welcomed medical science's claims to authority.[14] To the historian of medicine, however, it is abundantly clear that translating bench science into clinical intervention was not a straightforward exercise.[15] Exactly *how* medical patients benefitted from laboratory science was unclear and was rarely queried.

Still, it was vital for medical practitioners—and their instructors—to clothe their work in the mantle of science if their profession was to be distinguished from the mountebanks competing for patients. Even when qualified to be listed in the *Register,* medical men were never free from competition; mesmerists, hypnotists, and herbalists vied for clients in the marketplace of ameliorative cures. Licensed medical practitioners may have satisfied the qualifications of the royal medical colleges or a hospital medical school, but they received no medical monopoly along with the degree. Inclusion in the *Register*, then, only identified the specific practitioner as having received the appropriate credential; it did not exclude unlicensed quacks from plying their trade.[16]

Beneath the physician in social standing—at least in the eyes of the elite medical practitioner, if not necessarily in the eyes of the ailing Londoner—were surgeons and apothecaries. Although apprenticeship was the main vehicle for their training, surgeons often attended lectures at universities and especially at private medical schools. London's most successful eighteenth-century instructional entrepreneur, William Hunter, employed techniques gained by studying dissection in Paris to open his own private anatomy school in 1746.[17] Only a year earlier, surgeons had severed their tie to barbers and begun a long process of encouraging their brethren skilled in treating broken limbs, lancing abscesses, and bandaging to think of themselves as scientific practitioners. To physicians, trained to consider the internal workings of the patients' organs and physiology, surgeons were rightfully restricted to dealing with the external, to treating physical injury or abscess, discernible by the senses. But to ambitious surgeons, possessed with a degree of acquaintance with anatomy that made them unique among medical practitioners, any association of their craft with a trade was demeaning. Still, for all these practitioners' mastery of anatomical knowledge and newly acquired surgical skill, before the advent of anesthesia and antiseptic surgical conditions, certain parts of the body—arguably the most important ones—were beyond surgical intervention. Opening the abdomen, chest cavity, or head was off-limits, limiting the surgeons' ability to translate asserted knowledge and professed skill into demonstrable results.[18]

In time, surgeons succeeded in receiving a royal charter for a medical corporation of their own in 1800. Fifteen years later, apothecaries (whose role in the medical field was supposedly restricted to the mixing of ingredients ordered by the physician) also secured a royal charter. The Apothecary Act of 1815 recognized a formal means of licensing apothecaries, although they had long been in the practice of prescribing (and then mixing) remedies without first consulting with a physician.[19]

What Kind of Mad-Doctor?

Although metropolitan hospitals offered the first sustained point of contact with groups of patients that would aid in developing classification of diseases and subsequent variations in medical treatment, those establishments had been conceived as a means of caring for persons suffering acute or sudden ailments.[20] Not admitted were the long-term sick, the elderly, or the mentally deranged.[21] England, of course, had a long history of housing the mad; Bethlehem Hospital (Bethlem) was founded in 1247 and was joined by St. Luke's in 1751.

The late 1700s also witnessed a private trade in accommodating lunacy that featured medical men (and others) as proprietors of small madhouses —a cottage industry of sorts—in which they housed inconvenient relatives and annoying village residents.[22] Of the many professional struggles faced by physicians, surgeons, and apothecaries in establishing themselves as rightful caretakers of the mad, fixing the medical qualification as a prerequisite for madhouse keeping was among the first and certainly the most vexing. There was nothing, after all, self-evidently *medical* in the proposed treatment—or the etiology—of mental derangement. Religious leaders or compassionate, socially minded persons of any ilk could put themselves forward as caring, thoughtful minders. Scandals prompted by parliamentary inquiries into the care patients received at Bethlem kept the question alive: What exactly did medical supervision of the mad amount to?[23]

A century earlier, it had been Parliament that had helped to create a cultural acceptance of medicine's role in the care of the deranged. Indeed, the relationship between the state and the specialty that would much later come to be called psychiatry would go far beyond parliamentary recognition of the various medical corporations of all three divisions of medical practitioners. Beginning in 1774 with a requirement that the Royal College of Physicians thenceforth be charged with inspecting madhouses, a series of legislative measures strategically placed medical men in the position of assessing the quality of care in establishments that housed the mad.[24] The Madhouse Act of 1828, for example, required every asylum to receive weekly visits from a medical practitioner. If more than one hundred madmen were housed, the onsite presence of a medical officer was required. This level of governmental authority was extended to the criminal courts: medical examination of offenders charged with capital crimes was not made official until 1864, although almost a hundred years earlier, prison doctors were regularly employed to interview defendants awaiting trial whom the courts believed might be contemplating an insanity plea. This informal practice was replaced by an order from the Solicitor to the Treasury to conduct pretrial interviews.[25]

A specialty, perhaps the first of English medical specialties, was emerging with the active participation of the state. Certainly, there were other early forms of expertise claimed in medical practice—obstetrics and gynecology come quickly to mind—that invited practitioners to narrow their practice, in part, one suspects, to lay claim to possessing unique knowledge and skill. But these practices were not subject to regular parliamentary scrutiny, and eventually medical practitioners enjoyed a monopoly as private madhouses operated by lay persons were actively discouraged in the nineteenth century. What Parliament did not specify was the precise qualification the medical officer need obtain—whether he needed to be physician, surgeon, or apothecary. All three were in evidence in the emerging mad-doctor trade.

And all three were present in another, more public forum, that would offer the opportunity to lay claim to professional arrival. With the appearance of John Monro in the trial of Earl Ferrers, the madhouse superintendent became a feature of insanity trials at the Old Bailey. He was followed in time by the apothecary to Bethlem, John Haslam, and the surgeon to Newgate Gaol, Gilbert McMurdo, by far the most frequently appearing medical man in insanity trials up to *McNaughtan*. Claims to professional insight did not come from an understanding of mental (or brain) disease qua disease; it derived instead from supervision of the deranged in asylums, jails, or prisons. Testimony beginning with "Among my 850 patients at Hanwell Asylum," or "In many of the cases of insanity we see in the prison," underscored the experiential credential claimed by medical men as grounds for their professional opinion.[26] Systemic instruction in mental psychology would only appear in the second half of the nineteenth century, decades after the medical witness had become a fixed feature in the trial. A century before, however, it was the sustained familiarity gained in prisons and asylums that served to legitimate claims to unique knowledge.

Although prisons and jails afforded medical men numerous opportunities to observe and converse with the putative mad, there was little doubt that asylum superintendence afforded the most sustained contact with the mentally troubled. Still, the size of these institutions—Hanwell alone housed more than eight hundred patients by the time its superintendent testified at the Old Bailey in 1840—transformed medical supervision into an administrative function, as revealed in the professional association the asylums generated. This association—complete with its own journal—revealed how considerations of proper and orderly administration could eclipse attention to the medical management of the hospitalized. Whatever motivation these medical officers shared regarding treatment and cure, they had to first confront the daily challenge of installing order, routine, and sanitary conditions among a population for whom personal hygiene was a struggle. A setting whose exigencies would test even the most benevolent mad-doctor cum superintendent, the large-scale county asylum challenged administrators who wanted to duplicate the educational and training function that had come to define the nineteenth-century urban hospital. By placing asylums away from metropolitan areas in order to remove the deranged from the pressures of congested living, however, the institutions also had removed asylum medical men from the scientific activity pursued in the metropolitan hospital.

In giving medical men a monopoly over the lives of the mad, therefore, the state had also segregated the mad-doctor from Victorian medicine.[27] Mad-doctors had long struggled against popular perceptions that they were too ready to aid greedy relatives in extracting inheritances before their time. They would now have to confront their brethren in the medical community who were suspicious of specialization in general and in particular one that countenanced the "artificial construct . . . [of a] . . . scheme of mind."[28]

The Clash over Body or Mind

Although asylum work was not known for occasioning systematic study of mental patients, efforts to employ science to decipher an organic basis for mental derangement were not unknown. The asylum was often home to a medical specialist who owed his interest in madness not to defects of emotion or volition but to physical alteration of the nerves. As a nervous disease, madness was the proper sphere for medical men interested in neural function, starting with Thomas Willis and Charles Bell and continuing into the time of asylum construction that witnessed the writings of Thomas Laycock, William B. Carpenter, and James Crichton-Browne. Although they focused on nerves, filaments, and the spinal cord, neurologists (scientists who made the nerves their special study) were inevitably drawn into debate concerning the necessary connections between aberrant physiology and mental derangement. Since the Enlightenment, neurologists increasingly had invoked the nervous system in theorizing about melancholia, hysteria, and hypochondria.[29] Although not experienced in treating the insane, neurologists often lectured on medical psychology.

In many ways, the ease with which neurologists entered debates about the nature of insanity began with their sharing space with alienists in the asylum, which could serve as the professional launching pad for both specialists in the nature of madness. Alienists closely monitored and classified patients; neurologists performed autopsies in search of a lesion or other anatomical abnormality that the insane were believed to manifest. Willis had probably served as the exemplar when he anatomized the brains and nervous systems of executed felons. Asylum research, including cortical stimulation to discern localized brain functions, was pursued from 1866 to 1876 at the West Riding Lunatic Asylum under the supervision of physician Crichton-Browne, who invited neurologists and fellow alienists to the institution to foster research and stimulate cooperative inquiry into the brain and behavior.[30] On paper, the neurologist and the alienist shared obvious common interests and a parallel division of labor: one investigated the brain and the "why" of neural functioning, the other, emotional derangement and aberrant behavior. Indeed, it was sometimes not clear where neurology left off and alienism began. But always lingering just below the surface of professional comity was the looming question of *will*; at what point does the research on the brain and neural pathways eclipse the medical psychologists' belief that patients must, in the end, be able to respond to reason and effect a change in their own functioning?[31] Psychophysical parallelism had long respected the mind's independence from the body—its capacity to retain its integrity, to remain "untarnished." As the secular embodiment of the soul, the mind remained inviolate, eternal.[32]

Even as nineteenth-century medical psychologists and others recoiled at restrictively materialist renderings of human behavior—objecting when intentional behavior was reduced to (mere) sensory and motor responses— the belief remained that mental derangement must be expressing some alteration in the nervous system. That the connection between the two had yet eluded detection was freely acknowledged, and at times there were even expressions of resignation: "Why this link is apparent we do not know and may never know."[33] Those who adhered to belief in the mind's parallel sovereignty maintained that the mind, though not *itself* diseased, was compelled to work through a defective organ—the brain—resulting in impaired emotion or compromised volition.[34] Some of the more prominent voices within medicine, particularly those alienists hoping to gain acceptance among their brethren in general practice, abjured any discussion of the mind, dismissing its existence as metaphysical voodoo. With his characteristic approach to reasoned debate, Henry Maudsley observed, "No one whose opinion is of any value pretends now that [the phenomena of insanity] are anything more than deranged functions of the supreme nervous centers of the body." These understandings had allowed medicine to free itself from the "bondage of false theology and mischievous metaphysics."[35]

Other alienists were not so sure. Even so thoroughgoing a materialist as Crichton-Browne was not willing to relinquish the will as the central guiding agent of the personality.[36] The ability to hold both beliefs—that powerful reflexes and impulses acted upon a person without his or her conscious awareness *and* also that the same person had an intangible, metaphysical will, capable of reigning in untoward impulses and exercising rational control— seems a tall order, but to Crichton-Browne and others in his circle, believing in both was not impossible. After all, phrenology—clearly the most materialist conception of human character and difference—had reserved a prominent role for some force that could organize twenty-seven disparate functions and provide guidance in functioning and behavior. But even the acknowledgment of the existence of such a mysterious force was not enough to mollify phrenology's critics who recoiled at human functioning devoid of will, which they saw as an ungodly conception of human behavior, whatever place might be allotted for the nonorganic guiding agent.[37]

The medical elite's rejection of a physiological rendering of the mind would not last the century. Popular and scientific acceptance of degeneration and evolutionary theory placed biology at the center of abnormal behavior, whether the malefactor was criminal, epileptic, or insane.[38] In embracing evolutionary theory, medical men with a growing specialization in madness sought to reinforce their identification as men of science. Their claim to be the legitimate caretakers of the mad was never free from dispute; they could not identify a consistent etiology of madness, isolate a common lesion, nor claim success at treatment. Prevailing beliefs in failed evolution and doomed hereditary disposition were not, however, without some good news for mad-doctors supervising asylums. Their conspicuous failure to intervene successfully in the course of mental derangement could be attributed to natural forces beyond human control. Even so, it meant assuming a posture of administrative resignation rather than professional optimism. Furthermore, a full-throated endorsement of biology's cruel sentence threatened a much larger issue: if insanity was, at basis, a nervous disease, what distinguished the knowledge claims of medical psychology from basic neurology?[39] What qualified alienists rather than the clergy or moral philosophers to be the rightful caretakers of the mad? One question predominated: What precisely defined extravagant behavior or sustained dejection as medical illness?

To Name a Disease

By the early nineteenth century, oral testimony in front of a jury was firmly established as the preferred route for evidence to enter the jury's consideration and subsequent deliberation. When the court heard expert evidence, the defining element would be the medical man's diagnosis: how symptoms and the course of illness revealed to the skilled observer what species of madness possessed the putatively insane defendant. Similar to all witnesses' testimony, the mad-doctor's evidence was based on the sensory mechanisms of the observer—his sight, his hearing, perhaps even his touch. A further element was called into service by the classifier of a mental impairment, however; the mental pathologist had to concern himself not only with physical alterations of the body but with immaterial forces as well.

Given the range in educational backgrounds of practitioners in eighteenth- and nineteenth-century medicine, it would have been remarkable indeed if their disparate experiences had resulted in a consistent classification scheme of mental diseases. Medical men schooled in universities practiced in the same city as those trained in private medical schools or through apprenticeship, at home and abroad. They also witnessed during this time the waning influence of humoral theory and the increasing academic opinion that the nervous system held the answers to questions about aberrant behavioral functioning and mental processing. To this mix was added changes in descriptive psychopathology emerging from large-scale sequestering of the mad from other social deviants, a development that gathered momentum with the creation of county asylums in the first half of the nineteenth century.[40] By the 1840s, asylum work was fast becoming the predominant starting point for a career in mental medicine, with an attendant opening up of classification that broke with inherited categories of a century earlier.[41]

William Cullen's pioneering work in identifying and isolating nerves delineated the nervous system's role in regulating the fundamental processes of organic life: respiration, circulation, and digestion.[42] And yet, when considering the determining influence of the most dominant organ, the brain, Cullen retained traditional medieval categories of will, memory, imagination, and perception, steadfastly maintaining that those functions could not be understood mechanically. For some medical men, this belief originated in religious conviction: it was nothing short of blasphemy to conceive of human behavior as the result of nervous filaments and nonthinking reflexes. Leaving considerations of the will and reason aside, Cullen and his fellow nosologists based disease classification on symptoms and on the sequence of symptoms evident in physiological disturbance.

The names given to various types of nervous disease drew upon the long familiar categories of mania and melancholia in use since antiquity. Also represented in disease classifications was lunacy, a state of derangement current since at least medieval England.[43] Despite names being given to recognizable types, insanity was most often conceived to be a global delirium—mania and insanity were used interchangeably to denote the descent into madness. Still, the derangement was perceived not as having its own characteristics but as departing from the patient's conventional state of health. Attention was paid more to restoring his proper balance rather than curing him of a particular disease. According to medical historian Christopher Lawrence, this perspective changed in the nineteenth century, when medical men "developed a language for situating all people in relation to one another . . . measuring their deviation from the normal."[44] These deviations in time came to occupy their own space in the landscape of cultural perception.

It is in this regard that madhouse keeping was integral to the development of refinements in the classification of mental impairment. Parliament's role in this process cannot be overemphasized. As historian William Bynum has maintained, with the exception of public health, no other medical specialty has received as much legal attention and regulation as madhouse keeping, in particular, and psychological medicine by extension. Given the social and monetary consequences that could follow commitment to an asylum, Parliament, especially at the end of the eighteenth century, turned its attention to private asylums and the protocol for relatives stashing away an inconvenient, prosperous relation. Early in the next century, the Parliamentary Inquiry of 1815–16 exposed the insalubrious conditions found in Bethlem, prompting the dismissal of its well-known apothecary, John Haslam. To ensure standards of health and humane care, government action regulating madhouses stipulated that they be visited regularly by a medical practitioner and that any institution housing more than one hundred inhabitants must appoint a medical officer. Mandated along with regular medical supervision was the daily record of each inmate's progress.[45]

According to German Berrios, one can look to this newly mandated regimen of record keeping and observation over time as the impetus for the qualitative change in descriptive psychopathology; separation of "acute" from "chronic" cases would eventually follow. Asylum-based experience could also be seen in Pinel's departure from conceptions of insanity dating to Locke, which considered madness a question of cognitive impairment (alone). Citing his experience with patients at the Bicêtre and the Salpêtrière, Pinel proffered his own formulation, *manie sans délire*, to characterize the disease that described the lived experience of the population he observed daily: a manic derangement unaccompanied by delirium or delusion. His patients suffered no confusion but rather an abstract, autonomous force that had reportedly carried the afflicted "quite away." In time, emotional and volitional insanities would become the focus of medical texts and, tellingly for present purposes, medical testimony. From the late eighteenth through the nineteenth centuries, the point of contact giving form and substance to these innovative diagnoses expanded to include not only asylum supervision but medicine's growing presence at the arrest stage, in prison prior to trial, and, of course, during the criminal prosecution itself.

The history of forensic psychiatry is first and foremost the history of law: creating a place of expert opinion in the courtroom was the work of ambitious medical practitioners, eager to claim knowledge and legitimacy in the evolving market in health and personal services in London, as well as ambitious defense advocates and attorneys for the prosecution. From 1760 to 1913, medical practitioners appeared on both sides of the courtroom, often as a result of a subpoena (sent by the Solicitor to the Treasury as administrator of the criminal courts) or in their capacity as prison doctors or jail surgeons. Just as the mandated record keeping had stimulated medical interest in discriminating separate species of madness and speculating on the natural course of these discrete ailments within the population of asylum internees, the government's employment of medical men in jails, police stations, and prisons drew the medical gaze increasingly to elements in the crime commission itself: the social relations between the parties, the troubling absence of motive, the indifferent, indeed cavalier, attitude evinced by the alleged perpetrator immediately after the crime. Over time and over the participation of generations of forensic psychiatrists in the London courtroom, one sees a change from their attempting to explain the crime by the insanity to their discerning the presence of insanity itself by the inexplicability of the circumstances surrounding or immediately following the crime.

From Medical Practitioner to Medical Witness

Even if one were to argue that the state's increasingly prominent role in consigning the management of the deranged to the emerging specialty in mental medicine influenced a growing cultural acceptance that the mad "belonged" to medicine, it was not at all clear which specialty had first claim. Did the mad belong to physicians more than surgeons or to surgeons more than apothecaries? A derangement in nervous fibers, melancholic vapors, or disordered organs seemed to suggest a disease internal to the body, grasped most readily by the classically educated medical man schooled in natural philosophy and historical medical theory. Still, although surgeons may not have had the benefit of immersion in materia medica, their extensive experience with head wounds, falls, and other direct assaults on the body gave them an obvious perch from which to observe the ravages of delirium and the confusion attendant to physical injury. Apothecaries were also likely to claim sustained experience with mental derangement, as relatives of the mad routinely sought out medicinal remedies for their family members' histrionic or depressive episodes.

Social class further influenced which medical professional one sought out. The larger swath of London society consulted an apothecary. It certainly was possible for the middling classes to encounter one of London's (gentleman) physicians, but these interactions, when they happened, occurred in a large public hospital, not the physician's consulting room. Although ostensibly restricted to mixing prescriptions, apothecaries were well known to offer their services to clients as consultants. The use of laudanum (and its overprescription) also helped to reinforce the notion of the apothecary as possessing a possible remedy for emotional and behavioral excess. Physicians and surgeons, of course, had remedies as well, along with theories about the etiology of madness, its natural course, and possible cure. But none of the three branches of medicine enjoyed a particularly enviable record of success, and one's financial resources or street address therefore usually dictated the choice of practitioner. Living next door to a medical man was often the shortest path to the specialist's door, as spectators at Old Bailey insanity trials were soon to learn.

Recreating the historical process by which *mental,* rather than general, patients arrived at the specialist's door is challenging for a number of reasons, not least the dynamics of discerning the mental component in the physical ailment. Recognizing that a client's trouble was psychological was often gradual: physical and mental states were regularly intertwined in cases of head wounds, fever, and an oddly frequent debility—sunstroke, usually suffered in India. Depression following childbirth or prolonged sorrow following personal crises or illnesses initially framed as physical meant that psychiatric diagnosis, such as it was, was a latter-day inference. It could, of course, be interpreted as constituting a pathological entity in and of itself, having no necessary home in physical disturbance. The defendant's odyssey from physical to mental patient was therefore in the eye—and one suspects, the training—of the medical observer, whose experience with discerning states of madness may have been plentiful or not. For the majority of practitioners, the naming of mental problems depended on the type of formal education or apprenticeship he received. One suspects that nineteenth-century hospital medical schools and universities contributed some regularity to diagnosis over time, increasingly including the recognition of symptoms and the course of various states of madness in their curricula.[46] Although one finds in asylum registers the diagnosis recorded at intake, the questions posed earlier—how one first fell under the medical gaze and the resulting diagnosis received—is not a matter of record.

Fortunately for the historian of psychiatry, one class of the purportedly insane left behind a record of these two pivotal moments: the initial interaction with a medical practitioner and the array of symptoms that characterized the mental world of the deranged. Beginning with a Bethlem physician's appearance in 1760 and continuing to 1913, 375 physicians, surgeons, and apothecaries appeared at the Old Bailey, testifying either in hearings to determine if the prisoner was mentally fit for the trial or at the eventual trial itself. Contained within this group were the era's most prominent authors, lecturers, and practitioners in psychological medicine—Henry Maudsley, Charles Bucknill, Thomas Harrington Tuke, George Savage, Charles Mercier, and Edward Thomas Munro—as well as the superintendents of London's oldest public asylum, Bethlem, and its first establishment for the criminally insane, Broadmoor. The Old Bailey witness box, however, was also home to lesser-known medical practitioners whose initial point of contact was far removed from either the asylum or a Harley Street consulting room.

> I am the divisional surgeon and saw the body of the deceased child . . . I went to the station and saw the prisoner there. I told her I was a medical man, and I asked her if she complained of anything—she then made a statement to me, of which I made notes, she said, "I feel very impelled to do bad things, never to do good things. I wanted to do something for which they would hang me. I felt that I must take the child and drown it; I had no control over myself, so I just held the child in the bath and left it there. I have had a dragging pain at the back of my head and a lifting at the top . . . I should like to stab myself there so as to get from that which pains me . . . ever since baby was born I have been very low-spirited and depressed."

After reading his notes to the jury, the divisional surgeon looked up from his notes and delivered his diagnosis, "her condition was that of melancholia, a sort of puerperal mania, that often occurs during lactation." On cross-examination he added that her derangement "mainly results in suicidal mania."[47]

Assigned to police departments, divisional surgeons appeared at a critical moment in the career of the allegedly insane defendant. At this trial, the medical superintendent of a county asylum that had discharged the defendant two weeks before the killing and the prison doctor who interviewed all defendants awaiting trial followed the police surgeon in the witness box. Although both men could offer their impressions of the defendant's mental state sometime before and sometime after the fatal assault, only the divisional surgeon could comment on her manifest madness immediately following the crime. The asylum physicians' temporal distance from the time of the crime did not necessarily diminish the potential impact of their medical opinions, but it did reveal a weakness. As many medical men freely acknowledged from the witness stand, several days or even weeks in prison or an infirmary would be likely to induce calm in the defendant and a return, however incomplete, of reasonable composure and coherent conversation. Prison demeanor was of limited import, however; the issue for the jury was the state of the intellects or emotions at the time of the crime or shortly thereafter, and only the on-scene witness or medical men who treated the deranged soon after the crime in a hospital or a workhouse could supply this information. For this reason, the creation of the position of divisional surgeon was significant, and his testimony was especially compelling when he had recorded his impressions at the time and read the entries in the Occurrence Book to the jury.

Surgeons attached to police divisions were only one of a wide array of medical men drawn into the prosecution of allegedly insane offenders. In the century and a half covered in the present survey, medical practitioners testifying in 994 insanity trials gained their familiarity with the prisoner in any one of twelve separate occupational designations. Together, they make 1,120 court appearances (including "fitness to plead" hearings). Physicians, surgeons, and apothecaries might have met the prisoner in private practice, in a hospital, asylum, or workhouse infirmary, in the military, in jail awaiting trial, or in prison awaiting sentence. Medical witnesses were variously identified as "physician to the prison," "apothecary to the asylum," "medical superintendent," or "medical officer," which made identifying their branch of medicine difficult. Further, medical men often belonged to both the Royal College of Physicians and the corresponding corporation for surgeons, thus challenging their assignment to one or the other professional group. Sometimes a man designated "Surgeon of the Jail" listed MD after his name. Although the resulting frequency distribution of the twelve categories of medical participation presented below reveals change over the course of the time period considered in this survey, it is not always apparent whether a medical officer was a physician, a surgeon, or both. (Similar questions arise regarding the "medical officer" of a jail or prison.) It would be intriguing to know if there were discernible changes within these categories over time, but questions about the precision with which some medical people were listed limit one's ability to infer whether any of the three medical specialties came to be seen as the "rightful caretakers of the insane."

Fortunately, there remains a way to examine changes in medical encounters with the putatively insane that is not dependent on the specific specialty or credentials of the practitioner. Beyond classifying them by their training and title, medical witnesses can be separated by institutional affiliation and by their work as private practitioners. Table 3.1 gives these data.

Up to the trial of Daniel McNaughtan (1843), the most frequently appearing medical witness at the Old Bailey had gained his familiarity with the accused professionally, as his physician, surgeon, or apothecary, or casually, as his neighbor or social acquaintance.[48] The practitioner's services might have been sought for what was then termed a nervous ailment, but most often the doctor had been treating the accused for a physical condition—often pregnancy and childbirth—that in time yielded what were interpreted to be psychological features signifying a dangerous and potentially murderous condition. Most often, the crime was infanticide and the diagnosis, puerperal mania. In one such case, a seemingly uncomplicated pregnancy and delivery resulted in a "reserved manner, [she] seemed to have no affection for the child, say[ing] it was not her child; that it had been changed." But private physicians were also caught up with male infanticides: "I have known the prisoner for about eight years. [He] last called upon me for professional advice; he was suffering from dyspepsia. He had the delusion that he was suffering from venereal disease. I assured him there was no foundation for this. I saw him several times subsequently, and he persisted in his belief in spite of my assurances. He told me he was distressed about the poor condition of the baby, and thought it was due to his own diseased state." The physician's diagnosis of delusions were then given legal significance by the medical officer of Brixton Prison: "In my opinion, at the time he committed this act, it was under the impulse of his delusions, and he was in such a state that he did not know the nature or quality of his act."[49]

Not all private physicians, surgeons, and apothecaries had a relationship with the prisoner prior to arrest. Many were called to the police station to help with injuries sustained in failed suicide attempts or were enlisted by either

TABLE 3.1
From Medical Practitioner to Medical Witness (in percentages)

	1760–1843	1844–1859	1860–1879	1880–1899	1900–1913
Surgeons*					
Prison	7	7	7	2	
Private	28	27	19	4	2
Police	1	4	2	7	10
Hospital	2	4	4	3	2
Apothecary	6				
Physicians*					
Prison	1	1			
Private	15	11	12	8	8
Hospital	4	1	8	12	13
Asylum	9	7	4	5	2
Medical Officers					
Asylum	1				
Prison	2	2	9	17	
Frequent Witnesses					
Prison Surgeons					
Mr. McMurdo	15	19			
Mr. Gibson		11		35	23
Mr. Walker	3	8	32		
Prison Physicians					
Dr. Scott	10	1			
Dr. Dyer	11				
Dr. Bastian	5				
Insufficient data	11	4	4	2	2
$N^\dagger$	117	138	187	314	354

*Surgeons and physicians in these upper rows refer to individual medical men employed in these capacities. Apothecaries disappear after the first time period; they were grouped with surgeons because a number of them were often referred to as "Surgeon and Apothecary" in the trial narratives. The large percentage of "insufficient data" in this first time period is a by-product of the editors of the trial narratives being less than specific: "medical gentleman," "medical professor," "attends the compter" (a jail). Subsequent time periods have far fewer of these nebulous descriptions. By far, the most frequent court appearances were made by the six men named as prison physicians and surgeons. Their careers offer the clearest sign of which specialties dominated in court. Specific specialities are hard to determine in the last time period, as the designation "medical officer" is often given, without further specification. Army surgeons also testified, adding 2% and 1% for the periods 1760–1843 and 1844–59, respectively. Nurses also appear in the second time period, adding 1%.
†Number of appearances made by medical witnesses in each period.

the court or defense counsel to visit the defendant in prison before trial. These witnesses' defining character was their professional independence; they were not in the regular employ of a hospital or the state. Not surprisingly, the police station or jail cell provided the occasion for meeting a Henry Maudsley, Forbes Winslow, Charles Bucknill, and Thomas Harrington Tuke, as well as authors Charles Mercier and George Savage. That their renown as authorities on mental derangement had spread beyond the pages of medical journals and textbooks was clear when they were brought to prisons and then to court to advise juries on the characteristic features of different species of insanity. There is sometimes a certain deference paid them by the prison doctor, acknowledging and deferring to their greater expertise. Still, the court appearance of these eminent Victorian alienists was far outweighed by the decidedly nonspecialist voice of the prison surgeon and physician who proportionately made up most of the medical witness pool. Usually appearing at the behest of the court but also often subpoenaed to testify for the defense, these prison medical men displayed no automatic loyalty to the prosecution: they were as likely to declare the accused "not responsible for his actions" as "perfectly sane." Where they distinguished themselves from other medical men was in their assertion that they had detected sham or counterfeited insanity. With multiple opportunities to observe the accused, any lapse in histrionics or lifting of saturnine countenance was reported to the jury as evidence of fakery.

Data in table 3.1 reveal several trends in medical participation over time. Private association between surgeons and prisoners declines dramatically, from one in four to less than one in twenty. Private association with physicians slips marginally less, but it started out as a smaller proportion. Hospital physicians grow in frequency of appearance, the courtroom being the one venue where nonelite Londoners were likely to encounter a physician. The participation of prison surgeons Gilbert McMurdo, John Rowland Gibson, and George Edward Walker is immediately apparent; indeed, the frequency of their testifying at the Old Bailey reduces the proportion that had been taken up by private and hospital medical people in the early days of medical witnesses in insanity trials.

Still, there is one class of medical men that experiences the greatest growth over the course of these years: the police surgeon. Along with hospital physicians, police surgeons are the only practitioners who do not experience a decline in proportional participation, given the predominance of the jail and prison personnel. These were the two groups of medical men most likely to be called to the scene of the crime to treat the victim and perhaps the perpetrator. They alone were able to comment upon the offender's behavior immediately after the crime, and their testimony became crucial once the diagnosis was proffered and witnesses heard the judge advise that only one type of insanity concerned the law: the state of the offender's intellects at the time of the crime. Prison and jail personnel may have had more experience with offenders and could comment on repeated conversations with the defendant, but only on-scene medical witnesses could supply the court with impressions taken at the scene.

This wide range of experience with defendants and indeed with insanity itself reminds us that to speak of the medical witness as representative of some identifiable professional body is just as misleading as to speak of the medical professional until at least 1858. From jail surgeon to asylum superintendent, from hospital apothecary to university lecturer, medical witnesses represented the full range of experience and learning that characterized medical practitioners of their day. The flashpoint in court would be the diagnosis, the basis for the practitioner's inference and the implications the court would try to draw out. Disagreements between practitioners during trials revealed a difference not just of opinion but of the basis for how that opinion was formed. These courtroom debates revealed the tenuous state of knowledge claimed by the fledgling practitioner of mental medicine.

CHAPTER FOUR

The Diagnosis in the Dock

Professor T. Wallis Rogers, M.B.I.M.S. consulting phrenologist, medical hypnotist and mesmerist, electrical and hygienic practitioner, graduate of the Institute of Physicians and Surgeons in New York, USA.

Having, by his own admission, the skills needed to "grow a new heart, lungs, and liver," Professor Rogers assured parlormaid Emma Elizabeth Ling that he possessed the knowledge to grow her a new "natural eye" to replace her artificial one. Nine years later, Emma Ling stood in the dock at the Old Bailey, quoting Rogers's business letter (cited above) and reading from the defendant's initial offer of professional services: "You will see with your eye in six or eight weeks from the start . . . and will be sound for life without treatment. It will not affect the other eye, except by disturbing the magnetic conditions temporarily . . . kindly forward £10 on account as a guarantee in the matter." Elizabeth Ling's treatment consisted of being thumped on the back with "tapping movements upon her spine," required to "release those currents coming from the loins and particles of matter that got caught up on the spinal column." Despite repeated assurances that her eye was indeed growing back, Elizabeth Ling sought a second opinion at Middlesex Hospital, where a Dr. Harman regretfully told her, "There [is] no eye there." And that is how "Professor" Rogers found himself on trial at the Old Bailey under an indictment of fraud.

Called to testify, Dr. Harman found himself compelled to acknowledge the limits of medical science to the defendant, who conducted his own vigorous cross-examination of the hospital physician.

Dr. Nathaniel Bishop Harman: I am quite confident that it is impossible to "grow" a new eye after the original one has been removed. I base that view on my knowledge . . . of embryology . . . it is self-evidently impossible; you cannot put a person through her mother's womb a second time. You ask how I know it is impossible; the only man I have ever heard of trying to grow one failed—that is yourself.

Judge [to defendant]: Did you ever know a man with a wooden leg grow a real one?

Defendant Rogers: I would have you know that it is not impossible, in my judgment . . . it would take years; but it is not an impossibility . . . I know a great deal about magnetism and electricity. I know the story of Mesmer and his performances.

Judge: Have you ever attempted to prove through your own will or senses the power that there is a human magnetism to heal and restore?

Dr. Harman: I have used all the legitimate and all the knowledgeable arts of my craft. In the way you put it, your question has no meaning.

Judge: Can you tell me by what powers a child grows; take a child from birth; what is the secret of its growth, the law by which it grows?

Dr. Harman: If you can tell me that, perhaps I should be able to answer all the riddles of the universe.

Defendant Rogers: It is the riddle of the universe, and I claim to have solved it. Magnetism is the basis of life. The child grows by the law of magnetism.

In the end, it was the law of fraud, not magnetism, that convicted Rogers of "obtaining from Emma Elizabeth Ling various sums, amounting to £14 15s., by means of false pretenses." Had the sentence been immediately pronounced, there would be little reason to include his case in a survey of insanity trials, although it is always worth noting that London's alienists were not the only medical practitioners who could encounter close questioning on the witness stand. And, similar to the examination Dr. Harman faced, medical witnesses in insanity trials would often find their sharpest questioners—compelling them to justify the "knowledge arts of [their] craft"—to be the putatively mad defendants who took harsh exception to being diagnosed insane. Only at the end of Rogers's trial—after his conviction—did the deputy medical officer of Brixton jail approach the dock.

I have had prisoner under special observation since his admission. I think he is of unsound mind and incapable of knowing the nature and quality of his offence. In conversation he has told me that he is capable of giving people new hearts, livers, and kidneys; that he can raise the dead; that he can break bones and heal them in five minutes by . . . placing his finger on the bones they melt, then on removing his finger they solidify and become like shell; further, he does not consider that the substance of which his food consists has anything to do with nutrition, but that the colors in the food are what nourish him. I believe these are genuine insane delusions.

Asked by the judge, "You mean that he pretends to medical powers which you consider impossible and improbable and that shows he is mad?" The medical witness responded with a simple "yes," which the judge chose to ignore. Instead, he ruled, "the question of insanity [cannot] be dealt with here," and the defendant was sentenced to nine months imprisonment, to be kept under observation and if "found to be insane . . . treated accordingly."[1]

Eccentric or insane; mercenary or delusional? The trial of the mesmeric ophthalmologist reminds today's historian of forensic psychiatry that medical men were called to testify in insanity trials precipitated by indictments of libel, fraud, or counterfeiting, as well as the more usual charges stemming from child murder and attempted regicide. (Queen Victoria alone would suffer three attempts on her life by putative madmen.) As seen in the preceding chapter, medical witnesses represented the full array of hospital, asylum, and prison affiliations, the elite of medical school professors, celebrated authors, and the noncelebrated general practitioner. Their routes into court were similarly varied: some appeared through subpoena, some at the request of the Solicitor of the Treasury (serving as public prosecutor), some at the invitation of the defendant's family, and some on their own initiative, having read of the crime in the newspaper and eager to ensure the jury heard their evidence, even if it meant defending the prisoner themselves.

The deputy medical officer at Brixton jail, for example, had offered his testimony in the Rogers case in an official capacity, having had the prisoner "under special observation." Ever since the 1830s, it was standard practice for jail surgeons to be told, "mind you see that prisoner, for your evidence will be needed," whenever the Crown suspected a likely insanity plea. What is curious about this trial is the introduction of medical testimony *after* conviction. It was not unheard of for a judge to order a medical examination before pronouncing sentence, but that usually happened when the jury expressed concern that, though not legally insane, the defendant was clearly troubled. No such wish was recorded in the Rogers trial; indeed, no testimony bearing on his mental faculties was offered at all. When the jury doubtless ascribed the defendant's courtroom outburst ("I possess the powers which operate the law in human nature") to dramatics rather than delirium, it was left to the jail surgeon to frame the defendant's self-aggrandizement as delusion and then to give the grounds for his opinion.

Diagnosis

The essence of expert testimony is the framing of a judgment based upon knowledge gained through unique experience, specialized learning, or both.[2] Most often, scientific opinion is brought to bear on the ambiguous facts of crime—determining the presence of poison and distinguishing what kind, inferring whether a head wound resulted from a fall or the blow of a blunt object. Making these determinations was clearly beyond the ken of a community juror. Bloodless wounds, sudden infant deaths, or a patient's inexplicable turn from seemingly robust health to agonizing death called for an interpretation—an opinion—to make sense of the critical events surrounding the fatality.[3] Although few Londoners were sufficiently knowledgeable to state with any confidence the presence of poison or to explain how a wound came to be, no such reticence inhibited their readiness to form opinion when testimony touched on matters psychological. Who could *not* recognize which of his relatives was mad? Everyday citizens of early modern England employed a host of terms—lunacy, melancholy, and various forms of mania— that were certainly employed by medical men but were also routinely used in common conversation. For all the mystery that surrounded the origin and unpredictability of mental derangement, madness itself was legible; the terms used to identify its various forms were widespread and unproblematic.

The challenge this widespread use of terms and images surrounding madness posed to the would-be specialist in mental medicine was daunting. He had to convince the judge and jury that he possessed esoteric knowledge and professional experience that justified a privileged voice in the courtroom, and he had to persuade his listeners that they did not possess the knowledge they thought they did. It was an altogether delicate effort: invoking unique knowledge while avoiding condescension required the skills of a supple negotiator. Among the most pointed interactions in all insanity trials are those moments when the defendant, bristling at having the state of his intellects impugned, questions the medical witness pointedly about the grounds for his inference. In 1813, the apothecary to St. Luke's Hospital had just finished giving his evidence when the prisoner, heretofore mute, interjected, "From what do you form your opinion that I am insane?" The apothecary responded, "From your action, and ideas, and your general conduct told me you were an improper person to be at liberty." And the prisoner answered, "You judge from ideas; you have a good opinion of yourself."[4]

Ideas—not fever, wounds, or diseased organs—were the substance of the mad-doctor's testimony from the moment of its introduction in the mid-eighteenth-century courtroom. Insanity was therefore "imparted by the ear." Where most medical witnesses employed their senses (sight, smell, touch, taste) to discern the presence of disease, "judging from ideas" required something beyond simple sensory perception. The determination of a mental disease was "dependent upon evidence which is cognizable by the intellect alone, and upon data which the senses furnish to us only at second hand." Writing in 1858, noted authors John Charles Bucknill and Daniel Hack Tuke argued that the alienist "must not only be a physician, but a metaphysician, seeking to ascertain the laws of the mind, which are as regular as any natural laws."[5] Although they shared medical credentials with other members of their profession and could site parallel apprenticeships or university training as the unique experience providing the grounds for their informed opinion, it is nonetheless true that metaphysician and physician part company when their testimony turns to forensic evidence. The toxicologist or obstetrician (an "accoucheur") could speak to bodily symptoms and chemical tests, but the mad-doctor cum alienist was usually confined to reporting incoherent conversation and burlesque behavior, the sort of evidence that any neighbor could offer. To distinguish their expert inference from the neighbor's "surface" impressions, medical witnesses from the beginning of the nineteenth century put forward delusion as the essence of derangement.[6]

Hidden, Recondite, and Subterranean

In print, the early specialists in mental medicine openly disparaged the perceptions of lay observers, who were likely to mistake a "lucid interval" for a restoration to sanity. "Let the conversation be extended," averred the apothecary to Bethlem, let the conversation drift to "the favorite subject . . . afloat in the madman's brain, and [the observer] will be convinced of the hastiness of his decision." And, invoking delusion—the term that would eventually separate medical from lay testimony—John Haslam concluded, "the experienced [practitioner] will find that by some unaccountable association, even ordinary topics are linked to his darling delusions—the map of his mind will point out that the smallest rivulet flows into the great stream of his derangement." Adding graphic imagery to his description of delusion's subterranean nature, Haslam advised the easily mistaken casual observer: "[to] protract the discourse, let him touch the fatal string which throws his mind into discord ... draw the hair-trigger which inflames the combustible materials of his disease."[7] Gaining sustained experience with the delusions of the mad enabled medical witnesses to distinguish their experience-based knowledge from the erroneous perception of persons who might claim their own occupational experience with the deranged. The police, medical men in court argued, were likely to mistake delirium tremens for insanity; only the skilled practitioner could distinguish between the two. Even their own medical brethren who might have treated those arrested in general hospitals or infirmaries lacked the advanced learning and sustained exposure to the deranged that permitted penetrating insight into "the combustible nature of [this] disease."

Such proffering of privileged insight did not always go unchallenged. When asked pointedly by a judge in 1840, "Why could not any person form an opinion whether a person was sane or insane from the circumstances which have been referred to," a medical witness responded, "because it seems to require a careful comparison of particular cases, more likely to be looked at by medical men, who are especially experienced in cases of unsound mind." Although respectful and less dismissive than Haslam's opinions on lay observation, the message was clear: a careful comparison of particular cases was required to distinguish the sane from the insane. Also, by the 1840s, it would require even greater familiarity with particular cases in order to distinguish entirely new forms of derangement having little to do with the manifest madness of mania, delirium, and even delusion.

Although conventionally framed as a cognitive defect, from its introduction in criminal prosecutions in 1800, delusion always carried an insistent behavioral impetus *to act*. If one fatefully believed that one could effect the Second Coming by bringing about one's own state execution or that one could save one's children's souls by dispatching them to heaven before the devil could grab them first, one did not sit and deliberate the proper course of action. The fateful error in belief demanded some kind of action to relieve the sufferer from the unrelenting fear or all-consuming preoccupation. Courtroom testimony, however, left the criminal consequence at the level of inference for the jury to draw—medical witnesses rarely commented upon the blind force that delusion was believed to unleash. Still, the mention of profoundly mistaken belief was often sufficient: common-law jurisprudence conceived of delusion as a failure to understand the nature of one's act or its consequence; without a coherent understanding of the events surrounding the action, no choice to do evil could attend the action. The willingness of medical testimony to explore the issue of compromised self-control, however, found its expression in the trial of Daniel McNaughtan almost half a century after delusion's first use at the Old Bailey. As one medical witness stated, with no discussion at all about mental "confusion": "the commission of the act is placed beyond his moral control . . . the impulse was so strong that nothing short of a physical impossibility would prevent him from performing an act which his delusion might impel him to do."[8]

Already by 1843, however, medical witnesses were chafing at the stricture that only an insanity of intellectual impairment should carry exculpatory value. In print, medical writers had already taken issue with the narrowness of considering cognition alone.[9] Moral insanity and lesion of the will made their entrance at the Old Bailey three years before *McNaughtan*. Indeed, given the emphasis placed on knowing right from wrong—knowing the nature and quality of the act—it is tempting to see the *Rules* that followed the celebrated verdict as the judiciary's attempt to enshrine delusion as the sole medico-legal concept of significance for common-law trials featuring an insanity plea. By implication, a discrete derangement in volition had been conspicuously excluded. Although medical and legal texts continued to treat *McNaughtan* as the defining case in medical jurisprudence, it was rarely mentioned—and certainly not cited as definitive—from the mid-nineteenth to the early twentieth centuries. Delusion, to be sure, continued as the diagnosis of preference for medical witnesses throughout this period. Judges might indulge medical witnesses venturing into diagnoses of volitional or emotional madness, but they followed up the testimony by asking, "Has he any delusion at all?"[10] Some judges, however, were not so patient.

Taking exception to being pressed to answer whether the prisoner knew right from wrong, Superintendent of Hanwell Asylum John Conolly responded, "we medical men do not consider that a question of distinction at all—I should question the power of the mind in the state which the prisoner's had been to appreciate right and wrong." The prosecuting attorney countered, "You can perfectly well understand my question because, as you say, it is one that is often put to you, do you mean at the time he was beating his wife . . . he could not distinguish right from wrong?" Conolly replied, "I am perfectly aware that is the question." The judge then interjected, "If that is the question it can surely be answered," prompting the medical witness to respond, "I do not think it can absolutely be answered; I think it can only in the manner in which I have answered it." Again the prosecutor asked about the prisoner's ca-

pacity to distinguish right from wrong, and again Conolly demurred, reintro-
ducing the prisoner's dubious power of *appreciating* the moral dimension of
his action, adding for good measure his attendant impairment in the "power
of controlling or resisting a train of thought tending to criminal actions."
If the court believed the *McNaughtan Rules* would circumscribe insanity's
meaning to the cognitive faculties, it was in for a rude awakening. Despite
having made the participation of medical witnesses standard fare in a Victorian insanity trial, the court did not possess the skill in keeping asylum
doctors like Conolly on script.[11]

Aside from Conolly's adamantine refusal to confine the definition of insanity to an inability to know right from wrong, there are two features of this
cross-examination that are worth noting. First, his testimony appears to be
the first intimation in court that knowledge of one's act did not signify the
moral appreciation of *why* the act was wrong. From *McNaughtan* forward,
medical men explicitly separated knowledge from appreciation. They might
freely acknowledge the defendant's rudimentary recognition that he or she
had committed a physical act, but then they might describe the accused as
having "no definite conception of the real nature of his acts: I mean the moral
nature of his acts: [he] thought he was justified in killing his child."[12] Most
often, it was the moral gravity of the act that eluded the prisoner: "I think
he knew he had killed a man but I do not think he regarded it in light of a
crime—[he] seemed to think it was a rather praiseworthy act."[13] Yes, the prisoner "knew" the difference between right and wrong, but "[she] did not know
the act was calculated to take away life: she answered simply: [she was] taking
the child to heaven to see its father."[14]

Oblivious to the "enormity of her deed" or "suffering from melancholia
[so as] . . . not in a condition to know the nature and the quality of his acts,"[15]
defendants might also be described as "not conscious of the wickedness of the
act," "perfectly unconscious of what she is saying," or "not conscious of the
moral guilt he was about to commit."[16] Medical witnesses therefore accounted
for seemingly purposeful, though (legally) unintentional, behavior: "I have
found in lunatics a most intense earnestness of purpose . . . and whatever
reasoning is applied to show them they are wrong has no effect whatever."[17]
The Old Bailey jury was therefore asked to consider the possibility of a state
of suspended consciousness that could allow purposeful though curiously
nonintentional acts. When asked by judges to clarify these mental states, the
medical man responded, "she was not conscious of the act having been committed, that is to reflect upon the circumstances," or "the basis of their reason-

ing is very often quite false and delusive."[18] In the years following *McNaughtan* then, medical witnesses continually cast doubt on what "knowing" actually signified: the prisoner had not failed to grasp the inherent difference between right and wrong, but his state of distraction decoupled the physical doing from the mental comprehension of the act. Medical testimony therefore engaged the fundamental meaning of intention: what the actor meant to do. If "not conscious of the moral gravity of the act," could the act be one of choice at all? What will to harm could possibly be present?

"The Memory is Blank, the Brain Stands Still"

Perhaps the most graphic separation of physical act from intent was put forward in mid nineteenth-century England in cases of "doubled consciousness": sleepwalkers, automatons, and those afflicted with a form of insanity that left them in a state of absence, or *vertige*, as French clinicians termed it.[19] With all the outward appearance of engaging in some purposeful activity, those diagnosed with *vertige épileptique* were in fact in a state of suspended consciousness that separated two attacks of convulsive epilepsy. Again, to the untrained eye, the patient's capacity to converse and perform acts of considerable physical dexterity seemed to show recovery from the unconscious state. A second fit, however, soon revealed that all that had transpired between the two convulsive episodes was lost to the afflicted and that a state of unconsciousness had prevailed, allowing for the outward, misleading behavior perceived by onlookers as a sign of *return*. Recorded in medical writing as early as 1817, states of doubled consciousness acquired by midcentury the diagnostic label of *dédoublement de la personnalité*. Confronted with evidence of a person having made an inexplicable assault on beloved children or a cherished friend, medical men at the Old Bailey informed the court, "They are purely automatic acts, the patient is perfectly unconscious . . . this is not convulsive epilepsy . . . an automatic act and an unconscious act are identically the same."[20] The state was perhaps best characterized as: "the memory is blank, the brain stands still, and the muscular action goes on."[21]

Although epilepsy provided perhaps the most vivid graphic imagery of involuntary, unconscious movement, the years following *McNaughtan* had provided medical witnesses with the opportunity to assert the existence of volitional chaos that stayed far away from *moral insanity* and *lesion of the will*, terms that could provoke contemptuous dismissal by the judiciary. They could also incite a judge to admonish the attorney, "The juryman's attention is diverted from [points of law] by elaborate, mock-scientific examinations on delusion, illusion, hallucination and morbid imagination; and the replies are dissected with metaphysical subtlety, till the witness is as much at a loss to understand himself as counsel or jury can be to arrive at his meaning."[22] Still, there was little doubt that unruly, not just unresisted, impulses had entered into courtroom deliberations. It had also entered into legal commentary written by the most authoritative voice in common-law jurisprudence, James Fitzjames Stephen. In 1863, Stephen revealed a qualitative change from his earlier rejection of impulsive insanity. "It would be absurd to deny the possibility that such impulses may occur," he wrote, referring to the sudden, uncontrollable impulse to kill or, in short, "impulsive insanity."[23]

Still, the distance between legal commentary and courtroom practice could be quite an expanse. After alluding to impulsive insanity, a medical witness was advised by a judge, "It is stated in a book of authority that with regard to impulsive insanity or irresistible impulse, the doctors who present the theory should be able to form a distinct conception between impulses that are irresistible and impulses that are unresisted." The witness moved from the metaphysical to the physical: "I think the only way in which such a line can be drawn is to take the physical concomitants, and if I find the man who commits the crime is at the time in a state of physical suffering, with staring eye-balls, in a state of great excitement, and has at the same time a tendency to epilepsy, which in this case . . . I believe, I should put that down probably, not certainly, as an irresistible impulse."[24] The "tendency to epilepsy" had been discerned from family testimony attesting to the likely inheritance of a vulnerability to the disease; the "physical concomitants" refer to the far-away stare, the racing pulse, and, on occasion, an actual fit. As graphic as such testimony might be, judges could mitigate the evidence of an involuntary fit with signs of continuing consciousness evident in a prisoner leaving the crime scene before the fit had ended or taking care to remove incriminating evidence.[25]

For all the efforts undertaken to expand the scope of diagnostic terms in court to include "doubled consciousness" and indeed, the lack of consciousness at all, *delusion* remained the most frequently invoked medico-legal term in medical testimony. The graphic image of a sleepwalking murderous housemaid or a knife-wielding mother in a trance may have provided more vivid, indeed haunting, specters of insane criminality, but still it was the fateful confusion in the nature and consequences of one's act that defined the alienist's grounds for inferring insanity. "I believed he was labouring under a delusion— he said that a mesmerist was downstairs below him who was trying to throw him out of the window by force, trying experiments, and there were wires from the window below to his room, that he was cutting these wires, and while he was cutting them he was interrupted, and that he was very sorry he had shot the policeman—to the best of my judgment he was suffering under a delusion at that time, he was evidently insane." In this trial, the accused—a surgeon— provided evidence of florid delusion in his courtroom defense: "The room was filling with vapour sent through the floor, and [I] tore up the carpet, and put the mattress on the boards to keep the vapours from coming through, and at that moment the door was being broken and at open [I] fired . . . to deter the man from entering, having no idea he was a policeman."[26] Although few tormentors appeared in such a culturally topical incarnation as a mesmerist, illusory persecutors like the one surgeon Grimes feared rank as the most frequent of delusory beliefs. Fears of being poisoned, of having certain persons "leaguing" against him, or of one's spouse entertaining lovers were cited as reasons for a crime, as well as grounds for the medical witness's inference of madness.

Although delusion far outnumbered all other terms invoked by medical witnesses in the years following the *McNaughtan* verdict, Old Bailey juries became familiar with myriad species of madness that one might also encounter in contemporary medical texts. Thus, hysteria and neurasthenia, *furor epilepticus* and epileptic mania, scrofula and brain disorder were each invoked, spanning the spectrum from the psychological to the organic, from the traditional—delirium, insensibility, imbecility—to the contemporary: moral insanity, irresistible impulse, *vertige épileptique*. Table 4.1 lists the terms used most by medical witnesses in post-*McNaughtan* insanity trials.

Second only in frequency to delusion in Victorian medical testimony was melancholia, the affliction supposedly consigned to the diagnostic ash heap early in the nineteenth century. Cannibalized by Jean-Étienne-Dominique Esquirol to fashion the neologism *monomanie*, the centuries' old ailment *melancholia* made a surprising return to the Old Bailey in the last decade of the nineteenth century and the first decade of the twentieth.[27] Indeed, two-thirds of all courtroom mentions of melancholia were made in these years alone. But although melancholia was culturally familiar, its clinical features no longer resembled the sorrowful despondency long associated with mourning and free-floating despair: "I came to the conclusion that he was suffering from melancholia . . . [He] had lost the natural instinct of self preservation . . . I do not think of the fact that he had killed his own children rather than his step children but it strikes me now that it is a natural instinct to preserve one's

TABLE 4.1
Number of Trials Featuring Specific Medical Terms, 1844–1913

Delusion	121
Melancholia	36
Homicidal Mania	30
"Women's Issues"*	29
Epilepsy	26
Desponding/Nervous	26
Puerperal Mania	16
Delirium Tremens	12

*"Women's Issues" include "change of life" and "suppression of menses," in contrast to the specific diagnosis of *puerperal mania* and *puerperal melancholia,* which were specific to confinement, delivery, and postdelivery mental states. Added together, they would rank second only to delusion in terms of the number of trials in which insanity was framed in medical testimony.

offspring and that instinct has obviously gone—my opinion is that at the time he committed these acts he was prevented by mental disease from controlling his conduct."[28] Usually associated with suicide, the diagnosis of melancholia had, by the turn of the century, expanded to include the addition of homicidal impulses. In the latter 1800s, the diagnoses of puerperal melancholia, melancholia with homicidal tendencies, and delusional melancholia were all linked to lethal violence.

In addition to the novelty of melancholia being cited in cases of male violence, the testimony cited above includes an emphasis placed on instincts: "the natural instinct of self preservation is inborn . . . I consider that a man who takes away the life of those he loves must do it from an insane point of view." Instincts had rarely been invoked in medical testimony and had never before been pictured as overridden by "mental disease." Puerperal mania had been a matter of depleted energy or nonspecific physiological reflex causing one to drown one's children or to poison their rice pudding. The instinct of loving one's children—of self-preservation—was conspicuously absent until its association with melancholia by the witness, a medical officer at Bethlem. This was years before Freud would pair the two in his seminal essay, "Mourning and Melancholia" (1917).[29] Indeed, the asylum doctors invoking an "instinct of self preservation" could easily have informed the famous essay, prompting one to question whether medical testimony influenced medical writing or vice versa. Clearly, both resonated with cultural anxiety over the individual's capacity to withstand self-destructive (as well as other-destructive) forces let loose by mental derangement. One wonders if the ease with which the medical witness introduced instincts in testimony about (male) melancholia is to be attributed to his rhetorical skill in the courtroom or to the likelihood that the medical man's clinico-academic psychology accommodated well the folk psychology of the jury.

Among the other frequently cited terms in medical testimony, *epilepsy* in its various forms figures prominently. In addition to *vertige épileptique* and *furor epilepticus*, one also finds in the early 1900s a variation very much in keeping with parallel developments in melancholia. Testifying in 1903, a private physician informed the court: "the prisoner . . . was brought to me . . . on referring to my book I find he had had epileptic fits . . . I have had such persons in my house—they show a homicidal tendency."[30] An early intimation of this homicidal cast can be found in the more nebulous category of *epileptic mania*, revealed by the "motiveless nature of [the] act."[31] Most often, however, epilepsy was cited in the context of depression and despondency. "A certain lowness" of spirits normally followed a seizure; homicidal tendency was a rarity until late in the century.

The only gender-specific derangement, puerperal insanity, joined non-specific "women's complaints" like suppressed menstruation, lactation, and "change of life" as commonly heard elements in Victorian medical testimony. Often associated with delusion—"she was convinced her milk had turned to water"—and melancholy amounting to "suicidal mania," various states of depression and despondency described states that ranged from gauzy consciousness to frenzy.[32] Standard to these infanticides was a display of affection shortly before the killing. "The prisoner was particularly anxious that the lady who held the infant [during vaccination] should not hurt the arm which she held, and asked her to be very careful," testified a health officer in a trial for the willful murder of an infant in 1894. Quoting from Taylor's *Medical Jurisprudence,* the witness continued:

> extending over some weeks, a woman is peculiarly liable to excessive emotional disturbance, which is likely to take the form of revulsion of feelings toward children and an attempt to murder—I should call that an instance of puerperal mania; that may come on suddenly without apparent cause—it may as suddenly cease—a person may be observed to be calm and collected, say at 8 o'clock, and yet have an access of mania say an hour before . . . a woman who was the victim of such an attack would certainly not be a free agent during the existence of the attack.

Pressed by the judge to articulate the signs of this particular derangement, the witness replied, "There are no symptoms by which we can ascertain the approach of puerperal mania, and why frequently it is impossible to observe any except from what afterward takes place—there are no symptoms recognizable by medical skills, either before or after."[33]

Although ostensibly limited to women killing beloved infants, puerperal mania introduced a range of elements regarding criminality, diagnosis, and courtroom testimony that were not limited to suppression of milk, of the menses, or of maternal feeling. The suddenness of attacks that appeared to come out of nowhere—motiveless and purposeless, out of character and sometimes out of consciousness—would characterize women's insanity throughout the Victorian era, as explained by the array of medical witnesses at the Old Bailey, public and private, elite and ordinary, institutionally based and self-employed. Increasingly, they would maintain, as did the medical witness above, that the crime revealed the derangement; the evidence of madness was manifest in the nature of the violence and the nonrandom choice of victim.[34]

There was nothing "natural" in the predominance of "women's issues" in accounting for women's insanity; before the mid-nineteenth-century elision of reproductive ills with all of women's derangement, a sort of "equal-opportunity" derangement obtained for men and women: stealing, shoplifting, and forgery were actively engaged in by putatively mad men and women. Women before *McNaughtan* suffered from melancholy, not women's melancholy; they could be delusional, delirious, or insensible, much like their male cohorts. Women's biology was implicated as the etiological agent in women's insanity in the medical literature, to be sure, but not on the witness stand. Puerperal mania was invoked in the early decades of the nineteenth century only in cases of infanticide. For all other offenses, women and men resembled one another in diagnosis; only with the coming of Victorian alienism was women's madness routinely ascribed to biological disruption.[35]

The Crime and the Medical Inference

That the medical witness in the child murder case cited above quoted from Taylor's *Medical Jurisprudence* was a somewhat controversial practice because, by legal stricture, oral testimony was not to be replaced by reading to the jury the words of an acknowledged authority. A published text—even if well regarded—could not be cross-examined, a forensic ritual fast becoming the hallmark of the nineteenth-century adversarial trial. Oral testimony required oral witnesses, and yet this convention was respected more in the breach than the practice: medical witnesses often quoted Taylor verbatim. Indeed, Taylor's text might also be mined by defense attorneys in cross-examining medical men reluctant to find evidence of insanity. Although Taylor himself "appeared" only in print, other authors well familiar with contemporary medical practitioners (and jurists, too, given the reference to medical ideas found in Stephen's legal commentary) testified in person at London's central criminal court. Charles Mercier, George Savage, and Arthur Luff referred to their own writings as the grounds for their opinions.[36]

Beyond citing a familiarity with published medical tracts, practitioners called to the Old Bailey referred to their sustained familiarity with the deranged gained through supervision in a workhouse, infirmary, or asylum, as well as through encounters with distracted patients in the course of traditional medical practice, particularly obstetrics. In the case of derangement attending reproductive ills, medical men had an extensive body of folk psychology to draw upon. *Puerperal mania* may have been the approved medical term, but few Londoners familiar with the physical upheaval of childbirth needed a courtroom diagnosis on the psychological effects that might attend even the most unproblematic delivery. When medical witnesses were called to testify in cases having nothing to do with child murder animated by "women's problems," they were asked to justify their opinions. In response to judicial or prosecutorial inquiry then, how did they frame their testimony on the stand? How was diagnosis explained and defended?[37]

Although medical testimony from 1760 to 1913 brimmed with a robust array of physical and psychological ailments, only the most frequent diagnoses appear in table 4.1. London's medical practitioners throughout these years often spoke of generalized insanity rather than specifically naming moral insanity, monomania, or melancholia. For many, the testimony amounted to, "I have looked upon him as a man insane." The only term mentioned more than *insanity* or simply "unsound mind" was *delusion*. Other, seemingly discrete, mental ailments were described in Taylor's compendium, first published in 1865. It would go through six editions by 1910, complete with guides to diagnosis and suggestions about the forensic-legal implications of each. But for all the particulars offered in print, it was generic insanity the witnesses spoke to in court, and they did so in language exquisitely sensitive to the forum in which they found themselves. They may have been tempted to draw on the more adventurous species of insanity offered by Taylor (or Mercier, Savage, or Luff), but they knew the court was listening for cognitive impairment, whatever emotional and volitional insanity was offered in testimony. While some medical witnesses tried to dismiss the restrictive stricture of "knowing right from wrong," others incorporated that exact phrase into their testimony by using the criterion as evidence of insanity, describing the prisoner as "unconscious of the fact of the crime" (a symptom of epileptic vertigo), lacking "sufficient control of his mind to know he was doing a wrong act," or failing "to understand he was doing a criminal act." Sometimes the medical witness could bring out this issue by pointedly inserting appreciating for knowing: "There is nothing consistent with his being perfectly unable to appreciate the act he was doing . . . at the time, they may be perfectly oblivious of the act, before and after."[38]

Employing such phrases in testimony revealed how skillfully medical witnesses had learned to speak in the coinage of the law. They not only invoked the legal formula of an inability to know the nature and quality of the act, they employed the precise language as the grounds for their inference of insanity. Tellingly, when asked directly, "Do you mean to say that you think he was not aware that killing a man was wrong?" the witness could respond, "I do not say that, but I say I do not think him conscious of the moral guilt he was about to commit—I do not think he was aware of the enormity of the act he was doing—I do not say that he did not know that the act of killing a man was wrong, many lunatics do . . . I have found in lunatics a most intense earnestness of purpose, and whatever reasoning is applied to show them they are wrong has no effect whatever."[39]

Although the caseload at the Old Bailey included sleepwalkers, automatons, and persons described as submerged in episodes in which they were literally unconscious of the knife in their hands, most medical witnesses employed *unconscious* in the context of being oblivious to the *moral* significance of one's acts. "She seemed to have no definite conception of the real nature of the act—I mean the moral nature of the acts: [she] thought she was justified in killing the child." This delusory belief was sometimes made explicit: "she said the children would . . . become angels."[40] Conscious that they had a lethal weapon in their hands and fully aware of the consequences at the time they committed the act, these defendants were nonetheless diagnosed as insane, with medical witnesses offering opinions such as "no sane mother would take away the life under such circumstances" and "there is insanity which surrounds the unconsciousness of an act."[41]

Increasingly, medical men asserted that it had been the prisoner's moral obliviousness to the true quality of the act that led to their opinion. As cited earlier in this chapter, but now with renewed emphasis since the diagnosis invoked the crime itself, the failure to appreciate the consequences of the act was invoked to reveal the lack of moral sense, of an understanding of *why* an act was wrong. "I think he knew using a knife would produce death or a serious wound but I don't suppose he was in a condition to consider whether it was right or wrong to do that . . . [he] was merely acting under the delusion that the man was going to kill him."[42]

Did the testimony of the medical witnesses reflect medical opinions expressed in print? Authors of contemporary medical texts also included references to insanity as generic derangement, but the reader is likely to find insanity as a subheading (Partial Insanities) rather than a diagnosable condition. One finds instead the signs and symptoms of specific disease entities. In melancholia, for example, "no mental disease stamps itself more legibly upon the physiognomy and demeanour . . . the sad and anxious eye, the dripping brow, the painful mouth."[43] Mania, on the other hand, reveals a face "pale or flushed, the skin dry and harsh, the pulse accelerated."[44] Focus on characteristic functioning and the decidedly uncharacteristic florid mania was a constant theme in diagnosis; a conspicuous change in temperament, in natural feeling, or in accustomed behavior were each grounds to suspect insanity. Whether the behavior was labeled as a form of mania or melancholia, whether it was accompanied by hallucinations or delusions, or whether it was sudden or gradual was of potential significance. The diagnoses appeared to reflect the classifier's idiosyncratic perceptual frame rather than the use of some diagnostic guide or manual. The one characteristic that united medical opinion was the protean nature of madness, a theme one can trace to antiquity. Now, in the nineteenth century, it was emphasized again: "No class of diseases with which man is afflicted is so various in their manifestation as those known under the general term of insanity."[45]

Perhaps because of the maddeningly imprecise nature of diagnostic symptoms one finds in contemporary medical texts, medical witnesses in court stressed behavioral signs of manifest derangement. Although one still finds witnesses mentioning "his eyes—his expression was very vacant, the pupils . . . rather unequal," and reference to an abnormal pulse, the reasons for diagnoses given in court increasingly highlighted elements surrounding the criminal offense rather than the accused's physical or biographical makeup.[46] As the medical officer of Holloway Prison explained to the jury, "in considering the act itself, one first considers whether there was motive or not; also the way the act was done, and whether it was done in such a way as would ensure detection . . . also whether unnecessary or outrageous violence was used."[47]

Evidence of appalling brutality was a constant theme in diagnosis. Witnesses remarked that "unusual violence in a crime like this would lead me to look very carefully for insanity," or "I consider an act of this sort the climax of . . . mental disease," or "[it is] a very common occurrence to have many wounds committed by an insane person."[48] In addition to the grievous nature of the attack—the extraordinary violence, even for a homicide—the second element referenced in the prison doctor's evidence also resonated in testimony offered by his medical brethren. Thus, medical witnesses might say, "the chief reason [for diagnosis] is the absence of any discoverable motive for such a terrible crime," or, put another way, "I should persist in my opinion he did not know what he was doing, being so thoroughly without a motive." Another witness might conclude insanity "from the lack of motive of the deed, the absolute difference between the man's real character suddenly taking place . . . culminating in such an act."[49] Of course, the absence of motive might also reveal a sane depravity, as one doctor acknowledged: "I do not think a man would have an intelligible motive for killing his brother, unless he was insane, or a very great criminal, especially with such antecedents as the prisoner's."[50] As a history of epilepsy in the family was also evident, this final element may well have prompted the jury to opt for insanity over evil.

Still, the absence of any discernible motive exposed a weakness in medical testimony that hinged on the inability to find a sane reason for the killing. The failure to discover delusion, medical men argued throughout the century, did not mean that no delusion existed. The essence of deeply hidden and fervently held obsessive beliefs lay in the fact that they were lodged far below the conscious surface; they resisted discovery precisely because of their subterranean hold on the prisoner. Since the motive of the putatively mad defendant was clearly given shape and urgency by delusory beliefs, it is not at all surprising that someone not privy to the prisoner's subjective world would be unable to detect discernible motive, or in any case, a sane one.

CHAPTER FIVE

The Witness Takes the Stand

From 1760 to 1913, Old Bailey juries listened to the testimony of 375 individual medical witnesses, making a total 1,110 courtroom appearances in 994 trials. Not all of these were full courtroom proceedings, as many prisoners were found unfit to stand trial. Medical men were present at these hearings and offered opinions regarding prisoners' capacity to understand the proceedings and advise in their own defense, but only the medical men's appearance is noted: no testimony is recorded in the courtroom narratives. These abbreviated hearings normally included a prison surgeon or physician, often accompanied by one other medical man. Participation of jail and prison surgeons was so frequent that prison medical officers comprised at least half of all the medical witnesses that appeared in the court, rising to over 60 percent in the early twentieth century. How did other prisoners come under the medical *gaze*? These data are to be found in table 5.1.

How the Prisoner Met the Doctor, 1760–1913

In the latter decades of the eighteenth century, defendants' private acquaintances—neighbors, coworkers, and casual friends—supplied almost a third of the opportunities for observation and inference that found their way into Old Bailey.[1] By the time of *McNaughtan* (1843), testimony by witnesses with a private, personal association with the defendant had already slipped to barely 10 percent, and it fell still further to 1 percent by the beginning of the 1900s. There was a similar precipitous decline in testimony by witnesses with a preexisting professional acquaintance—those who had treated the accused for physical or psychological ailments, who had attended the accused in a hospital (including an asylum), or who had been initially called to treat a patient and found his attention turned to the bizarre histrionics or doleful brooding of the family member (now the accused) in the corner of the room.

The disappearance of a prior association between the medical man and the

TABLE 5.1
How the Defendant Met the Doctor (in percentages)

	1760–1843	1844–1859	1860–1879	1880–1899	1900–1913
Private	13	1	4	2	1
Professional	32	20	14	16	7
Crime Scene	4	10	12	11	20
Hospital	3	4	3	8	
Prison/Jail	44	55	56	59	60
No Previous Contact	2	5	9	3	1
Insufficient Data	5	6	1	6	3
*N**	117	138	187	314	354

*Number of appearances made by medical witnesses in each trial period.

accused would have direct implications for diagnosis. With the medical literature's conspicuous emphasis upon the madman's change in behavior, mood, and affect, courtroom witnesses after *McNaughtan* were at a loss to contrast the prisoner's current demeanor with his customary state, to comment on the inexplicable alienation of affection, or to account for sudden, out-of-character brutality. That medical testimony would shift to other grounds for inferring insanity given the change in how the prisoner met the doctor thus highlights the importance of social setting in eventual diagnosis. Why this shift in meeting place should have taken place is not immediately obvious; the rapidly growing commerce in medicine and an expanding middle class able to afford medical services left London with a brisk trade in all things physic.[2] The precipitous decline in medical witnesses' private, informal association with defendants may simply reflect the sharp rise in institutional affiliation—the state's increasing use of medical men at every stage of criminal justice processing. Perhaps also the type of offender who predominated in the later years of the study was less likely to have visited a medical practitioner, although the reason for this was unlikely to be social class. Crimes of petty theft—more likely committed by the poor or barely employed—constituted the majority of cases at the beginning of these years. The crimes that animated insanity trials after *McNaughtan* were violent personal assaults; these may have been more frequent among the poor but not necessarily.[3] Insanity trials throughout the century featured violent personal attacks between spouses who were of considerable social standing: physicians, schoolmasters, and the well-to-do (if shiftless) sons of the bourgeoisie.[4]

By far the most frequent association between prisoner and medical man began in Newgate or Holloway in the days (and sometimes) weeks during which the accused awaited trial. In the last half of the 1700s, no prisoner met a medical man in Newgate or any other jail; by the time of *McNaughtan,* almost half of all encounters began in the confinement awaiting trial. One particular jail surgeon, Gilbert McMurdo, distinguished himself in terms of frequency and consistency of opinion, finding suspected insanity defendants to be almost invariably sane, with an apparently visceral proclivity often reaching risible levels.[5] Confronted with a ship's captain in 1833 who was in the habit of stripping off his clothes, breaking windows with his bare fists, dancing a jig on the broken glass, and once, on hearing the name of his supposed nemesis, completing the episode by jumping on the back of a passing whale, McMurdo informed the court, "I have no knowledge of any symptom which he has exhibited to make me come to the conclusion of his being of unsound mind."[6]

McMurdo's participation in these trials was instigated by London's lord mayor, who ordered the Newgate surgeon to gather impressions of prisoners suspected of contemplating an insanity plea. McMurdo was succeeded by another surgeon, John Rowland Gibson, and eventually by physicians who served under an array of official titles, including Medical Officer at His Majesty's Prison, Holloway; Surgeon of Newgate Gaol; and Medical Superintendent of the [Workhouse] Infirmary. Although Old Bailey juries encountered a range of clinical practitioners, at least half of the early forensic-psychiatric witnesses were affiliated with a jail or a prison. The one exception was Henry Charlton Bastian, Physician to the National Hospital for the Paralysed and Epileptic, whose frequent participation was the direct result of a series of parliamentary acts. These legislative efforts aimed to define the role of a public prosecutor, a comparatively new innovation, which carried direct implications for the way medical evidence was placed before the jury. Attorney General Sir Henry James addressed the Commons:

> I have requested that whenever any accused person is brought before justices on a capital charge, the magistrate's clerk shall communicate with the Solicitor of the Treasury and that that officer shall take charge of the prosecution . . . in the absence of any . . . private conduct it will be the duty of the Treasury Solicitor, acting as Director of Public Prosecutions to see the evidence in every capital case be fully brought before the jury. I have also requested that, in those cases where insanity in the accused is alleged, full inquiry shall be made . . . in the absence of [the prisoner's] friends' ability to produce witnesses, the Treasury's Solicitor shall secure their attendance.[7]

The prescribed full inquiry enjoined the treasury solicitor "to apply to medical men of experience and repute, one of whom is usually the medical superintendent of the lunatic asylum for the county in which the accused is in custody."[8] Although this may have been the prescriptive directive, asylum superintendents testified in decreasing numbers as the nineteenth century progressed; their contributions in court were taken up by general and specialized hospital physicians who catered to nervous diseases and epilepsy. One such specialist was Edward Merrion, Physician of the Hospital for Diseases of the Nervous System, who offered vivid testimony in the trial of the mother whose epileptic vertigo resulted in the tragic death of her infant daughter.

Together with hospital physicians like Merrion, police surgeons and general medical practitioners assigned to jails and prisons expanded the diagnostic realm of mental medicine beyond the preserves of the asylum superintendents. Although these institutions were often the home of the most eminent Victorian alienists and offered the sustained interaction with the mentally deranged that could easily buttress claims to expertise—and hence professional knowledge—the testimony of the superintendents themselves was often unremarkable. John Charles Bucknill, coauthor of one of the era's most quoted medical texts, was superintendent of Devonshire County Asylum for eighteen years, and yet his familiarity with the deranged did not yield strikingly innovative diagnoses or particularly distinguished testimony: "I was obliged on the first occasion to make [the prisoner] stand up to the window to see his eyes, and yet he answered the questions sensibly—on the second occasion I came to the conclusion that his answers were those of a man deprived of sense—I have observed the same . . . in those who were decided lunatics . . . in my experience of traumatic insanity, I have found cases where a slight blow has been followed by insanity . . . hereditary influence is a great factor in producing insanity."[9]

Although he identified himself as the "Lord Chancellor's Visitor of Lunatics, and author of several well-known books upon insanity," there is nothing in Bucknill's remarks that could not be found in medical testimony in the mid-to-late 1700s, which also mentioned the appearance of the eyes, incoherent answers, head wounds, and heredity's probable effects. At most, asylum superintendents could offer evidence of the prisoner's manifest madness that was similar to what a neighbor or coworker could provide. Most notably for a prominent author, Bucknill failed to use the occasion of a high-profile trial to address mental medicine's continuing disaffection with the legal conception of insanity. This was left to medical officials employed by the prison service, as witnessed in the following testimony offered by John Scott, medical officer at Holloway Prison. In answering a judge's request to amplify his statement, Scott replied, "I cannot say that [the prisoner] did not know the nature of the act . . . I think there is hardly a lunatic who does not know to some extent the nature of his acts and also their quality. The whole point is what we include under the word 'know'; though a person may know to some extent, there may be lacking a proper appreciation of the character of the act; there may not be proper reasoning control."[10]

Asking the jury to consider whether the defendant was capable of appreciating the wrong committed was fast becoming a continuing theme in Scott's Old Bailey testimony, explicitly challenging the law's tacit assumption that knowing the nature of an act necessarily meant an awareness of its moral significance. Insane people, Scott once argued, "have colossal schemes: the mind in a way is always at work."[11] But to paraphrase the prison medical officer, the whole point is what one includes under the word *mind*. The law had long insisted that insanity was a matter of impaired cognition: an inability to know the nature and consequences of one's acts. But juries clearly had their own way of constructing what exactly the defendant knew about the consequences of his acts. James Hadfield's acquittal for an attempted regicide that he had undertaken because of its consequences underscored a growing separation of legal from moral wrong. There was no question that Hadfield knew he had a gun in his hand and the physical consequences of firing. He had committed a legal wrong, certainly, but his apocalyptic religious delusion obscured the moral turpitude one would attach to the regicide. His hope of engineering the Second Coming informed rather than obscured his *knowledge* of what he was up to.[12]

In lower-profile cases, prison medical officers drew attention to the defendants' superficial knowledge of the mechanics of crime. This focus on something beyond simple awareness for ascribing culpability had a long pedigree in the common law. Since the Middle Ages, at least, the acts of children and florid lunatics were considered special cases in terms of punishment and guilt fastening.[13] The resolve to do evil had long been questioned, not because children and idiots were confused about the nature and likely result of their acts, but because they were unable to appreciate those acts' inherent moral wrongfulness and their long-term consequences. A parallel effort to hold back on ascribing moral intention to the less floridly mad would prove challenging for the court as medical witnesses advanced defenses based on delusion. Delusion had left defendants like Hadfield aware of the nature and perhaps the consequences of their acts but—as was increasingly mentioned in medical testimony—woefully unaware of the social context of their actions. Consequently, mid-nineteenth-century juries increasingly heard prisoners described as "unconscious to the moral nature of their act": they "knew" at a physical level what they were doing, but juries were challenged to apply such a constrained notion of "knowing" to a standard for assigning culpability.

It is worth noting that this frontal assault on the law's grounds for ascribing responsibility did not come from asylum doctors or medical professors, who predictably might have sought to use the witness box in order to assert professional claims to unique knowledge. The law's criterion for defining the essence of insanity received its most direct challenge from prison medical officers, whose appearance in court had been at the direction of the state. "I made this report on his mental condition at the request of the Director of Public Prosecutions," prison physician Scott testified in 1901.[14] The independent spirit of witnesses was seen also among private practitioners who had informed the court that they had been "requested by the police sergeant to visit the prisoner in the cell" or "desired by the Solicitor of the Treasury to see the prisoner."[15] Henry Charlton Bastian informed the court, "I am frequently employed by the Treasury for such a purpose," an assignment, however, that did not translate into favoritism to the prosecution's case.[16] Being employed by the Treasury or requested by the Home Office to visit the prisoner and testify in court only ensured the medical man's appearance: he was just as likely to support the defense as the prosecution.

Still, sustained familiarity with prisoners could work in favor of the prosecution. John Scott, for example, was often the first to suspect shammed madness, disputing a prisoner's claim to have had a fit since no record could be found of either the seizure or the prisoner's prompt removal to a "special cell."[17] In like fashion, medical men in the employ of the Crown might point out the defendant's use of a mask and a weapon that "militate very strongly against the possibility of this being such an attack [of insanity]."[18] In one case, witnesses reported being called "in support of . . . [the accused's] defense of insanity" but decided the defendant's "unbalance" was due to irregular menstrual cycles, not an inability to know what she was up to.[19] Most often, though, denials of derangement were based on a perception of *counterfeited* madness, a constant challenge facing prison surgeons: "I am of opinion that he is acting; that his conduct is assumed . . . I have had a great many cases of persons feigning insanity, it is one of my greatest troubles."[20]

"Not in Any Way Am I a Partisan for Either Side"

Even when their testimony appeared to favor the prosecution rather than the defense, particularly in the suggestion that the putatively mad defendant "rather overact[ed] his part," medical witnesses often faced judicial suspicion regarding where their loyalties rested. "Having frequently been consulted by the Treasury in cases of insanity," Henry Charlton Bastian began his testimony with "I should like to say I am asked to give my impression," but he was interrupted by the judge and summarily directed "not to interfere as a Partisan." Bastian replied, "I have been a practitioner thirty-five years and have come to certain conclusions," at which point the judge again interposed, "declin[ing] to admit the witness's conclusions at present." Pressing on, Bastian continued, "I have opinions as to his sanity or insanity at the present time, and have sent those conclusions to the Treasury, contained in the report which you hold in your hand." Cross-examined by the prosecutor's attorney, Bastian underscored his neutral role: "May I say I go as a friend to the court to form an opinion . . . There was no reason why I should not accept [the prisoner's] statement."[21]

The issue of medical bias was also brought up by prison medical officer John Scott. "I have had [the prisoner] under very close observation in my capacity as an officer of the prison and not in any way as a partisan for either side—I did not suspect that he was shamming or that his convictions were not genuine . . . I was not instructed to keep him under very close observation—I should have done so under any circumstances."[22] Regular inspection of prisoners suspected to be contemplating an insanity plea had initially been prompted by the Home Office or Treasury solicitor, but by the second half of the nineteenth century, it was routine for prison doctors to visit regularly any prisoner facing a capital charge. The medical gaze, however, was described as one of detachment: "I simply approached the prisoner in the ordinary way as I do with all prisoners to test his mental capacity . . . unless insanity is forced upon me I don't believe it—I assume in the first place that a criminal is sane unless I find evidence to the contrary."[23]

Professional distance was also apparent in testimony that addressed "counterfeited" madness. As we have seen, of all specialist witnesses, prison doctors and medical men enlisted by government officials to visit prisoners in their cell were in a good position to report transparent episodes of shamming madness. Whether these detective skills increased their credibility in the court's eyes is hard to say, but such reports resonated strongly with the jail and prison surgeons' assertions that they began their conversations with the prisoners with the belief in their sanity, only finding madness when it "is forced upon me."

As if to disabuse the jury of suspicions that prisoners pretended madness to convince doctors to support their insanity pleas, medical witnesses informed the court that they had kept secret from the accused the real purpose of their conversation. Still, it seems hard to believe that prisoners being asked about the nature of their delusions would not have divined the identity of a questioner who was obviously neither their attorney nor their jailer (likely their only visitors). But since many prisoners evidenced greater reluctance to be labeled insane than criminal, the knowledge that the visitor was a doctor may have led them to try to give an impression of sanity rather than the reverse. To be sure, there is little evidence in the testimony to suggest active manipulation, other than the behavioral displays that appeared more theatrical than spontaneous.

There is evidence, however, of the medical witnesses' sensitivity to reporting the content—not just the histrionics—of their encounters with the accused in prison cells. After all, in explaining how they came to commit the acts for which they had been indicted, prisoners were divulging incriminating details about the killing or the theft, in effect doing the prosecutor's work for him. One might think that an insanity plea was an implicit acknowledgment of the prisoner's role in the offense and, hence, his or her culpability, but this was not necessarily the case. Juries were advised that their role was to determine the facts surrounding the alleged act and also to pronounce upon the state of the prisoner's intellects. If the former was not proven beyond a reasonable doubt, juries were perfectly justified in rendering a "not guilty" verdict, whatever their suspicions regarding the manifest madness of the accused. The content of the prison interview, which focused on the relation of delusion or homicidal melancholia to the crime, therefore could carry direct significance for establishing criminal responsibility, since it often affirmed the *actus rea*. If the prisoner's mental distraction did not rise to the requisite level of insanity, the plea was an obvious acknowledgement of guilt.

Although the precise questions that framed the prison interview—ostensibly the grounds for eventual diagnosis—did not often make their way into the printed testimony narratives, some conversations were recorded and recounted in vivid detail. Medical witnesses might read directly from the police station "Occurrence Book" containing daily entries of station business taken down by the officer on duty.[24] On other occasions, medical men referred to notes taken on their visits with prisoners in their cells. Showing exquisite sensitivity to the question of the accuracy of his recollections, a prison doctor informed the court, "I make a note of all cases in the prison and there is a note in this case . . . These are the original notes I jotted down; they are not copied from anything."[25] Most often, witnesses imparted some sense of the interview by referring to their opening interview question: "How came you to strike your child?" or "How were your shipmates *leaguing* against you?" Sometimes, the jury learned the range of questions asked and answers given:

Has anyone tried to injure you? He said, "I have thought so."
Has anyone tried to hang you?—"No."
Has anyone tried to cut your throat?—"No."
Has anyone tried to drown you or throw you in a pond?—"No."
Has anyone tried to poison you?—"I have thought so."
When?—"A good many times—I have many times sent my wife out of the room and changed the cup of tea and taken hers and given her mine."
Why did you do that?—"Because I was afraid she was trying to poison me."
Did you really believe it?—"I could not believe she would but I used to fancy so."
What made you think that?—"Because I used to think she was setting men to follow me wherever I went."

The medical witness then added, "He had pains in his stomach and used to think it was due to poison—he said his food was being drugged." The physician concluded, "I did not lead him by questions, because I have no interest in this matter but that of justice . . . I went to the prison to test the information I had been given—I wrote purposely for permission to have the interview with him—I did not go with a prejudicial mind; I had certain information which I had got at great trouble—I have no doubt he knows he is being tried for murder, but the insane know a great deal."[26]

The defensiveness inherent in a statement such as "I have no interest in this matter but that of justice" was not unusual; in addition to scornfully abjuring the role of partisan, medical witnesses unequivocally asserted their independence: "There is no motive in my mind why I should give a fake opinion on this matter—I am absolutely colorless; I came as a friend of the court—no hint was given to me as to what opinion I should form; I formed my opinion from the facts."[27]

It was not only the suspicion of bias toward one side or the other that the alienist had to confront. Their objections to courtroom questions sometimes revealed a prickliness on the part of general practitioners compelled to make fine distinctions between delusion and mistaken belief: "I cannot say if he was sane or not; you are asking me an impossible question."[28] While some medical witnesses cited the growing professional literature to reinforce the uncertain state of knowledge in the field, others announced their limitations by asserting what they did not know: "I cannot say that I have read Montgomery on the signs and symptoms of pregnancy—but I have had large experience in these cases—I have read extracts in a book by Esquiraux [Esquirol], but I must protest against being examined over the whole range of madness."[29] Such witnesses were not subject to judicial comments regarding partisanship; these were reserved for the prison doctor and the hospital physician, whose participation was requested by either the defense or the prosecution. When such a suspicion was lodged, it is worth emphasizing that judges did not reserve the charge only for defense medical witnesses. The bench seemed equally reluctant to assume independence on the part of medical witnesses regardless of which side solicited their opinions.

Given the aura of partisanship that could attach to medical testimony, one particular trial stands out for the activist medico-legal posture of the defense attorney and for the equanimity the bench displayed, given the novel role assumed by the medical man. Beginning his testimony by identifying himself as "author of two books on the subject of epilepsy and mental disorders and of numerous articles on the same subjects," Charles Mercier, lecturer on insanity at Westminster Hospital, explained his singular role in the trial of Matthew Bennett, indicted for assault with intent to commit grievous bodily harm on a complete stranger.

> My attention was first directed to the case by seeing an account of it in the newspapers—I read the evidence carefully and formed a distinct opinion about it and in consequence of that I am now defending the prisoner . . . [I] have carefully looked at the evidence and in my opinion it indicates a particular form of epilepsy called epileptic vertigo . . . Sudden unconsciousness is the characteristic feature of that malady, the sinking down on the knees, the dazed appearance, the pallor, the silence on being questioned, are all symptoms of the malady . . . If a person in [epileptic vertigo] finds in his hand an article which he has been accustomed to use, he will use it in the customary manner . . . without any relation to the circumstances.

On cross-examination, Mercier denied that "it is an exceptional thing for a medical man to undertake a defense"—although he was playing a bit loose with the term *defense*; it was indeed anomalous for a medical man to appear as legal advocate for the defense. He defended his role in the proceedings and the grounds for the diagnosis of epileptic vertigo by invoking unique experience and the knowledge he had thereby gained.

> I am a specialist . . . It was a matter that I thought would not properly occur to an ordinary medical man, and I communicated with the Colonel of his regiment—he said they were not going to undertake his defense, and I thought it was a view that should be placed before a jury—the view is, that the man having a rifle in his hand, automatically went through the movements customary to him, that is, loading and firing, and that he was oblivious to the fact that he was a sentry . . . he did not appreciate the act he was doing . . . not that he was insane but unconscious, that he had no mind at all at the time.

Acting as legal advocate, Mercier had obtained the defendant's "consent to this defense," soberly discussing with him the consequences of a "verdict of insanity," which would mean commitment to Broadmoor for an indeterminate term: "I did not hold out any promise to him that he might be got out." On re-examination, Mercier switched from defense advocate to medical witness: "There is no danger of such a thing occurring again unless the gun were in his hand." Stating that they were of the opinion that the accused "had no object in firing, that it was done on the spur of the moment," the jurors convicted him of simple assault, sentencing him to three months of hard labor rather than acquitting him on grounds of insanity and committing him to Broadmoor. It did not hurt his case that the defense attorney and the medical witness spoke with one voice.[30]

When Mercier disparaged the limited knowledge base of the "ordinary medical man," his effort to distance and elevate the testimony of specialists in mental medicine from lay and general *medical* opinion was well under way. First, he offered a criticism common to early nineteenth-century medical texts: the public's tendency to mistake mania's lucid interval for a restoration to sanity. The trained observer recognized such transitory episodes as a mere respite in the natural course of derangement. The untrained observer, writers alleged, drew liberally upon Shakespearean stereotypes of madness: distracted Ophelia, melancholic Hamlet, and furious Lear. As the diagnosis of madness migrated "inside," however—as observable derangement was replaced by the contents of consciousness and of delusion, circumscribed to a particular subject—the uninitiated were duped by surface calm, unmindful of the need to draw out the conversation.

The effort to distinguish and elevate specialist opinion over lay observation at the Old Bailey begins mid nineteenth century.[31] Even general medical training was not sufficient to comment knowingly on delusion: "a man who has experience in insanity is able to come to a conclusion in a case of this kind as far as the mental condition is concerned."[32] The untrained, the inexperienced, and those lacking a sustained exposure to madness could not make sense of symptoms because "nothing is seen by outside observers of what is going on in the mind."[33] Again, it was the misleading nature of surface calm that confused the uninitiated: "I don't know if some of the patients in Bethlehem are to all appearance rational to an ordinary person—we give balls and concerts there, and out-patients and visitors mix and dance with the patients—to the outside world they appear sane . . . there is no infallible preceding symptom before a patient becomes absolutely insane; you look for certain signs."[34]

George Savage, physician of Bethlem for ten years before giving the testimony above, exemplified the medical witness who disparaged the observations of the *uninitiated,* as lay people were referred to in court. When questioned closely about their opinions, the witnesses who were most defensive on the stand were not prison doctors, police surgeons, or general medical practitioners but rather the elite of the mental medicine practitioners. It is curious that their testimony focused more on dismissing the observations of the "uninitiated" and less on refining gross categories of derangement into forms of insanity that engaged the law most directly. It would fall to another type of medical witness to engage both the law's basis for assigning culpability and the jury's consideration of states of mental functioning that divided seemingly purposeful action from apparent consciousness.

Taking the Courtroom Temperature

Given the dearth of specialized medical terms in the early decades of courtroom testimony, it is not surprising that physicians, surgeons, and apothecaries claiming unique experience and insight into madness faced few hostile questions in court. Initially, they were testifying about a neighbor or a former patient; their use of terms like *lunacy, delirium,* and *insensibility* was immediately comprehensible to judge and jury alike. Even the first term to distinguish medical from lay testimony, *delusion,* was hardly mysterious or in any way opaque. After all, *delusion* had been introduced to the criminal courtroom by an attorney. As we have seen, the few moments of raw contentiousness seem to have been particular to a specific witness or medical term, not to the appearance of specialists in mental medicine per se. Thus Dr. Luis Leo in 1800 faced insulting judicial comments because of either his religion or his making a second appearance "to get someone off on insanity."[35] John Conolly faced a judge who insisted he answer a question not of his choosing; the asylum superintendent's responses suggest a rather imperious attitude that the judge seemed happy to curb. Conolly's preferred diagnosis, moral insanity, could engender sharp rebuke from the judiciary, even when the witness appeared more deferential to courtroom protocol: "Experts in madness! Mad-doctors! Gentlemen, I will read you the evidence of these medical witnesses—these 'experts in madness.' And if you can make sane evidence out of what they say, do so; but I confess it's more than I can do. Of course I do not say you don't understand it, but I say 'place what value upon it you think it worth.'"[36]

Although extreme in tone, the judge's dismissiveness of a diagnosis based upon a derangement of morals, independent of any cognitive defect, seems to have been sparked by a particularly heinous crime and medical testimony that sought to explain the crime *by* the crime: a derangement of how one "ought to feel" rather than a failure of knowing that homicide was a crime. Clearly, a diagnosis of moral insanity was a hazardous undertaking, not least because it was only revealed by the crime itself. To be sure, the legal community was not the only quarter that raised alarm; autonomous diseases of the will and emotion had their own detractors in the medical community.

Apart from the occasional eruption from the bench, the other courtroom actors—attorneys for the prosecution or defense—showed little hostility in questioning medical witnesses. Very often, the attorneys' questions were so tendentiously phrased that medical witnesses need only respond with a simple yes or no: "Do you believe, supposing it should be proved to the satisfaction of the Jury that she threw this child into the Thames, that the delusion in her mind might have induced her to do it to prevent its having a life of suffering?"[37] Although one is hardly surprised to find attorneys asking leading questions, it is the deft pairing of delusion with an inevitable murderous action that underscored the predictive behavioral result of delusory beliefs. Even without such prompting, medical witnesses were deft at placing the crime squarely at the foot of obsessive fear, with the defendant described as "under the influence of insane delusions when he committed the offense with which he was charged."[38] Medical men were keen to stress the impelling nature of false beliefs eclipsing a "general sense of right and wrong" when the accused was in the throes of overwhelming false beliefs: "It is quite possible that in insanity there may be delusions which overcome the moral sense and self control, and yet some functions of the mind may perform their ordinary operations . . . [asked then by the judge to amplify this point] I think his power of judging right and wrong generally, would have been interfered with by reason of these mental delusions . . . at the time he would have no adequate control over his actions and therefore he would not have known properly the quality of his act."[39] What did it signify to inquire whether the deluded defendant was *conscious* of having a knife in his hand or a distracted mother had *purposely* mixed rat poison into her children's pudding? When prosecuting attorneys and judges attempted to ascribe jealousy or revenge as the motive for a killing, the medical witness was quick to ground the jealousy in the unyielding conviction that one's spouse was trying to poison him. This was no ordinary green-eyed monster: this was an insistent, propelling delusory belief that "overcame moral sense and self control."

Defending the Diagnosis . . . to the Defendant

Although medical witnesses could expect sharp questioning by prosecutors and sometimes judges, they also encountered antagonism in an unexpected quarter. The author of dismissive comments mentioned earlier—"You judge from ideas; you've got a good opinion of yourself"—that cast aspersions on the self-aggrandizing confidence of the medical man, was neither judge nor attorney but the defendant.[40] In the second half of the eighteenth century when defense attorneys (if they were in court at all) were restricted to asking questions of witnesses, the defendant spoke at the end of the trial, the testimony recorded in the trial narratives as the "Prisoner's Defense." Normally a claim of innocence—either a complete denial of involvement or a forceful justification for the act—was a vestige of the earlier type of trial, in which the victim confronted the alleged offender in open court. As the adversary trial emerged, both the prosecutor and the defendant were replaced as courtroom questioners by their legal representatives.

As the insanity trial became populated with attorneys and medical witnesses on either side, the prisoner's defense statement became abbreviated and, in time, all but disappeared completely. Occasionally, the prisoner would speak up during the trial, to question a medical witness: "Did you not say before the Magistrate at Worship Street that you considered I was of unsound mind?" While this courtroom dialogue between the prisoner and the doctor often took the tone of urging the medical witness to support the prisoner's insanity plea, far more colorful questioning characterized the defendant's refusal to accept the doctor's diagnosis of madness.

Heated dialogue between defendant and doctor might concern a specific diagnosis. In 1854, Hugh Pollard Willoughby listened as first Gilbert McMurdo and then Forbes Winslow, a prominent alienist, proffered delusion as the cause of the defendant's attack on a barrister. The jail surgeon was the first to testify and sidestepped the judge's question about the defendant's ability to distinguish good from evil: "His case is peculiar—your Lordship is aware, quite as much as I can be that many persons of unsound mind are particularly shrewd upon many points, and that unless you have the thread given you, you cannot draw out of them just cause to form your conclusions . . . I believe he is laboring under a most horrible delusion; a settled delusion, which renders him perfectly unsound at this moment."[41] The defendant, however, was unconvinced, and protested that delusion was simply a matter of *whose* version of the events was true. If the events surrounding the offense really had happened, the behavior was justified; if they had not, Willoughby would accept the diagnosis. In any event, he had no use for the jail surgeon. "If they were not done, then I am stark mad; I am under a delusion; they either did happen, or they did not; if they did not, I am under a delusion and I am mad; it is no use my talking to you." Still, he asked the prison surgeon, "Do you consider me to be of unsound mind in any other respect?" Apparently bristling at the prospect of sparring with a man he considered delusional, the jail surgeon directed his response to the court instead of the prisoner: "His unsoundness of mind is to such extent upon this point, that I should consider him of unsound mind on any point."[42]

The jail surgeon was followed to the stand by Forbes Winslow, who had treated the defendant some years before at the request of the family. He concurred with surgeon McMurdo that the diagnosis was delusion. The prisoner objected.

Defendant: Did not you tell me you would be of the opinion that I was not laboring under a delusion, if my statements were corroborated by [the judge] and others?

Forbes Winslow: I mentioned to you, that if you could establish total satisfaction that the circumstances you alleged actually occurred . . . they would be facts and not delusions, and that, of course, would considerably modify my opinion—you said that the judge was in a position to establish all the facts.

Defendant: Not all the facts; the leading facts—did I object to see you?

Forbes Winslow: Not at all; not to answer any of my questions—what you stated I considered a delusion—if those things can be proved to be facts, then of course, they would not be delusions . . . you told me it was a delusion, you must be mad—I asked you whether it would not be better to plead insanity, in order to avoid being transported—I endeavoured to persuade you that you were under a fake impression; and I said, with a view to comforting you, that it was quite possible, in the course of time, that those impressions might be removed.[43]

But the impressions were not removed. The defendant's deft questioning of the medical witnesses regarding the possible relationship of "true facts" and a false diagnosis of delusion were eventually effaced by a rambling, incoherent, religiously themed prisoner's defense that went on for pages in the *OBSP* and resulted in the one outcome the defendant did not want: not guilty on the grounds of insanity.

Defendants could also question the basis for medical diagnosis, writ large. In 1906, an asylum physician had just finished discussing the basis for this finding of "unsound mind" and its having "produce[d] the effects we have heard of." For the first time in the trial, the prisoner spoke up.

Prisoner: Did a Catholic priest tell you that I broke your images?

Physician: No, my servant said she saw you there—I did not say "breaking images,"—I said "statues."

Prisoner: You are demented—you had better go back to your native Ireland; you are no use here—the doctor who recommended you came and looked me in the eye, and said he could tell a lunatic by looking in his eye—what a precious fool he must be.[44]

Since the late eighteenth century, it had been common practice for medical witnesses to speak of the peculiar look in the madman's eye or the well-referenced "lunatic's ear." With remarks like "you judge from ideas, you have a good opinion of yourself," defendants alleged insane called attention to the utterly subjective grounds for the medical inference of insanity. The medical witness found himself with precious few grounds for divining organic brain disease—hence, the prisoner's lampooning the alienist's diagnosing from *ideas*. The alienist had only his experience of continued interaction with the deranged to buttress his claim to a knowledge base, but the ephemeral nature of this experience cum knowledge was always in danger of being dismissed and never more emphatically than by the allegedly mad defendant. "They want to prove me insane," a prisoner said in his prisoner's defense, "I think I can prove a good many of them insane."[45]

On trial for assault, a prisoner listened as the medical superintendent of Peckham House Asylum described the delusion he believed had animated the attack: "I was quite unable to convince him that he had in any way committed an offense. I could not get any reason except his delusion that even now it would be quite possible to get [the woman] to marry him . . . that idea seemed to dominate him. He was very threatening to me. He threatened lawsuits and became very emotional . . . My opinion is that his mental disease will be progressive—that he will deteriorate." When the prisoner interrupted the asylum doctor, suggesting that he had permitted him to escape, the doctor replied, "I did not allow you to escape purposely. You seized the opportunity. I have had nearly twenty years' experience of insanity and have been medical superintendent at Peckham for twelve years." The asylum physician was followed to the stand by the medical officer at Holloway Prison, James Scott. After completing his testimony, Scott was in turn grilled by the prisoner, to whom he replied, "I have had much experience of insanity. I have examined for the Courts of London for fully ten years and had previous experience in other places." The prisoner lost little time turning the two witnesses' experience to his advantage in crafting his prisoner's defense. As related by the recorder, "The Prisoner said that Dr. Halstead and Dr. Scott may have observed him, but he also observed them, and it was generally admitted that people who had to do with insane people were apt to become a little touched. The germs of insanity saturated them."[46]

The trial narratives abound in examples of defendants resisting the label of *mad.* "Is there any appeal against this," protested John Tuck, "I am a good many years old to [be] found out insane."[47] His disquiet at being so labeled was shared by another prisoner, who insisted that he be sworn and examined by his defense attorney rather than let the prison doctor's testimony about his delusions go unchallenged. He stated, "A great deal of trouble was in connection with the loss of my daughter . . . I suggested that Dr. Savage, a specialist should see her. Instead of allowing that, they persecuted me, slandering me everywhere, were continually sending writs and sheriffs to me. It is ridiculous nonsense to suggest that I myself once suggested I should go to an asylum. I challenge you or the prosecution to bring into the box anyone who has known the way I have carried on business during the last 5 years to say that I am insane."[48]

One cannot help wondering if there was a method to the mad defendant's madness. There could hardly be a more crafty strategy for convincing the jury of one's derangement than to spar with a medical witness, adamantly denying one's madness, while all the time appearing unhinged. Although there are numerous examples of such confrontations, few defendants went to such lengths as William Tebbitt to avoid the label of madman altogether. In 1912, Tebbitt pointed a pistol at Leopold de Rothschild, a family friend who had taken an interest in the young man. The bullet missed the intended target but struck a policeman nearby. "I intended to shoot Leopold," he reportedly said at the police station shortly afterward. As his defense attorney explained to the court, "He thought that Mr. Rothschild had for some reason conceived an enmity towards him, and that using the great influence which prisoner supposed him to possess, he had influenced the instructor at the college to mis-instruct him and to prevent his progress in his studies. Prisoner's view was that the only way in which he could put a stop to that interruption to his studies . . . was to put an end to Mr. Rothschild's life."[49] The precise nature of the delusory intrusion was explained by a private practitioner, Theophilus Bulkeley Hyslop, who interviewed the prisoner in Brixton Prison. As the medical witness informed the court, the defendant believed that "a tutor of chemistry at King's College has been indirectly influenced by Sir Leopold to make a wrong equation of some chemical formula . . . and [the accused] thought he was duty bound to retaliate."[50] Cross-examined by the defense attorney to describe the defendant's demeanor in the interview, he replied, "He is in some respects fairly intelligent. I know he very strongly resents the suggestion that he is insane and desires his sanity to be established in the course of this inquiry . . . that does not shake my belief; 99 out of 100 persons who are suffering from mental disease deny the fact . . . he desired to be examined by another expert . . . He did not accept my view that he is insane."[51]

Rounding out the medical witnesses was the medical officer at Brixton, Sidney Dyer, who concurred with the privately retained witness's diagnosis of delusional insanity. Dyer testified, "He is so diseased with delusions that they rather seem to percolate into other topics. He talks coherently and intelligently on labour matters and politics . . . then these delusions of persecution seem to come into them." Silent throughout the trial, Tebbitt's prisoner's defense came in the form of a statement made to the chief inspector of the city police, written down and initialed sheet by sheet by the defendant. (He complained that two different kinds of paper were being used.)

> I have reason to suppose that there is a general impression that I was insane at the time I made my attempt on the life of Mr. de Rothschild. I consider I was perfectly sane and think that an impartial reading of the police evidence

will support my opinion. I am completing a full statement of the motives for my action, which are mainly political, and which I will read to the judge who tries me. I take this opportunity of saying that no reliance can be placed upon any report, speeches, statement, etc. of other people which purport to contain expressions of my view.[52]

Tebbitt concluded his defense by preemptively pleading guilty to the two indictments of felonious shooting with intent to murder. With this, the trial came to a close, placing the judge, by his own admission, "in considerable difficulty by the course which this case has taken. Although personally . . . I am of an opinion that you are not responsible for your actions . . . I am bound to consider you, for the purpose of today, as a sane man, responsible for your act, and to pass the same sentence upon you that I should pass on a sane man."[53] Still, the diagnosis of delusional insanity had its effect on the judge, no matter how vigorously the prisoner had abjured the medical man's professional opinion. Acknowledging that the twenty-year sentence he had just announced to the court was "more or less a formality," the judge explained, "I am satisfied, and you may be satisfied, that the sentence will not be carried into effect, and that your state of mind being inquired into, the result, in fact will be that you will be detained awaiting His Majesty's pleasure."[54] This is, of course, the same disposition the defendant would have received had he been found "guilty of the act but not responsible," as the judge affirmed in his remarks.

One is struck by the judge's remark to the prisoner: "and you may be satisfied." In his work on the evolution of the adversary criminal trial, John Langbein highlighted the judicial discouraging of guilty pleas, dating at least to the seventeenth century: "The trial court's role in sentencing and clemency . . . militated strongly against guilty pleas, even in cases in which conviction was certain."[55] Was the trace of vinegar in the judge's comment referring to the difficulty in which he found himself—being forced to sentence a man he personally believed bore "no moral blame" for his conduct? Or did it acknowledge the court's pique at the prisoner's refusal to accept a diagnosis put forward by the expert witness representing contemporary medical practice? Whatever displeasure lay behind the judicial summing up, one thing was clear. Although his hands were tied "for purposes of today," the sentence was, in his mind and in his words, a formality. No guilty plea was going to rob him of his authority in guilt fastening (or guilt acquitting) and sentencing.

And what of the medical witness's authority? What insights do the *Old Bai-*

ley Sessions Papers offer regarding the professional voice of the mad-doctor cum private practitioner cum alienist? His parrying with the putative insane from the witness box no doubt provided gripping theater for the Old Bailey gallery and the readers of the testimony narratives, but it is doubtful that the medical man's sense of professional gravitas suffered any lasting damage. Nor do the sessions papers suggest that medical men faced rough seas with attorneys for either the defense or the prosecution. Certainly, one reads of "close questioning," but the testimony narratives reveal no evidence of general suspicion or hostility toward the self-described specialist in court. Above all, there were few if any slurs cast upon the knowledge base of psychiatry. Even in its efforts to expose conceptual narrowness, cross-examination appears, perhaps inadvertently, to have elevated specialists in mental medicine above the general practitioner. A phrase like "perhaps you are familiar with the works of . . . " functioned just as easily to lend authority to a witness's opinion as to diminish the opinion of the medical man whose background did not include sustained experience with the deranged. This is not to suggest that all medical witnesses were treated with kid gloves. An attorney might ask, archly, "Are you a licensed keeper of an asylum?" (knowing full well the physician was not) in an effort to dilute the effect of a diagnosis offered by the inexperienced, though medically qualified, witness. Questions could also be worded to express incredulity at the medical man's opinion—"You do not consider, for a moment, that this man has not understood right from wrong"—but again, one senses this was a rhetorical strategy, not an effort to denigrate the specialist's claim to unique insight.

Overall, cross-examination in insanity trials did not attempt to probe the grounds for witnesses' medical inferences as much as to compel medical men to address how their diagnoses affected the defendants' capacity to know the nature and quality of their acts. Whatever baseless suspicions, paranoid fantasies, or conspiratorial plots had led the medical man to infer insanity, the attorney—and sometimes the judge—was bound to return the court's business to determining the defects of cognition. This was the ultimate question waiting at the end of innovative medical testimony that included derangement of the volitional faculties: moral insanity, lesion of the will, and irresistible impulse. As predictable as the judge's final question, "Has he any delusion at all?," was the prosecuting attorney's "Do you mean at the time he was beating his wife . . . he could not distinguish right from wrong?"

It was not the alienist's claim to knowledge that was on trial. Much more threatening to his professional integrity was the judge's intimation—and, at times, explicit suggestion—that the medical man appeared as a partisan whose knowledge had been contoured to fit the needs of the side that paid him. Even without the judge expressing doubt, medical witnesses were moved to state, "I have no interest in the matter but justice," or "I go as a friend of the court." The somewhat maladroit protestation "I give evidence on both sides" doubtless was intended to convey a lack of partisanship but could lamentably reinforce that the medical witness was an expert for hire. This charge was also leveled at other nineteenth-century expert witnesses, particularly chemists on their way to becoming toxicologists. That a professional's services were enlisted to bolster the claims to innocence (or guilt) of either side always left open the suggestion that his opinion as well as his services could be purchased.

The vulnerability medical witnesses in insanity cases faced was unique, however; the toxicologist had chemical analyses to discuss, the surgeon had bodily signs of trauma to draw upon to distinguish a homicidal from a suicidal wound. The mad-doctor cum alienist had only ideas, uncharacteristic behavior, and rambling conversation. The grounds for diagnoses were, as the disgruntled defendant pointed out, eminently subjective and perhaps had contracted a madness all their own. As the allegedly mad defendant had described his classifiers, "the germs of insanity [have] saturated them."

CHAPTER SIX

Homicidal Mania

Provenance and Cultural Context

I am a qualified surgeon, and have been thirty-four years in practice . . . I have
seen a good deal of insanity in hospitals . . . I know there is a species of insanity
known as homicidal mania—that takes the form of an attempt on a man's life
or the life of another person—that may break out in either or both ways, and in
the case of a man who had not been previously suspected of being insane—he
may recover completely after the attack, and may or may not have any recollection of it—in the case of a man whose relatives had died in an asylum . . . would
have to be taken into consideration . . . insane persons show great cunning and
in planning and often show a spirit of revenge.

In addition to being a qualified surgeon, George Robertson brought a further
credential to a murder trial at the Old Bailey in 1894; he had been the first
medical man at the scene. He found the victim "flat on her back with the
throat cut . . . I came to the conclusion, as there was no blood on her dress, that
the wound had been inflicted when she was on her back—the left side of the
wound was jagged, the edges pointing to the right side."[1] Mr. Robertson did
not just happen upon the body; he was divisional surgeon of police. His inferences about the cause and manner of death would be critical to the Old Bailey
because of his firsthand experience with the crime scene.

Although his medical knowledge had usually been called upon to attend
to victims who might be saved, his position with the police afforded him the
opportunity to encounter the likely offender, apprehended immediately at the
scene or within an hour or two after the offense. The surgeon routinely jotted
down in the police station's Occurrence Book his impressions of the suspect's
demeanor and account of his role in the crime, and he often delivered these
observations at the trial. Whether reading from his personal notes or the
station record, medical men called to the scene (most commonly surgeons
assigned to a police division) moved seamlessly from making cause-of-death

determinations based on position of the body and blood evidence to drawing inferences regarding the suspect's mental condition. In the last decades of the nineteenth century, jurors familiar with delusion and melancholia confronted another diagnosis, often delivered by police surgeons. Homicidal mania's defining feature, jurors learned, was the "killing or destroying [of] some person most commonly dear to the person so affected." Those afflicted were described as "more dangerous [than other deranged offenders], as the delusion may recur."[2]

Delusion and melancholia may have been diagnosed more frequently in medical testimony, but neither type of madness led inevitably to crime. The delusional and the melancholic often suffered profound depression, leading them perhaps to suicide, if to any specific act at all. But homicidal mania contained criminality in its name: the inevitable result was murder. The diagnosis and its proffering in court and in print sit at a critical moment in the histories of madness, forensic psychiatry, and the (then-emerging) advocacy bar, affording a critical window into the reciprocal relations between law and forensic medicine.[3]

"Unable to Resist the Animal Functions of the Brain"

"A person may have reason and know the wickedness of what he is going to commit, yet he is unable to resist," explained James Duncan at the 1860 trial of his footman, charged with murder.[4] Homicidal mania had first been introduced at the Old Bailey three years earlier by John Gibson, surgeon of Newgate Gaol, in a case of child murder. The mother's delusion, Gibson explained, was her belief that "her milk had turned to water—I believe she had been suckling the child immediately before [the killing] . . . she told me there was a large hole in the child's back, into which she could place her fist."[5] In an apparent state of despair at the child's imminent starvation, she twisted a piece of linen around its neck to preclude an agonizingly slow death.

When Gibson cited the centrality of delusion to his diagnosis, he articulated a common feature that subsequent medical witnesses invoking homicidal mania would include in their courtroom testimony. In the second half of the nineteenth century and into the early twentieth, forty-three medical men in thirty separate trials based their inferences of insanity on homicidal mania, with half citing prisoners' delusions in their diagnosis. One defendant believed he bore an unmistakable resemblance to Oliver Cromwell, another that his mother was an imposter, a sailor that his shipmates were conspiring to kill him, and yet another defendant claimed to have been served poisoned tea and to have tested the theory by switching cups with the suspected mur-derous spouse.[6] Also making an appearance in the testimony was the centu-ries' old fear of the "power of darkness, overshadowing" one, a conception of delusion that dated to classical antiquity.[7]

First introduced into common law at the beginning of the nineteenth cen-tury, delusion had attained a pride of place as the court's preferred medico-legal form of derangement. Attorney Thomas Erskine, who first enlisted de-lusion in a criminal defense in 1800, had maintained that the mere presence of a delusion was not sufficient: a direct, logical link must connect the fateful misapprehension with the criminal act. His fellow jurists and certainly most medical men did not adhere to this stricture. What did it mean to say that no *logical* connection could be found between the act and the deluded be-lief? For medical witnesses, the "mere" presence of delusion was evidence enough of a profoundly deranged individual, one who could not exercise choice because of the profound confusion surrounding the nature of what he was doing. Jurists also had tried to circumscribe delusion's significance by referring to it as a partial insanity, but there was nothing partial as far as medical opinion was concerned. Delusions carried inevitable consequences. When the "thread to the darling delusion was pulled," the individual was no longer in control of his own thought and behavior. This loss of self-mastery would prove the most fundamental challenge to the common law's notion of culpability. In terms of its implications for jurisprudence, delusion had mi-grated from an inability to know right from wrong to a "loss of moral liberty."

Called to the scene of a murder in 1872, surgeon Joseph Moore encoun-tered the suspected assailant, whose demeanor he recounted to the court. "I have had under my notice a species of insanity known as homicidal mania; it is sometimes called melancholia—I have known cases of 'delusion' pushed into action by an uncontrollable impulse . . . I believe it is occasionally the case . . . that the victim has been the person most loved by the person com-mitting the crime."[8] The surgeon's testimony is noteworthy for the naming of an "uncontrollable impulse," propelling the deluded into action. Impulses—irresistible, uncontrollable—had been spoken of before at the Old Bailey but were invoked in discussions of moral insanity, engendering withering con-tempt from the bench. During the first two-thirds of the nineteenth century, such "clear-thinking" insanities were conspicuously removed from jury con-sideration. Only delusion and other errors in knowing merited the court's indulgence.

But delusion always carried an involuntary consequence, not always articulated but always implied. James Hadfield's unyielding belief that his own execution was required for Christ's return could not find resolution in his imagination: only the king's death and his own execution would quell the insistent, hectoring delusion. Daniel McNaughtan's belief that Robert Peel was out to destroy him did not lend itself to quiet reflection about possible courses of action: "Nothing short of a physical impossibility would prevent him from performing an act which his delusion might impel him to do."[9] Juries were not always told of this uncontrollable drive, but they were presented with involuntary actions propelled by delusory fears and obsessive beliefs. The murderous impulse had to be rooted in cognitive error, however; free-floating, autonomous impulses were kept from the jury's consideration because of their association with moral insanity. Medical witnesses became much more explicit about the behavioral consequences attending delusion when they invoked homicidal mania in their testimony.

Trials that featured this innovative diagnosis shared another characteristic: the victimization of persons closest to the offender. Indeed, the choice of victim became a defining element in cases that introduced homicidal mania for the jury's consideration: "She did not attack her lover [who abandoned her] as a sane person would have done; she had a spite against him, and had every cause to be offended with him; she attacks her dearly loved child; it is not the act of a sane person to do this; homicidal mania is a species of insanity that takes the form of killing or destroying . . . most commonly those who are most dear to the person so affected."[10] Children had certainly been targeted before, as had beloved spouses and friends. Infanticides, in particular, had often resulted from a visit by Satan: "you must and you shall kill your child" (or the devil would take him first). Delusions about spousal infidelity have never been uncommon, but specialist testimony in the late 1800s described attacks of a sudden, impulsive nature, sometimes having little to do with the content of the delusion lodged in the prisoner's mind. The fateful error in belief seemed to anchor the new diagnosis in traditional legal thought regarding a lack of culpability. It was not preoccupying anxiety or gnawing fear that had precluded the capacity to make a choice: medical witnesses spoke instead of the impelling force of an impulse that bypassed reason altogether. Also bypassed was any moral awareness of the nature of the crime. "I should think a person moved by such an impulse would probably not be capable of judging right from wrong," one witness offered, while another testified, "She suffered from an uncontrollable impulse to kill, not conscious of the nature or quality of the act, or conscious that she was doing wrong."[11]

Medical men who based their testimony on homicidal mania were unequivocal in their dismissal of the defendant's capacity to retain powers of volition. When a judge asked physician Henry Charlton Bastian what homicidal mania was, the doctor replied, "A man having certain tendencies will occasionally, without warning or provocation, commit a certain act of violence or something comes over him abruptly, suddenly without any apparent reason, leading him to commit some act of violence . . . he being absolutely unconscious of the act, he may know what the act is, but not the quality of it—a gust of impulse comes over him so suddenly that he is not in a position to weigh or balance whether such a thing is right or wrong." Asked to elaborate, the physician described the afflicted as "deprived of reason, loss of will, and loss of controlling power, that would practically be his mental condition; bereft of reason and power of control."[12] Medical witnesses defended their diagnoses by incessantly invoking the specter of motiveless violence—the insane defendants were "unable to resist the animal pressures of the brain," and thus destroyed those most near and dear.[13] Juries were presented with incredulous, inconsolable mothers, horrified by what they had done. The diagnosis left only the sudden "gust of passion" as the culprit. Again, this was passion triggered by no "sane" revenge or understandable animus. In most cases, the fury had no reason; it was based on nothing at all.

Not all defendants diagnosed with homicidal mania revealed lapses in consciousness. Some recalled the attack with dread. But theirs was a curious sort of consciousness, revealing the chasm that could separate knowing from appreciating, a distinction to which medical witnesses had alluded earlier in the century. An appreciation of why the act was wrong had eluded the defendant: "He may be in such a state to form murderous intentions to know that if he shot [the victim] it would be murder, but yet he may be so dissociated from the world he has not a grasp of the act."[14] Similar to prisoners earlier in the century whose unconscious state of being resembled sleepwalking, persons afflicted with homicidal mania could be described in court as being in the "condition of post-epileptic automatism; he is another person altogether."[15] Although few medical witnesses addressed the phenomenon of doubled consciousness directly, the difference between a mother naturally disposed to suckle and nurture her infant and the defendant who followed such feedings with strangulation could not have escaped a juror.[16]

Medical witnesses who chose to address the common law's announced criterion of whether the defendant was "capable of judging right from wrong" stressed the vagaries of consciousness when in the throes of an overwhelming impulse to kill. Called to the police station to speak to a mother suspected of child murder, the police surgeon reported his observation to the court: "She then seemed to be totally insensible to the gravity of the crime with which she was charged, and totally regardless of the effect of it on herself . . . looking at the whole case [a family history of insanity] I am of opinion that at the time this was done the prisoner was certainly suffering from an uncontrollable impulse to kill, and therefore was not conscious of the nature and quality of the act which she was committing, or conscious that what she was doing was wrong."[17] Was it possible for a person who committed a crime in the throes of homicidal mania to retain a recollection of what she did? For some medical men, memory revealed the presence of a conscious state, suggesting both knowledge and intention. And if one was even minimally aware of killing someone (particularly a loved one), how was it possible not to know it was wrong? These were the moments when the law's unrelenting standard of "knowing" was most directly under assault. As one medical witness averred, "I do not know if the element of [knowing] right from wrong is very strong—a patient might know it was wrong to murder, but he might not think it wrong to kill a particular person—it may be a delusion that the object of their hatred has injured them."[18]

Revenge, of course, was an all too understandable motive in murders committed by the sane; for those afflicted with homicidal mania, evidence of premeditation would seem to have reinforced rather than precluded the forming of mens rea. At these moments, delusion returned to center stage. One who killed out of self-defense—delusory as the belief may have been that one was in danger—was no different from someone raising an affirmative defense of duress. Even evidence of premeditation could be well explained by the delusion. What could *not* be explained easily by delusory belief was a defendant whose demented construction of the circumstances surrounding the act left him with sufficient understanding to know the precariousness of his position. Medical witnesses were frankly incredulous when confronted with such obvious design: "if the act was committed during a paroxysm of insanity, I should not expect to find a man purchasing a revolver and cartridges some hours before the act . . . to understand enough to say, 'Oh yes it will be used in evidence against me.'" To the medical witness, this was a clear sign that the defendant knew the act to be *criminal* and the consequences that would follow upon arrest.

But why should it matter that the defendant had planned the crime by careful design and even knew the act to be punishable? Hadfield, after all, had also secured a firearm and ammunition in the throes of delusional insanity. His saying to the policeman who wrestled him to the ground, "Did I get him, did I get the king?"—suggested a grasp of the consequences that resonated with the sentiment, "Oh yes, it will be used in evidence against me." And yet Hadfield had been acquitted; his capacity to procure the weapon and ammunition necessary for the *intended* assassination did not militate against the jury's conviction that he was well and truly deluded. At the end of the century, prison surgeon George Walker affirmed the same argument, this time at the trial of a thirteen-year-old boy on trial for fatally stabbing his mother: "I seriously mean that he would go to the shop, select the knife, bargain for it, and buy it while under the influence of mania; under the influence of homicidal mania these crimes are done with great deliberation."[19]

Such a statement likely perplexed the Old Bailey juror as much as it does today's reader of the *OBSP.* Was homicidal mania a sudden, overpowering gust of passion, or was it a state of consciousness in which calm, purposeful, deliberate action had been dictated by impulse? Furthermore, what level of consciousness attended this species of insanity? Some offenders diagnosed with homicidal mania could recollect their attacks, while others could not. Some defendants seemed oblivious to having committed any outrage at all, others willingly surrendered to police, and others, like the thirteen-year-old mentioned above, tried to conceal their crime, clearly revealing that they knew the act to have been wrong. Much like melancholia, puerperal mania, and insensibility, homicidal mania was a capacious diagnosis, capable of hosting a range of effects. Like other persons diagnosed with mental derangement, the deluded followed no script in terms of predictable behavior. Some patients did nothing about their fears, others ended their own lives, and still others arrived at the Old Bailey, having destroyed their suspected tormentors.

The one element medical men could agree upon was the strategic role of the criminal act itself as the marker of this particular species of insanity: "I look upon the act as a symptom of insanity—in cases of homicidal mania you may have no definite symptoms of insanity before the commission of the act, or after the act, yet the act itself may be an insane act . . . probably she would know the effect of cutting the child's throat would be to kill it, but she would not think it was a crime to kill it at the time the crime was committed."[20] Medical witnesses throughout the late Victorian era thus cited the absence of an appreciation of the act's moral nature—the inability to recognize the outrage to social convention that the act represented—as the defining element rather than the consequence of insanity. Homicidal mania was distinguished from other diagnoses not as confusion or a failure to understand one's behavior but as being "driven by a morbid, uncontrollable impulse."[21] Courtroom inquiry about finding a discernible motive or the importance of recollection was beside the point for the medical witness. His testimony centered on one feature: "in homicidal mania you may have nothing but the criminal act."[22] The utter inexplicability of destroying those nearest and dearest and, afterward, the killer's unearthly calm—indeed, indifference—did not reveal doubled consciousness, unconsciousness, or cloudy consciousness. Medical witnesses described instead the tragic mental state that had left the defendant in the throes of an impulse that carried them "quite away."

Medical Text and Medical Testimony

Morbid mental states were, of course, the subject of medical texts as well as testimony. In some trials, their authors also participated in the proceedings at the Old Bailey, sometimes quoting their writings. Forbes Winslow, George Savage, Charles Mercier, and Henry Maudsley were well known within medical circles and beyond; their contributions to gentlemen's magazines and intellectual quarterlies delivered their views on insanity to a wide audience, especially their views on insanity and the law. Although these printed works were often mined to formulate questions by defense and prosecuting attorneys alike, by tradition and by principle the court preferred viva voce witnesses who could be examined in real time. There was no way to cross-examine a printed work; its author needed to take the stand.

An exception to this convention was the most widely circulated text of forensic medicine: Alfred Swaine Taylor's *The Principles and Practice of Medical Jurisprudence*. His work brought medicine into the dynamics of the courtroom, offering ways of determining evidence of and distinguishing types of poison, differentiating a suicidal gash from a homicidal slash, or deciding if a hanging had taken place before or after death. In time, Taylor's comprehensive efforts grew to fill two volumes, the second consisting of the most inclusive treatment of insanity to appear in the Victorian era. Definitions of different species of insanity, the testimonial capacity of lunatics, and the civil commitment of the insane received full treatment. Given the attention this period paid to lunacy in criminal matters, one expects to find in Taylor's work a detailed examination of tests of responsibility and the plea of insanity in criminal cases, and it does not disappoint. Taylor himself appeared at the Old Bailey just two years after his book first appeared. His testimony concerned the characteristics of a suicide by knife, placing the time of death according to his knowledge of "the period when rigidity commences and when the body commences to cool." The advantage of having Taylor and not just his text present was clear when the jury was able to follow up his testimony by asking, "In your judgment would the blood spurt out in such a quantity as to produce what you have seen?" Taylor responded, "That would depend on the person making the blow; the moment the carotid artery was cut the blood would spurt out—there might be some in front of the clothes of the sufferer if standing up, or on each side if lying down."[23] Although he made no further personal appearance at the Old Bailey, his opinions about blood evidence and manner of death would find resonance in subsequent insanity trials, uniquely those that featured homicidal mania, the era's newest and most crime-specific diagnosis.

Having been first upon the scene of a grisly killing, police surgeon Hugh Davis testified about the indentation he had discovered in the razor blade responsible for inflicting the fatal wound. "In my opinion this was caused by contact with the spinal bone, which was cut in two. It would require very great force for such a wound to be inflicted and the blood would immediately spurt all over the place." The police surgeon also suggested the probable placement of the assailant—as Taylor had also done in court—and the impossibility of the wound being self inflicted. In response to a question regarding the "very extraordinary force [that] must have been used, the surgeon invoked the author's authority.

> I agree with this statement in Taylor's "Principles and Practice in Medical Jurisprudence" under the heading "Impulsive Insanity": "Occasionally the act of murder is perpetrated with great deliberation and apparently with all the marks of sanity. These cases are rendered difficult by the fact that there may be no distinct proof of the existence of the past and present of any disorder of mind, so that the chief evidence of the disorder is the act itself. Of the existence of insanity in the common or legal acceptation of the term before and after perpetration of the crime there may be either no evidence whatsoever or it may be so slight as to amount to proof. Sudden restoration to reason is not infrequent in such cases of homicidal mania."

The witness declined to apply Taylor's lengthy quote to the defendant since he had not examined him, choosing instead to highlight the defendant's reported consciousness and recollection of the deed. The police surgeon concluded by affirming the existence of the new disease entity and how it was diagnosed: "Homicidal mania occurs in persons who have had suspicions, have threatened persons, and then in a sudden fit of mania committed homicide."[24]

Medical witnesses were not the only courtroom participants to ground their opinions in Taylor's authority. Four years after *Medical Jurisprudence* appeared, defense attorney Serjeant Sleigh asked a surgeon who had treated a prisoner during her pregnancy the following questions. (The judge joined in.)

Attorney: Is your opinion (*reading from Dr. Taylor's work*), that "In a person labouring under puerperal mania the killing of a child may be the result of an uncontrollable impulse seizing her at the time the act is done with a knowledge on the part of the mother that the act she is doing will cause death"? Knowing that the act of giving poison or cutting a child's throat would cause death, might she still be under that uncontrollable mania which would cause her to do it?

Surgeon: Yes.

Judge: You say that she would know the result of what she was doing?

Surgeon: Yes . . . I believe that in this form of mania they would be conscious that they were doing wrong, and still not be able to prevent themselves from doing it.

Prosecuting Attorney: Where you find puerperal mania, do you often find acts of violence?

Surgeon: In both sorts of puerperal mania [melancholy or non] you may have infanticide—more kill their children than kill themselves—I draw a distinction between puerperal mania and homicidal mania—I did not observe these symptoms before she was confined [late pregnancy]—not till about a fortnight after; there was a peculiar expression of the eyes, but no other symptom.[25]

The importance of the testimony lay in the surgeon's drawing together puerperal and homicidal mania. The former, implying a consciousness of the act but an impossibility of intruding upon the impulse, was familiar to the court. That a person under the control of an uncontrollable impulse could still manifest seemingly sane planning of the offense was suggested by an attorney's question of Dr. Henry Letheby. "Would you expect [such a] person to go to a shop, converse reasonably there, and buy poison?" Dr. Letheby answered simply "yes," with no elaboration; apparently he believed none was required.

Whether quoted directly by a witness or used to frame an attorney's question, Taylor's *Medical Jurisprudence* was the nineteenth-century medico-legal text cited most often in courtroom testimony. His work was particularly quoted in the diagnosis and explanation of the forms of homicidal mania: a propensity to kill, related to an actual delusion, an absurd motive to kill related to no known reason, or an impulse to kill that was "sudden, instantaneous, unreflective, and *uncontrollable."* Even when his name was not invoked specifically in court, the imagery and word choice were unmistakable. Testifying at a trial of a father for the murder of his young daughter, a medical witness concluded his testimony with "I agree that one of the degrees of homicidal mania is where the impulse to kill is sudden, unresisting, unreflective, and uncontrollable."[26] One finds other Taylorisms throughout the era's medical testimony that incorporated homicidal mania: "sudden impulse," "absence of motive," "unable to resist."[27]

At a certain point, Taylor's text and courtroom testimony begin to inform each other. His expansive work makes reference to the more celebrated contemporary insanity trials—*Hadfield, McNaughtan,* and *Oxford*—but also the lesser-known cases of deluded forgers, a sleepwalking woman who threw her children out the window of a top floor apartment she dreamt was on fire, and a devoted mother who poisoned her children's dinner.[28] These cases provided Taylor with graphic examples of manic criminality as real-world evidence of his disease typology, and his text in turn provided medical witnesses with a creditable published source to lend authority to their diagnosis. Each supplied the other with examples and legitimacy in an endless feedback loop.

"Instead of a Fit, They Get Homicidally Maniacal"

In addition to delusion, medical witnesses attempting to establish homicidal mania's bona fides in court had a second, thoroughly familiar, mental impairment to enlist in explaining the basis for this new diagnosis. Cases of homicidal mania not associated with delusion were presented to the jury in the following way: "I especially lay stress upon the epileptic character of his appearance at the time the deed was committed, the staring eyes, the fixed expression, and afterwards a sudden recovery—these are exactly the characteristics of an epileptic sudden mania . . . the general former history of the prisoner; his gentle manner and demeanor and the whole history of his former life as an affectionate man suddenly terminating in this horrid crime seems to me to be another element in the case." Thomas Harrington Tuke cited fixity of expression, a common element in testimony that invoked epilepsy. When asked by the trial judge to expand on his use of the term *irresistible impulse,* he gave a standard response.

It is stated in a book of authority that with regard to impulsive insanity or irresistible impulse, the doctors who present this theory should be able to form a distinct conception between impulses that are irresistible and impulses that are unresisted—I think the only way in which such a line can be drawn is to take the physical concomitants, and if I find that the man who commits the crime is at the time in a state of physical suffering, with staring eye-balls, in a state of great excitement, and has at the same time a tendency to epilepsy . . . I should put that down probably, not certainly, as an irresistible impulse.[29]

Long familiar to the Old Bailey as "fits" in the years before *McNaughtan* and as *vertige épileptique* when that term was introduced at the Old Bailey in 1876, epilepsy was one of the few physical ailments presented to the jury in considering the mental consequences of an organic disturbance. Since the beginning days of medical witnesses testifying about mental derangement, juries had been presented with the probable effects of head injuries, brain fever, fractured skull, and sunstroke. In addition, the psychological upheaval that attended all sorts of reproductive ills was commonplace in infanticide cases. Puerperal mania, puerperal melancholia, and melancholia with homicidal tendency were common diagnoses throughout the 1800s, although only the first two were particular to gender. Still, the features shared by homicidal and puerperal mania—sudden, explosive violence, the destruction of a beloved member of one's intimate circle—leads one to suspect that in some ways puerperal mania served as a template for homicidal mania. Again, one encountered physiological disturbance generating a violent gust of emotion. When medical witnesses like Tuke turned the jury's (and the judge's) attention to the staring eyes, the fixed glare, and the epileptic character of the accused's appearance, a space was opened in insanity trials to consider anew the issue of voluntarily chosen action.

Although connecting the violent act with an organic impairment (often referred to generically as "fits") had been standard in medical testimony since the early 1800s, homicidal mania would introduce an entirely new variant of epilepsy for the jury's consideration: "Then something seemed to snap in my head and I jumped up and caught her by the throat . . . I felt as if I was holding a very strong, battery . . . I wanted to leave go and I could not. When I did leave go she fell. I realized in a moment what I had done . . . I held a mirror to her mouth to see if she was breathing, and she was not."[30] On trial for murder, William Philpot was one of the few prisoners in the late 1800s who described his mental state to the jury. Some prisoners denied involvement point blank; others tried to sidestep culpability by pleading provocation. The *OBSP* also reveals prisoner's defenses containing reference to a gauzy sort of consciousness—"it was like a dream to me," or "something came over me as I sat by the fire." The idea of something snapping in one's head was topical: this was an age of fascination with reflexes and electrical energy.

The defendant was followed to the witness stand by a police surgeon who commented on the defendant's surprising composure immediately following the killing. "One of the characteristics of a person who is subject to such fits when the fit is not on is to be perfectly rational. After a fit they usually go to sleep, and on waking appear quite normal." Again, fits were not new to the court, nor was the return to normalcy upon waking or simply on regaining consciousness. But medical witnesses who drew upon the lack of volitional control associated with epilepsy presented an entirely new variant of the falling sickness.[31]

> Persons having epileptic tendencies may discharge the ordinary duties of life quite normally for years without the brain showing any weakness of the kind, and when subject to attack give way to uncontrollable fury. When the attack has passed over they appear quite cool and collected. This is called epileptic automatism. Persons suffering in this manner I have known to commit violent assaults and then be seized with remorse. I found no epileptic tendencies in prisoner, though he was closely watched. It would be possible for him, however, not to betray them. Of all the classes of weakness masked epilepsy is the one form that is so often concealed in a person.[32]

Automatism was not a new feature in the prison medical officer's testimony. What was novel was his use of "masked epilepsy," which was fast becoming the lynchpin for a diagnosis of homicidal mania when delusion was not in evidence. Bénédict-Augustin Morel and Jean-François Falret had introduced masked epilepsy, or *l'épilepsie larvée,* to the French medical community.[33] This "silent" form of epilepsy was part of the theorists' attempts to identify and calibrate states of epileptiform disorders in terms of their degree of impairment. Clinicians had been drawn to the form of epilepsy widely believed to be connected to murderous fury but "masked" by quotidian, normal functioning. Without (apparent) motive, the sudden, brutal assault was often committed in broad daylight with no effort to escape. Indeed, these offenders were likely to surrender themselves to the police once they had discovered the "enormity of the deed."[34]

Masked epilepsy found a responsive audience in England, and no one was more enthusiastic than Henry Maudsley, editor of the influential *Jour-*

nal of Mental Science from 1860 to 1878, prolific essayist on medical and literary topics, and sometime witness in Victorian insanity trials. Maudsley's approach to mental derangement was unequivocally physicalist. He seized upon masked epilepsy in an effort to "group the reported cases of homicidal mania to exhibit . . . morbid states of the nervous system."[35] Over the course of an extended professional life that included an early acquaintance with asylum work, he never relinquished his belief that a study of the deranged would eventually reveal a cerebral lesion at the root of the madness. In masked epilepsy he found just such an organic grounding for involuntary behavior, as well as a ready explanation for the lack of any sign of mental disease prior to the sudden, uncharacteristic, violent outburst. Insanity had been hidden—masked—by the seemingly customary behavior of the prisoner up to the moment when a convulsion—not of limbs, but of ideas—took hold, catapulting the hapless sufferer into murderous assault.

Although forms of masked epilepsy varied, its defining element was the substitution of crime in place of the standard convulsion: "the character of the disease changed; instead of epileptic attacks the afflicted was seized with an irresistible impulse to commit murder."[36] In court, medical witnesses stressed the phenomenon of substitution; "it is a disease in which the fact of epilepsy is replaced by an impulse to do some outrageous homicidal act."[37] Accordingly, a divisional police surgeon informed the jury, "In masked epilepsy there is not the frothing at the mouth or the twitching of the arms or limbs."[38] A prison medical officer several years later continued this theme, stating, "There is no outward sign, there is no convulsion or apparent lack of consciousness—the patient does not fall down."[39]

The most unsettling element mentioned in many trials was the inability of even the person's intimates—indeed, of the person himself—to know he was in danger of attacking a cherished loved one. As he stood over the body of his dead wife, Ernest Partridge realized to his horror what he had done. Upon arrest, he explained to the medical officer at Brixton Prison the following: "He remembered absolutely nothing else until he heard a knock and the shout "Milk, 3d. a quart." He then suddenly came to himself, and discovered . . . his wife . . . was dead with her throat cut. 'Doctor, if that milkman had only shouted "Milk, 3d. a quart" one minute before my dear wife's life would have been saved,' which I considered very strong evidence of the unconsciousness of his act." Sydney Dyer, medical officer of Holloway Prison, confirmed his diagnosis by citing the blank memory of the attack itself. "This attack which he had is called 'masked epilepsy' . . . his acts are automatic . . . on regaining consciousness . . . [he] does not remember the things that have happened." Asked by the judge to account for the form the dream had taken, Dyer explained, "Sometimes instead of a fit coming on they will get homicidally maniacal . . . From a criminal point of view, these are the worst cases."[40]

The connection between a particular criminal impulse and hidden disease was occasionally made explicit in court—"this is a case of impulsive homicidal mania, from masked epilepsy."[41] At other times, the two states were simply cited in close proximity with one another. Both homicidal mania and *l'épilepsie larvée* shared an absence of recollection, an absence of motive, and a history of epilepsy in the family. Of the three features, the absence of motive appeared to weigh heaviest in the diagnosis: "I do not think a man would have an intelligible motive for killing his brother, unless he was insane, or a very great criminal."[42]

Motive, purpose, and intention—the contents of conscious resolve—all belonged to a conception of human behavior that rested on cognition, on knowing the nature of one's acts. But the consequences of delusory beliefs and the convulsive effects of masked epilepsy presented the jury with actions without identifiable agency. *What*, not who, had been responsible for the outrageous crime was fast becoming the mystery the trial turned upon. The years that witnessed homicidal mania's increasingly prominent role in medical testimony revealed a further receding of the law's conception of psychological man: a sentient being who intends his behavior. The casualty of this patently involuntary behavior was volition, the capacity for self-control.

A Very Victorian Alienist: In Print and in Court

To some medical minds, the loss of will was no casualty at all; it had never existed in the first place. According to Henry Maudsley, the sooner mental medicine jettisoned metaphysics, the sooner it would ensure its place in general medicine. A thoroughgoing Lamarckian and a man of his age, Maudsley emphasized the inheritance of acquired characteristics, particularly the predisposition to crime, insanity, and vice. Biological weakness and immoral behavior in progenitors was lamentably passed along, dooming their offspring to suffer a proclivity to mental deviance with all the material force of a blow on the head.[43] "No one can escape the tyranny of his organization; no one can elude the destiny that is innate in him, and which unconsciously and irresistibly shapes his ends, even when he believes that he is determining them with consummate foresight and skill."[44] Put another way, the body "was like a (family) tree whose age, history, health could be read in cross-section."[45]

It was the nervous system, not the individual's consciousness of right and wrong, that was at issue. Past experience "moved down through the generations and was inscribed in the body. Experience passed beyond consciousness, eventually reaching the nervous system, the reflex, the organic."[46] Malevolent, particularly criminal, behavior easily conformed exquisitely to Maudsley's schema: "[the] body becomes an organic machine set in destructive motion by a morbid cause." He thus stressed the role of the unconscious, the reactive centers in the nervous system that operate with no guidance or intervention by the will. The brain "not only receives impressions from without unconsciously . . . but it responds as an organ of organic life to the inner stimuli of the organism unconsciously."[47] With all mental processing going on below the level of consciousness, volition as a human faculty was a fiction. Whether his unyielding devotion to materialism stemmed from a desire to remain firmly in the company of general—not just psychological—medicine, or whether he found psychological approaches to be prescientific or just intellectually bankrupt, Maudsley's organicism put him on a collision course with the legal construction of criminal responsibility. Maudsley collided also with the notion of a jury, "a singularly incompetent tribunal," deciding any matter of scientific data. "Medicine asserts that a theoretical study of mental diseases and defects is necessary to a proper understanding of such diseases and defects; Law denies this, and says that insanity is a fact to be determined by any dozen of ordinary men."[48] Judges did not escape his censure either: "Instead of urging [jurors] to throw off all prejudice, and aiding them with right information, they sometimes strengthen their prejudices by sneers at the medical evidence, and directly mislead them by laying down false doctrines."[49]

Not all jurists were wedded to the "false doctrines" of consciousness and will; James Fitzjames Stephen, for example, acknowledged by the second half of the nineteenth century the existence of an insanity of uncontrollable impulse (alone). However, the enduring criterion of "knowing right from wrong" remained the courtroom's basis for considering a plea of insanity. To Maudsley, this idea was nonsensical; since reflex and the involuntary activity of the brain lay behind mental functioning, what logic was there in speaking of a consciously chosen act? "The morbid idea may become irresistible . . . the characteristic of unsoundness of mind is the loss of volitional control over thoughts, in other words, the reflex involuntary action of the brain."[50]

Maudsley's was not a lone voice. Emerging biological research on reflexes was driven by a conception of an organism's reflexes serving its own physiological needs without any guidance from some conscious, self-equilibrating mechanism. The implications of such a model clearly threatened the centuries-held conception of the mind-body nexus. Mind, in this latter formulation, however, was simply superfluous: reflex action was automatic, carrying an "in-built purposiveness [that] functioned in terms of the law of organismic self-conservation."[51] With consciousness and will removed from the equation, Thomas Laycock and William B. Carpenter provided Maudsley's generation with a model of human functioning that relegated mental elements—conscious resolve, purpose—to the status of epiphenomena of organic processes. Incorporating Laycock and Carpenter's research, Maudsley argued, "it is perfectly well known that an idea may cause action quite independent of volition—a class of movements known as *ideo-motor*."[52]

Resisting an impulse to kill was therefore not a test of character or evidence of heightened powers of self-control but a question of how degenerated was the nerve element.[53] Maudsley drew on the graphic imagery supplied by epileptic seizure to position the nervous system at the center of his conception of responsibility. When there is a disease of the spinal cord, one observes convulsive movement that the will cannot restrain, whatever "level of consciousness" might attend the seizure. And when moral weakness, caused by the accumulated experience of dissolute, intemperate forebears, becomes written upon the biological inheritance of future generations, the residua leaves one powerless to resist the impulse to destroy. None of this goes on at the conscious level: the perpetrator is "*alienated* from himself, [the crime] was not truly *his* act, any more than convulsion is an act of will."[54] With behavior independent of "mental elements" such as intention, design, and purpose, how could moral responsibility attend any action?[55]

For Maudsley, the common law's approach to ascribing culpability to action was simply an anachronism: "they would search for a statute of Elizabeth to apply to a steam engine." The behavior of man was the result of natural force, of unconscious reflex. The "fundamental defect" in legal thinking about responsibility, Maudsley contended, was its foundations in consciousness: "every book on mind published in the present day [admits] that the most important parts of our mind operate unconsciously."[56] This error in conception, this refusal to consider insanity through the lens of objective (not subjective) science, had produced the current uncertainty: "it is a matter of accident whether a person is hanged or convicted on a plea of insanity." It was, Maudsley maintained, "quite absurd for lawyers or the general public to give their opinion on [insanity] in a doubtful case, as it would be for them to do so in a case of fever."[57] In the last analysis, insanity was a question of volitional control, not conscious awareness of the wrong being committed.

Beyond volition, Maudsley commented on two other foundational elements in ascribing criminal responsibility: motive and delusion. Discerning the presence of a motive would seem to convey purpose and design, at least, and premeditation at most. With obvious disdain, Maudsley cited a judge whose instructions to a jury stated that credible evidence of insanity was completely vitiated if an equally credible motive could be found. What, Maudsley asked, does the "appearance of design" reveal? Suppose a melancholic patient kills his tormentor—it is still an action dictated by a delusion. The insane kill "not really from passion or revenge—or enmity of any kind, but as a discharge which he must have of the terrible emotion with which he is possessed."[58] And delusion, that staple of common-law acceptance in insanity trials, was both misunderstood and too restrictively applied.

Ever since *Hadfield*, the law had accepted the medical opinion that it was possible for an individual to be fatefully confused on one subject or in regard to one person's designs, while on all other subjects, the individual enjoyed the full range of his or her faculties. Attorney Thomas Erskine, who introduced delusion to the criminal trial, averred that for the delusion to have exculpatory value, the crime had to be the direct offspring of the delusion, implying that any action unconnected to the cognitive error left the prisoner culpable.[59] This was patent nonsense to the editor of the *Journal of Mental Science*, who thought that an unsound mind expressed itself in delusion. The error was not localized to one subject but rather revealed how unsound the thought process was, period. "The fact of the delusion betokens a fundamental disorder in organic processes as the condition of its existence."[60] Even if the law did understand this, insisting on the presence of delusion as the grounds for a successful insanity plea ignored a whole range of deranged states more dangerous and "grave" than delusional impairment.

Rather than engage the question of "how much damage" the delusion revealed, Maudsley returned to the subject of involuntary reflex of epileptic convulsion. His contribution to the literature on the nature of homicidal mania centered on the role of masked epilepsy, "a transitory mania" that took the place of the (usual) seizures affecting the motor centers. Instead, "it fixes upon the mind-centers" resulting in a "paroxysm of mania . . . an epilepsy of mind."[61] It seems odd even to engage the notion of mind, given his investment in reflexes, but Maudsley did not appear troubled by this contradiction. Nor did he address the "reach" in epilepsy's standard association with physical construction. Instead, he argued that the disturbance commonly associated with unconsciousness, enfeeblement, and convulsions was best thought of not as a single disease but as "a series . . . of psycho-physiological disturbances which less or more affect the soundness of reason." Those enduring the convulsion of ideas that defined masked epilepsy, like those suffering the "unmasked" variety, experienced sudden, violent spasms and involuntary convulsions. Rather than dropping to the floor and frothing at the mouth, however, the felon had picked up a weapon; "the character of his disease has changed, and instead of epileptic attacks he was seized with an irresistible impulse to commit murder."[62]

In these episodes, persons afflicted with masked epilepsy resembled another enigmatic offender: the sleepwalker. Epileptic patients had undertaken journeys, contracted marriages, and recognized persons and places "utterly blotted out from consciousness." Manifesting a similar state of suspended consciousness, those suffering masked epilepsy were homicidally maniacal, unable to resist the impulse to kill and destroy. When Maudsley's audience was not readers of the *Journal of Mental Science*, the *Journal of Psychological Medicine and Pathology*, or his celebrated monograph *Responsibility in Mental Disease* but judges and juries at the Old Bailey, one wonders how forcefully he made his claims to have unraveled the mystery behind mentally deranged criminal behavior.

The Author in the Dock

Beginning in 1855, Henry Maudsley made six appearances at London's central criminal court. Most of his testimony was offered from 1898 to 1902, long after his publishing career had attenuated. In his first trial, he is identified only as "house surgeon, University Lodge Hospital"; he attended the victim on admission and was present at the subsequent postmortem examination. Describing the fatal wounds to the jury, he inferred, "they were such [fatal] injuries as would be produced by a cart going over the body—the injury to the head I should say was produced by the fall; the rupture to the spleen itself might account for death."[63] Fewer than twenty years later, his professional identity and his testimony took a decidedly different direction: "I have paid good attention to the disease of insanity, and have written a work on the physiology and pathology of mind—I was lecturer at St. Mary's Hospital, on the subject of insanity—I was at one time resident physician of a lunatic asylum in Manchester, where there were usually one hundred patients of the middle classes."[64] The one-time resident physician of the lunatic asylum could not have chosen a more notorious trial during which to burnish his credentials as an exert witness in mental medicine.

"Horrible Murder by Clergy man," ran the 1871 broadsheet carrying the account of the brutal death of Anne Watson at the hands of her husband, the recently discharged headmaster of Stockwell Grammar School and parish priest. After beating his wife to death and leaving her in her room for three days, John Selby Watson attempted suicide by swallowing prussic acid, after leaving a note for the surgeon whom he believed would find his body: "I have killed my wife in a fit of rage to which she has provoked me; often, often has she provoked me before, but I never lost restraint over myself till the present occasion, when I allowed fury to carry me a way. Her body will be found in the room adjoining the library, the key of which I leave with the paper. I trust she will be buried with the attention due to a lady of good birth."[65] Because of his social position and the religious connection, the trial caused an understandable sensation. The prosecution summoned four prominent medical men—Maudsley among them—to visit the prisoner in prison, supposedly to counter a defense strategy of mental distraction amounting to insanity. Of all his appearances at the Old Bailey, Maudsley was at his most voluble in this trial.

> The symptoms I observed in him were such as in my opinion would follow an attack of melancholia—a person suffering from melancholia is liable to outbursts of mad violence, and while these outbursts prevail his mind is diseased; gone; his reason is in abeyance, and he is nearly unconscious of what he is doing . . . it is a disease accompanied by dangerous propensities; it is not so much homicidal as suicidal . . . supposing a person is laboring under melancholia, a slight provocation or a provocation of any kind, will have a powerful effect in exciting the disease in him.[66]

When his own printed work was read back to him during cross-examination, Maudsley responded defensively, "I am sorry to say there are a good many omissions in my work which has been referred to," although it is not hard to see why the defense attorney would have found the witness's testimony curious. Having written unambiguously eight years before the trial, describing homicidal mania and homicidal insanity as their *own* disease entities, Maudsley in his trial testimony lodged the homicidal attack as a propensity result of melancholia. While it is true that melancholia had recently taken on a possible association with aggression and even violence, it was more traditionally connected to despondency and depression. Maudsley tried to distinguish melancholia as a "morbid aggravation of melancholy," but even when cloaked in morbidity, it had little of the graphic specter of homicidal mania. Furthermore, the witness pointedly abjured the isolation of a propensity to kill: "I object to adopting the term homicidal impulse as a disease by itself—I hold it to be but a symptom of the disease," referring to it instead as a "subdivision" of "affective insanity, affecting the passions, feelings, and propensities. He certainly did not object in print; homicidal mania sits at the heart of his writings. In court, however, he shied away from a full-throated defense of homicidal impulse "as a disease in itself."[67]

The difference between Maudsley in print and Maudsley in the dock becomes increasingly glaring in four cases at the turn of the century. In two, he employed masked epilepsy in his testimony, emphasizing its close kinship with the more familiar form of the disease: "I believe he had [on the day of the crime] the mental disorder which sometimes takes the place of an epileptic attack." Concerning the prisoner's weakness in resisting destructive impulses, Maudsley averred that "he has inherited an excitable nervous system which accounts for his erratic, loose, and irregular life . . . which has predisposed him to an outbreak of a mental nervous disorder—I do not think he would be conscious of the nature or quality of his act, or discover the difference between right or wrong in what he was doing."[68]

Conscious of the nature of what he was doing? *Conscious* of the difference between right and wrong? Is this the same Henry Maudsley who wrote with apodictic conviction that insanity was not a matter of consciousness but rather of an inability to resist impulses? In cases that did not feature masked epilepsy, Maudsley announced that he found no insanity because he "found no evidence of delusion," the medico-legal concept that he disparaged in print as the law's preferred basis for a finding of insanity. Of course, no one expects Maudsley in his trial testimony to have been as critical and dismissive of judges and other "uninitiated" persons who commented easily about insanity, although other medical witnesses did just that. In the trial of the grammar school headmaster, Maudsley had been followed to the witness stand by George Fielding Blandford, author and fellow of the Royal College of Physicians, who responded to questioning regarding the basis of his diagnosis with, "I have expressed dissatisfaction with the law as laid down by the Judge [referring to the *McNaughtan* judges] on the question of knowledge of right and wrong—I have said 'such questions are totally irrelevant and beside the issue, which is, was he of unsound mind when he committed it.'"[69] Far from objecting to the law's criterion of "knowing right from wrong," Maudsley incorporated it into his testimony with a nod to delusion's significance as well. This is not the first time medical writing and medical testimony diverge so conspicuously, although the occasion of the acerbic author striking a compliant posture once in court brings a wry smile. The marked difference reminds the historian of forensic medicine that, for all the opinions authors expressed regarding the types and indications of various forms of mental derangement, medical texts provide at best only an approximation of any era's conception of madness. As mentioned earlier, Nigel Walker maintained that the authority one might be tempted to invest in a historical text as revealing a particular way of thinking must be tempered by one's inability to know whether it was the thinking of the age or (just) the writer's opinion about what he or she *believed* the thinking of the age should be.

Trial narratives are critical for gaining insight into what juries heard in court from the medical men, and such testimony stands quite apart from what one might find in historical medical tracts. Maudsley, Forbes Winslow, George Blandford, George Savage, and Charles Mercier left behind sustained treatments on insanity, as well as trial testimony. The courtroom narratives, however, also reveal that in addition to authors and asylum superintendents who referred to extensive familiarity with the increasingly specialized subfield of mental medicine, jurors were just as likely to hear from the nonspecialist, the nonpublished, and the noncelebrated medical men who introduced innovative diagnoses informed by direct experience with the criminal suspect rather than the literature of their day.

Maudsley lamented, "The conflict indeed between law and medicine is painfully obvious—there is even a gloomy diversity of opinion between experts." Especially, but not only, in testimony regarding epilepsy, medical witnesses differed along familiar lines. Was consciousness necessarily suspended during a convulsive episode? Did later recollection of the attack militate against its being considered a true fit? Must some earlier evidence of insanity exist, or was the crime itself sufficient evidence of debilitating pathology? When medical witnesses differed, they were unfailingly polite, phrasing the contradiction with respect for the more eminent witness's standing. Still, acknowledging that an authority on a particular disease had given a differing opinion did not require obeisance. After a medical superintendent of an epilepsy ward had delivered his testimony, referring several times to his long-standing professional familiarity with the disease, a prison medical officer called attention to his own unique frame: "I do not suggest that I am an expert in epilepsy, but I see a great deal of it. I dare say that Dr. Toogood knows more about it than I do, but I do not think he sees the amount of epilepsy in criminal cases that I do . . . I have had three cases of epileptic automatism in crime within the last seven or eight weeks, two being for murder."[70] The assertion of relying upon a different basis for knowledge was respectful, measured, and yet unmistakable.

The Cultural Context and the New Diagnosis

Gentleman, such a thing as a person not being able to control himself or the doing of an act which he knows to be wrong is a phrase that is not known to the law of this country.

Thus the jury was instructed in the trial of Mary Ann Brough, charged with slitting the throats of her six children. Although the judge cited earlier judicial opinion that a "knowing but uncontrollable impulse was unknown to the common law," it was certainly true that Old Bailey jurors had often been confronted with defendants helpless to resist uncontrollable forces resulting from delusive fears and overwhelming anxiety. The difference between a knowing action that was beyond the defendant's power to control and the uncontrollable impulse proffered in the trial of Mary Ann Brough was the possibility of an impulse not rooted in delusion. As mentioned in the *Lancet,* the trial judge specifically rejected the notion of an uncontrollable impulse. In his opinion, this was "a most dangerous doctrine, for undoubtedly every crime is committed under some impulse and the object of law was to control impulses of that description and thus prevent crime."[71]

The judge's remarks continued in the vein of the scornful dismissal earlier in the century of medical testimony that put forward an insanity of affect: *moral insanity.* And medical men were not the only practitioners singled out for derision when juries were presented with defendants who knew what they were about yet were presented in court as the conduit, not the origin, of crim-inogenic forces. "The forensic subtlety of our lawyers and the metaphysical dexterity of our modern physicians, have combined to complicate the discussion and [to] leave the uninitiated in hopeless perplexity."[72] It should be stressed that such outbursts from the bench were rare and largely reserved for the more ambitious disease categories that targeted the will, bypassing cognitive defect.

James Fitzjames Stephen, who acknowledged the existence and consequences of impulsive insanity, did not share the trial judge's sentiments. Several years earlier, he had taken up the issue in an address to the Juridical Society, specifically allowing for the possibility of an uncontrollable impulse: "Guilt turns upon the willfulness of an act, and not upon the sanity of the prisoner."[73] The jurist's comment renews Henri de Bracton's thirteenth-century stricture that "a crime is not committed unless the will to harm be present . . . in misdeeds we look to the will and not the outcome."[74] To the extent that medical witnesses could speak to issues of the will—something that Maudsley was loath to do, since reifying volition opened the door to metaphysics—their opinion could inform the jury's verdict. But the issue at hand was always the voluntary choice to do evil. Juries were traditionally challenged to apply testimony concerning mania, delirium, delusion, and melancholia to the derangement discernible in the offender's conduct in the particular case at hand. Was the defendant's mental state, even given the diagnosis, clear enough for the will to harm to have been present? Homicidal mania, however, would seem to have settled the matter, as the disease and the crime were one.

In the years that witnessed the proffering of the new diagnosis, London society was haunted by the specter of social deviance—crime, madness, and epilepsy—as evidence of a backward slide in civilization's evolution. Maudsley may have saved for print his exposition of how experience passed beyond consciousness (eventually reaching the nervous system and reflexes), but by invoking masked epilepsy in the courtroom, he spoke directly to the possibility of uncontrollable impulses—criminal convulsions—propelling the defendant to murder. The suggestion of biological inheritance in madness had been part of expert testimony since the early 1800s. Medical witnesses routinely referred to a defendant's relatives dying in an asylum as evidence that the family had a proclivity for madness. But in the years after On The Origin of Species was published, the effect of inherited debility took on a materialist grounding: "All consciousness was enmeshed in history and the socio-biological past."[75] Decades before Freud then, uncontrollable impulses were making their way into medical writing; in medical testimony, it was masked epilepsy that gave such unaccountable impulses a home. Stephen advised juries to seek evidence of impulsive insanity in the act rather than try to ascertain the sanity of the prisoner. This advice was given precisely when medical witnesses defended their diagnoses by invoking the inexplicability of the crime. Motiveless, senseless, and ultimately ensuring the defendant's own self-destruction (not only psychologically but physically), the act was ascribed to an impulse beyond the prisoner's will—a doomed, relentless degenerative predisposition to deviance.

Given the introduction of involuntary, criminally propulsive impulses in medical diagnosis and testimony, it is noteworthy that the originator of masked epilepsy was also the author of the totemic text on degeneration.[76] Bénédict Augustin Morel's influential 1857 tome drew together a vast array of physical, social, and moral-pathological diseases and disorders that resonated with contemporary debates on evolution and the inheritance of destructive characteristics. Deterioration of the brain along with the body necessarily corroded the intellect, condemning future generations to social marginality, manifested in any number of forms. By turns criminal, epileptic, mad—and possibly all three at the same time—social deviance (and social *deviants*) had effectively been recast in biological terms, although not for the first time. Madness had long enjoyed an association with a host of physical agents, from black bile to "fuliginous vapours of the menstrual blood"[77] to a too-rich diet, and it was also connected with reproductive ills. What was unique to Morel was his discussion of epilepsy as not only a degenerative physical disorder but a degenerative disorder in social personhood, with the epileptic *character* defined as irritable, menacing, and, at its most extreme manifestation, homicidally maniacal. Similar to their cohort of criminals and the insane, those afflicted with masked epilepsy revealed the effects of forces, suggesting that the afflicted were, in the words of an eighteenth-century Old Bailey judge commenting on insanity, "a mere instrument in the hands of Providence."[78]

Combined with emerging evolutionary thought that situated criminals and the insane apart and below the fully evolved, the individual deviant was now a member of a *class* of social deviants that had failed to mount the last step in phylogenetic evolution. One Old Bailey defendant was described as "unable to resist the animal part of the functions of the brain."[79] By the late nineteenth century, uncontrollable impulses did not need to draw their energy from delusive fears, although some did: half of medical witnesses who invoked homicidal mania in their testimony put it in close proximity with delusion. The other half based the diagnosis on the presence of masked epilepsy. Instead of a fit coming on, the afflicted would become homicidally maniacal, and criminal violence might take "the place of an epileptic attack." By turns referred to as "epileptic automatism" or "epileptic mania" and described in unmistakable imagery of involuntary action and clouded (if not occluded) consciousness, the condition left the prisoner a bystander rather than the perpetrator of the crime. In consequence, the common law was left bereft of the essentials for ascribing culpability for action: cognitive soundness and the capacity to choose. Without these, no intention could attend the act.

As historically significant and culturally penetrating as Morel's work may have been, there is no way of knowing if members of the jury—much less the judge and bar—were walking into court with dog-eared copies of Darwin's *Origins* or Morel's *Traité des dégénérescences.* The ideas contained therein, along with those in Cesare Lombroso's *L'uomo Delinquente,* were rife in social commentary and debate. Still, it is not at all obvious that conceptions of social deviance were actively transferred undiluted to the social deviant. Daniel Pick has argued effectively that England's embrace of degeneracy theory was at the level of the process of "failed evolution," not at the level of individual human character; the notion of a social "degenerate" was an unpalatable cultural morsel, at odds with the country's liberal social and political beliefs.

Still, there is little doubt that commentary about "Outcast London" was subject to an increasingly biological frame.[80] Perhaps it was the fear of social degeneracy that penetrated courtroom debate as masked epilepsy and homicidal mania increasingly became the medical witness's stock in trade. In examining the trial narratives, one finds none of the imperious judicial derision that greeted moral insanity and lesion of the will decades before. The court's posture was inquisitive, not dismissive. There is a world of difference between inquiring, "What is homicidal mania?," and stating unambiguously, "Uncontrollable impulse [is] unknown to common law." Apart from contemporary efforts to reframe social problems as stemming from biological "unfitness" and to establish legal acknowledgement that uncontrollable impulses "did occur," one suspects that sober courtroom consideration of homicidal mania may have been prompted by the institutional affiliations of those medical witnesses proffering the new diagnosis.

How the Defendant Met the Doctor, 1856–1913

Data presented in chapter 4 reveals the changing basis of association between medical men and the accused in the years that spanned 1760 to 1913. Detention in a jail or prison in the days or weeks awaiting trial comprised between half and 60 percent of the interactions between medical men and prisoners by the turn of the twentieth century. Most noticeably, private, social contact had fallen dramatically, as did preexisting professional acquaintance. Other than the prison interview, the category of association that grew most was the on-scene encounter between the prisoner and the surgeon affiliated with the police division or a private medical man called to the station. Medical practitioners assigned to a police division were first at the scene of a crime. Together with surgeons and physicians in private practice who were also called in to try to save the victim's life, these "on-scene" associations are prominently represented among the witnesses putting forward the diagnosis of homicidal mania. Although asylum physicians and hospital lecturers certainly appeared in the Victorian insanity trial, few of them mentioned homicidal mania in their testimony. Given the conspicuous institutional base from which these medical men were able to consider the full range of insanity's species, what inference might be drawn about the particular occupational perch from which this unusual diagnosis was made, and the court's willingness to entertain this curious malady, especially when earlier versions of this diagnosis had been summarily rejected?

By the early decades of the nineteenth century, the Old Bailey had grown accustomed to the person and views of the first prison surgeon called to testify multiple times in an insanity trial. Gilbert McMurdo, surgeon of Newgate, testified repeatedly at the Old Bailey by the time of *McNaughtan*. He had no particular expertise in mental medicine; his biography in the Royal College of Surgeons lists his specialty as ophthalmology, leaving out any mention of his multiple appearances in court. Although Bethlem superintendent John Monro, the first forensic witness to testify about insanity as a medical disease, was indeed retained by the defense—and examined by the defendant himself—the Crown's repeated use of McMurdo seems to have initiated the widespread employment of medical men called by the defense to answer the jail surgeon's usual testimony: "I saw nothing of insanity about the prisoner." When McMurdo was succeeded by George Walker in 1837, there began the standard employment of prison and jail medical men who received the instruction, "Mind you see that prisoner, for it is very likely we shall want your evidence."

Given their employment by the Crown, surgeons assigned to police divisions also knew their evidence would be wanted, but as with jail and prison surgeons post-*McNaughtan*, there was no pronounced pattern of "leaning" against the prisoner. To be sure, these witnesses were far from gullible and reported their success at "piercing the smokescreen" of (alleged) insanity to the jury, "I came to the conclusion he was shamming—I told him that if he did not get up I would use the galvanic battery—he got up immediately."[81] They might also earn credibility by acknowledging the courtroom division of labor, reporting the defendant's verbatim statement at the police station and following it with a statement like, "I think it is for the Jury to say whether she is of sound mind or not rather than a medical man."[82] Still other police surgeons flatly found the prisoner free of delusion or any other state qualifying him or her for insanity. Even those jail surgeons who mentioned homicidal mania in their testimony did not always assert that the defendant qualified for the diagnosis. But when they did support the defense's claims to debilitating states of madness, their evidence was vivid and timely: alone among the cohort of medical witnesses, they had been present soon after the crime. When a judge reminded the jury of the utility of the specialist's testimony—"there is only one type of insanity and that is what was the condition of his mind at the time [of the crime]"—the divisional surgeon, whatever he might have lacked in formal training in mental medicine, was ideally suited to satisfy the judge's insistence by reporting the signs of insanity he was able to grasp at the scene.

In explaining the features of homicidal mania as detailed by Alfred Swaine Taylor, and by affirming how the diagnosis fit the features of an inexplicable crime, the police surgeon provided the jury with a recognized species of insanity exquisitely suited to the motiveless, purposeless destruction of loved ones. Of course, not all cases of alleged homicidal mania targeted family members; revenge sometimes played a role when framing self-defense as a form this type of insanity might take. Still, the diagnosis was invoked most often in trials centering on child and spousal murder. A caution again with verdicts: perhaps any or even no diagnosis would still have led to an acquittal, given how gruesome and senseless some crimes appeared. Indeed, juries had been known to acquit by reason of insanity when no medical testimony was entered at all. (See chapter 7.)

Beyond verdicts, however, the temperate questioning, the judges' solicitous requests for elaboration, and the constant affirmation by police surgeons and prison medical officers that homicidal mania was indeed a recognized species of insanity suggest the arrival of a form of madness that (only) found its expression in crime. Supported either by delusion (the common law's preferred medical term) or masked epilepsy (a new entity but conceptually connected to convulsive, involuntary seizure), homicidal mania's novelty resonated with long familiar topics of courtroom testimony and jury deliberation. Far from following in the footsteps of the first prison surgeon, subsequent medical men revealed an increasingly assertive forensic voice, independent of partiality for the prosecution or the defense. Each time a medical witness secured by the defense pronounced the defendant insane, or the police and jail surgeon found the opposite, a critical step was made toward the emergence of a profession. Each of these medical men furthered the claim that unique experience and learning, rather than patronage and obligation, supplied the knowledge that distinguished professional judgment and opinion.

CHAPTER SEVEN

The View from the Bench

Judicial Discretion and Forensic-Psychiatric Evidence

> She clutched at my throat and got hold of my collar saying, "finish it, oh finish it." I noticed a cut on her throat, and she was bleeding a little from the cut. I took my razor and finished the job. I little thought last Monday when I read about Crippen, that I should be so near him.

Testifying at the trial of Oliver Smith for the brutal murder of his girlfriend, the inspector from New Scotland Yard read to the jury the statement the defendant had given upon arrest. Pointing to a scar on his forehead, Smith had told him, "This was done when I was a little boy; it makes me feel dicky sometimes."[1] The prosecuting attorney did not follow up by asking the inspector to give his impression of the prisoner's mental state. In fact, nothing in the Crown's case against Oliver Smith pursued the question of the defendant's intellect, even though acquaintances of the accused were in court who could have spoken to the defendant's allusion to mental waywardness. After a divisional surgeon speculated about the violence that had produced the gaping wounds to the victim's throat, the Crown brought its case to a close. Oliver Smith's defense consisted of family members describing his history of erratic, violent outbursts as a child, his chronic inability to tell right from wrong, and episodes of frothing at the mouth. This vivid testimony managed to engage all the standard features of madness without once mentioning a plea of insanity. After the last defense witness alleged that the defendant was never "quite right in his head," the defense rested.

The prosecutor, however, did not. He asked the judge to call the defendant's social acquaintances in court to ask if their experiences with the accused mirrored his family's accounts of emotional and behavioral excess. He also expressed his intention to call Sidney Dyer, the medical officer of Brixton Prison, who had maintained watch over the defendant in the weeks preceding the trial. The defense attorney immediately objected, arguing that the prosecutor "must be confined to the evidence they had placed before the jury as their completed case." In response, the counsel for the Crown referred to a recent Resolution of the Judges (referring to the twelve judges who deliberated on matters of law raised in common-law trials): "it was not for the Crown to call evidence of sanity, even though the cross examination of their witnesses pointed to the probability that insanity would be raised." The prosecutor inferred this to mean that the Crown's evidence "should be reserved until a case of insanity was set up by the defense, either by cross examination or by substantive evidence," and in the latter event, the Crown evidence could only be introduced by way of rebuttal.[2]

Up to the moment this knotty legal point landed in the judge's lap, Smith's trial had followed the formulaic course of a late-Victorian insanity trial. A grisly, inexplicable murder between two people with no history of domestic discord was laid before the jury, police officials recounted the prisoner's bewildered statement, and family members provided haunting tales of the accused's history of mental derangement. The only usual character missing was a divisional police surgeon or prison medical officer, who, along with other members of London's medical community, was fast becoming a regular participant in trials that turned on the question of insanity.

Medical testimony at the Old Bailey has received so much attention by historians of law and medicine, however, that the one person who served as the conduit for how and whether medical testimony bearing on mental derangement reached the jury is often relegated to the shadows. The historian's lens is usually fixed on the colorful debate between legal practitioners and emerging specialists in mental medicine. Indeed, whatever attention is *not* directed at the medical witness is taken up by the rise of the defense attorney and his attempts to craft a more rigorous construction of evidence and a refining of "guilt beyond a reasonable doubt," both of which affected the proffering and possible reception of medical evidence.

But medical evidence only entered the courtroom at the sufferance of the judge. When Mr. Justice Darling ruled on the prosecutor's request to call witnesses in rebuttal, today's student of the history of medical jurisprudence is reminded that it was the judge alone who decided not only what the jury heard but, most significantly, what the jury heard *last*. When the prison medical officer eventually appeared at Smith's trial, the family's description of the defendant's history of frothing at the mouth was challenged by the prison doctor's forcefully rejecting the application of epilepsy to this case. In answer to testimony that expressly mentioned the defendant's inability to tell right from wrong, the medical man issued an unequivocal denial: "he did know the nature and quality [of the act] and that it was wrong."[3]

One can hardly think of much more damaging testimony just as the jurors were about to deliberate Smith's fate, and yet one has little way of knowing the weight they accorded Dr. Dyer's opinion. Indeed, it is also a mystery what impression medical claims to expertise in general carried for jury deliberation or whether medical terms and diagnoses resonated with contemporary beliefs about madness that jurors brought into court with them. Still, trial procedure had become well established by the nineteenth century; the standard of guilt beyond a reasonable doubt had been coupled with a sequence mandating that the last element of the criminal prosecution would be the defense argument. Indeed, until the rise of the defense attorney, it was the prisoner's own words that the jury took most immediately into deliberations. The judge's decision to admit rebuttal evidence could therefore amount to a fateful determination. The intentional placement of the defense attorney's construction of the events surrounding the crime—including the prisoner's mental state—might easily be compromised by prison doctors, whose testimony was chosen to be the last the jury would hear before the judge's instructions. How had this alteration in the sequence of courtroom testimony come about?

"In Every Case, a Matter for [My] Discretion"

The prosecutor's gambit to call Dr. Dyer in rebuttal enjoyed a lineage that stretched back at least to the years following *McNaughtan*. In 1847, a prosecutor's request to call medical witnesses to comment on expert evidence offered by the defense prompted the defense attorney to object to the Crown having the opportunity "to give fresh evidence in contradiction of the prisoner's case." The judge's eventual decision to permit new testimony represents an idiosyncratic and, one suspects, momentous reading of the *McNaughtan Rules*: "The learned judges expressly stat[ed], that after all the witnesses had been examined, and after all the facts had been stated, persons of skill might be called upon to give their opinion whether, assuming the facts disposed to be true, the accused was sane or insane at the time."[4] The judge's interpretation of the (*original*) intent of those who crafted the *Rules* strikes today's reader as somewhat singular. It is one thing for the court to turn to medical witnesses to comment upon the facts supplied by lay persons; it is quite another to invite doctors to comment on the observations of their medical brethren in what could easily devolve into an endless cycle of assertion and rebuttal. Still, according to this judge's reading at least, the *McNaughtan Rules* left the door open for medical witnesses to be called in response to the expert opinion offered by the other side.[5]

Although rebuttal evidence after *McNaughtan* was in no way common, it was not unheard of either. By the time of the Smith trial in 1910, it was apparently reaching sufficient notice that the court of appeals, responding to Smith's defense attorney's appeal, found it necessary to rule: "No general rule can be laid down at which stage of the trial it becomes the duty of the prosecutor to proffer evidence of sanity, where there is reason to believe that insanity will be relied upon as a defense."[6] The appellate judges cited an earlier decision allowing a prosecutor to introduce rebuttal witnesses, this time in a trial in which the defense attorney had employed no witnesses to argue insanity but rather had elicited testimony regarding mental derangement in his cross-examination of the witnesses for the Crown. In that ruling, Lord Coleridge asserted, "It would be highly unsatisfactory for any evidence of the prisoner's mind should be excluded, and therefore [the prosecutor] had better call any evidence he had."[7] When Mr. Justice Darling allowed the calling of such witnesses in the Smith trial, he was therefore on sound judicial footing, maintaining that "the rule as to rebutting evidence is that it really is a matter for the discretion of the judge presiding at the trial." With the provision that "no injustice is done to the accused . . . it is a matter, in every case, for the discretion of the judge."[8]

Also at the discretion of the judge were questions asked of specialist witnesses or, indeed, of any witness. When a medical witness in 1871 was asked his opinion of the prisoner's mental state when the act was committed—a frequently asked question—the prosecutor immediately objected: "the question could not be put, it referred to the state of the prisoner's mind at the time when the witness was not present . . . to answer this the witness must direct his mind . . . to circumstances deposed to by other witnesses and thus he would be asked to give his opinion on the very point it was the province of the jury to decide."[9] The judge agreed: the question could not be put. Several years later, when a judge refused to allow the question, he borrowed the previous prosecutor's language. In this case, a defense attorney had proposed to ask a medical witness if he had been able to form an opinion of the prisoner's mental state at the time of the crime, the judge interrupted: "this was the form of question often put and objected to, and it was in reality not a question of medical science, but was the question which the Jury alone could properly decide."[10] The witness was then confined to answering hypothetical questions regarding consciousness and violence in states of mental derangement.

Prominent professional credentials in no way deflected medical witnesses from courtroom admonishment, as no less a medical personage than Forbes Winslow was to discover. The well-known author and physician identified himself in court as "M.B. and L.L.M. of Cambridge, a member of the Royal College of Physicians, Physician to the British Hospital for Mental Disorders, and Lecturer on Mental Diseases at Charing Cross Hospital." But when he testified at the Old Bailey and moved from assessing the mental state of the defendant to addressing the legal consequences of his finding—"I formed the opinion that she is a person of unsound mind and not responsible for her actions"—the trial narrative reports, "The Court reproved the witness for making the latter observation, that being a question for the jury."[11] Had Winslow been the only Victorian doctor to venture an opinion on the legal consequences of his medical opinion, one might understand the reason for the judicial pique. But he was not: medical witnesses throughout the century often gave an opinion about the ultimate question of responsibility that followed their diagnoses. Indeed, they were sometimes asked directly by some judges to make this precise determination. Few, however, faced being reproved by the bench, leading one to wonder if in this case the witness's self-aggrandizing recitation of his credentials may have drawn the admonishment by the bench.

The variation in judicial reception of medical testimony is well worth noting. Although some judges reacted strongly to the medical witnesses venturing opinions about the defendant's criminal responsibility, others invited it, while still others advised caution. They certainly revealed no visceral distaste for medical testimony, but they jealously guarded the jury's prerogative to have the final determination. They also could bristle at the medical man's attempt to reconstruct the accused's state of mind at the time of the crime. For medical men to pronounce upon the defendant's intellects at a time when they were not present transgressed upon the role of the jury, and yet, this was exactly the question medical witnesses were in court to answer. Because the presence of insanity was an inference for the jury to draw, one might have thought medical witnesses would confine their testimony to diagnosis and the possible consequences of the named condition for mental disorientation and self-control. Instead, when they declared the defendant insane, they often employed the law's own construction of "knowing right from wrong" directly in their testimony.

Judges may well have worried if there was much for the jury to do when faced with medical specialists who framed the defendant's mental world in language exquisitely crafted to address the fundamental concerns of the law. They need not have been concerned. Juries were known to acquit on the grounds of insanity following medical agreement between the defense and the prosecution experts that the offender was perfectly sane, and they were known to convict in trials following unanimous medical opinion that the offender was mad as a hatter. This observation is not made to suggest that juries placed no import on medical testimony or held its conveyors in contempt. Rather, it is made to counter the facile notion that juries were obeisant in the face of scientific credentials, substituting the authority of a professional voice for their own folk wisdom and judgment. Medical witnesses like Winslow doubtless claimed insights based upon learning and experience, but theirs was one voice among many. In reading the courtroom narratives, one voice stands out—the judge's.

This chapter takes up the exercise of judicial discretion at three critical moments: the calling of rebuttal evidence, the effort to shape verdicts, and the direct questioning of forensic-psychiatric witnesses. Judicial decision making at the Old Bailey was exercised in real time; there was little opportunity (or inclination, one suspects) to consult precedent and established juridical opinion. Confronted with the ever assertive voice of the defense attorney and the increasingly confident forensic psychiatric witness's claims to an expanding body of knowledge, the judge was enjoined to strike a balance among the claims to professional expertise, the rights of the defendant, and the concerns of the Crown. Since it was the *McNaughtan Rules* that gave prosecutors the conceptual opening to argue the case for calling medical witnesses in rebuttal, the analysis that follows is focused on the years following the celebrated verdict that gave birth to the eponymous *Rules* (1843).

Witness for the Prosecution

Given the enduring conviction that no one could argue his or her innocence more persuasively than the defendant, the need for a defense attorney had been slow to gain ground. Common-law judges had long conceived their role as guarantor of the defendant's rights, claiming an expansive array of discretionary powers: ruling on the admissibility of evidence, commenting on the character of character witnesses, and advising the jury regarding the appropriate weight to be given to trial testimony. The introduction of a fully articulated role for a defense attorney would lead to sometimes acrid and sometimes veiled challenges to unbridled judicial gatekeeping, particularly in the area of ruling on hearsay, contested, and expert evidence.

As long as medical witnesses were called first by the prosecution and later by the judge, few evidentiary issues were placed before the judge. Like all expert testimony, medical opinion engaged the delicate question of courtroom division of labor, specifically, the need to protect the jury's prerogative as the sole arbiter in rendering courtroom opinion. Still, medical testimony that touched on "ultimate issues" such as the presence of insanity obviously threatened the courtroom division of labor. Permitting rebuttal testimony of courtroom evidence further threw into question the exclusive preserve of the jurors: only they could form an opinion about what they heard in the trial. Jurists after *McNaughtan* did not hesitate to point this out, and yet there were Old Bailey judges who clearly found expanded grounds for rebuttal testimony sanctioned by the *McNaughtan Rules*. This reading of the opinion opened the door to requests by prosecution attorneys to call medical witnesses—most often prison doctors—to challenge the evidence of medical men who had been privately retained by the defense solicitor.

How did the judge decide? If he conceived of his role as the traditional guarantor of the defendant's right to a fair trial, he could hardly look with favor on the calling of witnesses who would be quick to lessen the effect of the defense side's medical testimony. And yet the door had been opened for the medical consideration of courtroom testimony: Why should expert evidence *not* be subject to the same scrutiny and grounds for inquiry? Most often, judges grudgingly permitted the inclusion of rebuttal witnesses. Even though verdicts can be notoriously opaque with regard to the influence of expert evidence and the supposed cultural authority (and influence) of any particular participant, to the extent that medical testimony may have helped the prisoner, rebuttal evidence could easily have undermined whatever good the defense side's medical men may have accomplished. For example, when a defendant's courtroom collapse appeared to support medical testimony that he was prone to epileptic vertigo and states of unconsciousness, a rebuttal medical witness diagnosed the supposed convulsion as a simple fainting episode. Although one cannot attribute the prisoner's eventual conviction (and execution) to the rebuttal witness, it could hardly have helped the defense case.[12]

Insight into how judges regarded rebuttal evidence was perhaps best articulated in the Oliver Smith murder trial.[13] The ruling that sat at the heart of this issue—that the prosecutor was entitled to present evidence of the prisoner's mental condition *only* in answer to defense testimony—was also invoked in a series of trials in which the defense strategy was to call no medical men at all, presumably to preclude the prosecutor's use of his own medical witnesses (likely the prison medical officers) to counter the testimony of on-scene medical personnel who commented on the prisoner's erratic behavior or conversation. Unless the defense attorney introduced insanity into his questioning of witnesses, the prosecutor was theoretically barred by prevailing judicial opinion from presenting evidence that spoke to the defendant's purported incoherence and lack of self-possession.

Judicial response to this defense strategy varied. In the same year that Oliver Smith came to trial, another defense attorney listened, one suspects hopefully, as the defendant's father commented on his son's depression, his mother's suicide attempt, and the family's history of lunacy. The prosecutor proposed to call the medical officer of Brixton to report his conversations with the prisoner but added that it was not for him to call Dr. Dyer: "the burden of proof rested on the defense." And the defense rested, choosing to call no medical witnesses (and thereby precluding Dyer being called "in rebuttal"). Trying another tactic, the prosecutor referred the judge to a report written by the prison doctor that, although not formally a part of the case for the prosecution, could still be entered into testimony by his lordship calling the jail doctor to testify. But like the defense, the judge rested: "I shall do nothing; I shall leave it entirely to the counsel who defend the prisoner." The jury, however, did not rest: Bright was convicted of murder and sentenced to hang.[14]

Several months earlier, a defendant had met the same fate when his attorney had tried a similar tactic to preclude the appearance of the prison doctor. A physician called to the scene of the killing was asked under cross-examination by the defense attorney to comment on the mental state that might have accompanied the brutal attack: "A homicidal impulse may come very suddenly upon a person who had been up to that time quite sane; if anything of that kind is latent in a person, distress from a love affair [which spoke directly to the events surrounding the murder] or taking of an unaccustomed quantity of drink would be a pre-disposing cause." With such suggestive testimony offered by the prosecution's own witness, the defense attorney "intimated that he would call no witnesses." The prosecutor put it to the judge, however, to consider whether it was possible that the jury could base a verdict of insanity on any of the evidence the trial had already brought forward, and if so, he wanted to call the prison doctor, mindful that the Crown was not "to call evidence as to sanity until some evidence had been given [by the Defense] as to insanity." In this trial, the judge did not demur, considering it "highly unsatisfactory that any evidence directed to the condition of the prisoner's mind should be excluded in a formal hearing." Framing the on-scene physician's musing about homicidal mania as "hypothetical" (to blunt its effect), the prison doctor described his conversations with the prisoner, concluding that "he has never shown any symptom of homicidal tendency."[15]

The Resolution of Judges notwithstanding, when Old Bailey judges were asked to rule on the admissibility of rebuttal testimony, they gave lip service to the supposed insistence that it was up to the defense to introduce insanity. In court, judges exercised their discretion to allow any and all evidence that spoke to the mental state of the accused. The Resolution, as far as the Old Bailey judiciary was concerned, was not "an absolute rule . . . the prosecution had the power . . . to call a doctor in order that it might be seen whether there was any real foundation" in the witness's inference of madness.[16] And the judge had the discretionary power to determine when and where such rules applied.

Still, there were limits to judicial discretion; the judge could not rule evidence in or out if the defendant chose to plead guilty. In the 1912 trial of William Tebbitt for the attempted murder of Leopold de Rothschild (discussed in chapter 5), the judge had been faced with such a plea. From the beginning, the defendant strongly resisted the raising of an insanity defense; indeed, he rejected the mention of madness altogether. Similar to several other allegedly mad defendants, Tebbitt maintained that if his account of the events leading up to the shooting were absolutely true, his beliefs could hardly be diagnosed as delusional. Following an examination by the "mental expert" he himself had requested, the defendant opted not to put him on the stand, concluding, one suspects, that the physician was in agreement with the prison doctor's diagnosis of homicidal mania. The defendant elected to bypass any discussion of this mental state by pleading guilty to all counts, to the surprise of this defense attorney and annoyance of the judge, since the plea precluded the jury's function in announcing, in the judge's words, the "moral blame" attached to the defendant's conduct. It also removed the judge's capacity to exercise his own discretion, a resource he obviously relished. There would be no evidence to rule in or out, no medical witnesses whose diagnosis he could reinforce or dismiss by a carefully worded query—"do you seriously mean to suggest"— and most of all, no verdict to reject and therefore compel the jury to consider a finding more in keeping with the law's intentions. In short, although two hundred years of parliamentary decisions had served to constrain the scope of judicial discretion, few efforts were as successful as a defendant's entering a simple plea of guilty.

Revisiting *Bushell's Case*

Although Mr. Justice Coleridge was compelled to accept William Tebbitt's guilty plea, judicial discretion stretched far beyond evidentiary matters. Judges in Victorian insanity trials also had the authority to refuse to accept a verdict, insisting that jurors reconsider their reasoning in light of courtroom evidence and legal stricture. Although he could not threaten to imprison jurors in a room "without meat, drink, fire, or tobacco" until they reached a verdict more in keeping with his interpretation of the facts of the case—a practice judges apparently resorted to before the landmark *Bushell's Case* (1670)—Old Bailey judges managed to do more than signal their displeasure.[17] When a jury in 1889 convicted Edward Peters of arson, adding that they "did not believe him responsible at the time for his actions," Mr. Justice Channel "declined to take the verdict, no evidence to insanity having been called." The jury reconsidered, convicting the defendant with an unadorned "guilty" verdict. Sentencing was postponed pending inquiry into the defendant's mental condition, and the trial concluded with the judge pronouncing a three-year sentence.[18]

Directed verdicts also provide historians of law and psychiatry with enduring evidence of the influence judges could wield in their courtrooms. At times the trial narratives merely conclude with statements like "Mr. Justice Hamilton directed the jury to find a verdict of Guilty, but insane, and the prisoner was ordered to be detained."[19] Other times, a reason was given: "The Court directed the Jury to acquit the prisoner, stating that it was quite obvious she did not know what she was about."[20] Sometimes the verdict was arrived at indirectly but with the indelible imprint of the judge. In 1911, Amelia Horne was found "guilty, but not responsible for her actions at the time." The judge instructed the jury that such a verdict would result in the prisoner's incarceration in a criminal lunatic asylum, adding that "he did not think the jury intended that consequence." Horne had administered a fatal dose of laudanum to her newborn infant and swallowed the remainder herself. This once "happy and bright" woman had appeared depressed and weak after the child's delivery, "not in a state of health to appreciate what she was doing." Jurors reconsidered their verdict and, with a "strong recommendation to mercy," found the prisoner guilty. She was sentenced to five days imprisonment, which resulted in immediate discharge, since she was given credit for the time she spent awaiting trial.[21]

Although jurors in this case seemed confident in following the judge's lead that a minimal sentence was what he had in mind, they were taking a considerable risk. The judge had initially signaled his anger with the grand jury that first considered the mother's pitiable act. The use of poison is doubtless the clearest evidence of premeditation; a true bill of murder would have seemed the logical and expected course of action. Indeed, few defendants on trial for a purposeful killing in the nineteenth century faced indictments of anything short of "willful murder." In Horne's case, however, the grand jury stopped short of murder, returning an indictment for "Manslaughter of her infant child." In charging the jury at the trial's conclusion, Mr. Justice Scruttan lamented the case "coming before the Jury in an extremely unsatisfactory way, because it was idle to shut one's eyes to the fact that one of the possible or probable inferences to be drawn from the facts was that the woman meant to kill the child and herself." Her physical and mental condition may well have militated against her knowing the quality of her acts, and this, the judge believed, should have been investigated on a bill of murder. Such an action, however, had been precluded by the grand jury's "taking upon themselves to settle what crime she should be charged with."[22]

Of course, grand juries always decided the specific charge on indictment; what they were *not* supposed to do was decide for themselves the extent of the defendant's intention and to indict accordingly. The judge observed in court, "Juries must not allow their sympathies to interfere with their giving true answers to the question of fact." The reason for his disquiet was the objective of deterrence: "if it once got about that all a mother had to do was to go to the sympathies of a jury, and the jury to find that death was accidental, there would be a very large number of young babies killed immediately after birth in order to get them out of the way." Grand jurors, observed the judge, were not the only actors in court capable of having humane feelings: "they must do him the justice to believe that, although he had got on a red robe and a wig, he was a man with exactly the same feelings and sympathies as themselves."[23] Perhaps it was this last sentiment and his vocal displeasure at the less than truthful indictment that encouraged the trial jurors to believe the defendant would be in merciful hands when they voted an outright conviction.

The grand jury that heard the Crown's evidence against Leah Abrahams in 1905, on the other hand, had no difficulty returning a true bill of willful murder in the death of her newborn child, whose head had been cut off just after birth. Medical evidence brought forward during the trial threw the facts of the case into considerable uncertainty. Was the infant born alive? Could head trauma *independent* of the decapitation have been sustained when the infant had been dropped, post delivery? Did the mother's admittedly torturous delivery cause "such pain [as to render her] temporarily insane and unconscious . . . severe hemorrhage would produce unconsciousness"? Taking this evidence into account, the judge threw out the grand jury's indictment, "rul[ing] that the evidence of murder was not sufficient to go to the Jury." The defendant's attorney seized on the judge's comments, hoping to thwart any court action at all, asserting "that indeed there was no evidence [to convict] at all," but the judge was not about to see the mother's action go without legal consequence. There may not have been sufficient grounds for a finding of murder or manslaughter, but there was certainly evidence of concealment, and this offense, he maintained, must go to the jury. Convicted of concealment but recommended to mercy by the jury, Leah Abrahams was sentenced to one month hard labor.[24]

There were other occasions when a judge simply refused to accept a verdict's wording. Mentioned in the preceding chapter, Ernest Partridge's trial for the murder of his beloved wife had begun with the prisoner's own statement: "Something seemed to go snap in my head and I jumped up and caught her by the throat . . . I lost control of myself altogether; I did not know what I was doing exactly, I felt as though I was holding a very strong galvanic battery." Medical testimony suggested his lapse in consciousness was epileptic automatism, although the medical evidence would prove less than dispositive. The Brixton Prison medical officer testified, "Persons suffering in this manner I have known to commit violent assaults and then be seized with remorse." Still, he found no epileptic tendencies in the prisoner, although "it would be possible for him . . . not to betray them." Then again, that the prisoner gave him a "lucid account of the [crime], is not consistent with an attack of masked epilepsy." The jury's verdict reflected a less-than-confident determination of mental derangement, inviting the judge's efforts to shape their verdict.

> *Jury*: We find that the prisoner killed his wife, that he was sane at the time, that he acted in a fit of temper without intention of killing her.
> *Judge*: I do not understand what you mean by "without intention of killing her." A man is held to intend the consequences of his actions. Of course, if he does it in a fit of passion that is not "deliberate" intention in one sense of the word, but he is held to intend the necessary consequences of his act, in what sense do you use the words "without intention of killing her?"

Foreman: The Jury are unanimously and emphatically of opinion that at the moment of the act the prisoner did not realize the consequences of his act.

Judge: For what reason do you say he did not realize the consequences of the act he was doing?

Foreman: That we cannot say.

Judge: You must say if you please. If he was sane at the time there is no answer to the case.

Foreman: I cannot hold out any hope that the Jury will come to any other finding than that I have given.

After the judge directed the jury to retire "to reconsider their verdict," the defense attorney contended that their finding that "he did not realize at the time what he was doing" meant that a verdict of guilty could not be supported.

Judge: I do not agree with you. I think if a man flies into a passion and does a thing that might cause death . . . he is answerable for his actions (unless he was in a fit, which is characterized as insanity). I'm afraid I cannot hear you at the present moment. It must be discussed on some future occasion.

The jury returned to court, informing the judge, "We find that the prisoner killed his wife, and very strongly recommend him to mercy." In pronouncing a death sentence, the judge observed that the jury's former finding and the current recommendation would be "mercifully considered by the proper authorities."[25]

The proper authority was the Home Secretary, whose office reviewed sentences and dispositions, particularly in matters touching on insanity. In July 1907, the Old Bailey witnessed a bizarre trial of a woman accused of "obtaining money by false pretenses" involving the financier J. Pierpont Morgan: "There is no truth in the statement that I have had charge of her financial interests [the financier informed the court] and have obtained for her 12 per cent per annum on her investments or that I wrote to her . . . inviting her to join a syndicate in which I was interested." The prisoner was unknown to Morgan, who testified that he had "never seen her to my knowledge till I saw her at the police court." According to the prosecuting attorney, the prisoner had been confined in a sanitarium in America seven years prior to the arrest in London. Described in medical certificates as suffering from "hysteria and mania," although not insane, "she was of a highly neurotic temperament and at times on the verge of insanity." The judge remarked, "I have suspected it for some hours." He continued, "her conduct had been a puzzle to [me] ever since [I] listened to the case. On the one hand extraordinary acuteness was shown in sounding [out] these two people and making up her mind as to the kind of bait that would be likely to attract them. On the other the whole proceeding showed that she had a disordered mind, [committing the crime] in the crudest possible manner. A criminal in possession of her faculties did not commit fraud in that way." The judge's sentiment, "although it might appear severe," was designed to ensure that she would be "looked after for a considerable length of time." To this end, he chose to leave the decision of how long she was to stay and in what type of institution "to be determined by the Home Secretary, who had means at his disposal which the court had not." He therefore decided to give her a sentence of five years penal servitude "in order that the Home Secretary might have a full opportunity for considering . . . what was the best thing to be done with her."[26]

Not all judges exercised their discretion to encourage the jury to rethink a verdict. The medical witnesses who appeared at the trial of Ethel Harding left little doubt that delirium following delivery was responsible for her fatally stabbing her newborn. The jury's verdict sought to acknowledge the defendant's impaired mental state by finding her guilty, "with the strongest possible recommendation to mercy, as we consider that she was in a frenzied state of mind at the time the act was committed." The prisoner's counsel, who served at the court's request, submitted, "This was a verdict of Guilty but Insane." Mr. Justice Bingham, however, disagreed. "It was a verdict of guilty and he must act upon it." He addressed the prisoner, however, urging her "not to be anxious because he hoped and believed that the recommendation of the jury (to which his own would be added) would be received with sympathy and would be given effect by the Home Secretary." Nevertheless, he was "obliged to pass upon her the only sentence which was permissible for the crime of which she had been found guilty—namely the sentence of death."[27]

He may have believed himself obliged to pass the ultimate sentence, but he was not obliged to accept the verdict as stated. Late Victorian judges were known for encouraging juries to reconsider the wording of a verdict, the better to express their uncertainty regarding the defendant's possessing criminal intention. In this case, however, Bingham chose not to instruct the jury to reword its verdict, which would have saved him from sentencing the tragic woman to death. To declare that he was "obliged" to impose the only sentence permissible obscures the fact that he shared the bench with others who found creative ways to evade mandatory sentencing.

His judicial brethren were also finding ways to postpone questions of mental incapacity to the sentencing stage. Given the universe of deranged criminality one is likely to encounter in a survey of insanity trials spanning 150 years, it really does take an extraordinary trial to claim pride of place. It is even more remarkable when the offense was not a brutal killing but a rather ordinary, if imaginative, case of fraud. This trial, discussed at the beginning of chapter 4, concerned the "Consulting Phrenologist, Medical Hypnotist and Mesmerist, Electrical and Hygienic Practitioner" Thomas Rogers Willis. Even with the defendant's adamantine conviction that his magnetic powers would enable him to grow the plaintiff's eye, the judge chose to ignore the testimony of the prison doctor that this was all delusion. The judge asserted that he had witnessed no sign indicating a "want of intellect" in the defendant. Furthermore, "the question of insanity could not be dealt with here," since it had never been raised by the defense. The prisoner was duly sentenced to nine months imprisonment, to be kept under observation: "If he was found to be insane, he would be treated accordingly." The defendant's own attorney could easily have asked the jury to consider the prisoner's tenuous grasp on reality. Instead, the testimony of the jail medical officer is not given until after conviction. Even at that stage, the judge chose to ignore it as relevant for consideration.[28]

"Do You Seriously Mean to Suggest . . . ?"

Beyond deciding whether to admit rebuttal evidence and to instruct juries when verdicts did not comport with law or courtroom testimony, judges exerted powerful influence in establishing the courtroom climate for the reception of medical evidence bearing on insanity. Judges had long enjoyed an expansive voice regarding the credibility of lay witnesses—"these character witnesses rather seem to stand in need of character witnesses of their own"— and, on occasion, could disparage the common sense of expert witnesses. Confronted with an apothecary who permitted his professional partner to mix medicines for their clients, even though he was firmly convinced of his partner's madness, the judge asked archly, "How many of [your customers] might he have poisoned in the course of that six months?"[29] Still, whatever scorn jurists may have shown for medical men in print who ventured into ever more expansive diagnoses, the trial narratives reveal that juries rarely heard dismissive, discourteous comments emanating from the bench, although derisive comments were not unheard of and did not spare the feelings of even the most noted alienists.[30]

Judicial questions normally ranged from the simply inquisitive ("What do you mean when you say 'unsound mind'?") to close questioning that transported the more innovative diagnoses into the specifics of a particular case: "Did you ever know an instance within your own experience of a person being subject to epileptic vertigo who never before or after had a fit?"[31] Judges were particularly keen to learn about physicians' actual experience rather than hear about their training. After listening to detailed testimony outlining the effects of a brain concussion in terms of hallucinations and delusions, a judge asked, "Have you had any patients who have exhibited such symptoms?" The witness was compelled to acknowledge, "I speak more from reading than observation." The judge then pressed a second medical witness: "Might [the prisoner] without having committed willful perjury, have imagined this highway robbery. Do you consider [the delusion] consistent with what you said?" The witness agreed; the judge's apposite and well-timed question allowed the jury to reframe as delusion testimony suggesting perjury, prompting, one suspects, the jury's vote of a complete acquittal.[32] Judicial efforts to effect the best use of medical testimony remind historians that trial judges had not abandoned their time-honored role as protector of the defendant's interests, regardless of—or perhaps because of—the presence of a defense attorney.

Sometimes this posture led the judge to question the defendant and the medical witness. After listening to a defendant's co-offender testify that the accused was deranged, the judge turned to him and asked simply, "Were *you* ever insane?," compelling the co-offender to reply, "I have been in an asylum a few times."[33] Judges reserved most of their questioning of medical witnesses when they paired a diagnosis, as Forbes Winslow did in the case cited earlier, with the opinion that the accused "would not be responsible for his behavior." Still, many members of the judiciary went out of their way to draw explicit medical opinion on the subject of culpability. After a medical witness was asked if he had "not the slightest doubt that [the defendant] committed this act under a delusion," he responded, "There is not the slightest doubt about it." The judge then asked a question of his own: "Would that be the ordinary state of the progress she had gone through, for her brain to be in so excited a state that she would be entirely irresponsible for her acts?" And the witness replied, "I should decidedly say so."[34]

The one exception to the relative comity between medical witness and presiding judges has already been noted: an insanity diagnosis that engaged affect or volition alone, leaving the intellect intact, often invited sharp rebuke. When presented with moral, rather than cognitive, derangement, heretofore-obliging judges could turn noticeably acidic. In the case of a young boy who poisoned his grandfather by adding arsenic to the sugar bowl and was diagnosed by the medical witness to be suffering from moral insanity, the judge addressed the jury, saying he did not, "for a moment desire to disparage the evidence of the scientific man, but [I] must tell the jury that all they were required to do was to listen attentively to such evidence . . . they were not bound to pay a slavish obedience to it, but might reject it if they felt it did not accord with their own common sense and experience."[35] When the boy's conviction for murder was announced, the judge could barely disguise his pleasure: "This was a defense which was frequently made and which was too often successful, and [I] *rejoice* that the jury had thrown to the winds the idle sophistry by which the defense was sought to be made out in the present occasion" (italics added).[36]

Although it is hard to miss the obvious drama that took place in a courtroom when judges occasionally confronted diseases grounded in something other than faulty cognition, it is not clear if the judicial rejection was animated by the witness's threat to the courtroom division of labor or the changing content of the medical testimony itself. Medical witnesses had been appearing at Old Bailey insanity trials for nearly a century without being subjected to attacks on the specialization of mental medicine or an insistence that questions be answered with reference to delusion. Was it the language employed by Victorian alienists or their increasing presence in his courtroom that so vexed the judge?

Given the questions that one gleans from the *OBSP*, it seems that judges were inquiring into the nature of the proffered disease, not casting aspersions on its existence.[37] There is little defensiveness on the part of the medical witness, no attempt to convince the court that the affliction *really* does exist. This inquisitiveness on the part of the bench followed in the tradition of judicial questioning that sought clarification, not justification. Confronted with testimony about a defendant's blind impulse, for example, a judge in 1848 asked, "Do you mean that the convulsive action . . . struck you, or that she had powers of mind about her, and intentionally struck you?"[38] Judicial questions also functioned to keep the jury's attention focused on the business of the courts, quite apart from the announcement of a novel type of mental disease: "Should you say that she knew the nature and quality of the act she was doing . . . that it was prohibited by law . . . or was her mind so far *gone* that she did not know more than a natural idiot would have done?"[39]

These were hardly questions designed to ridicule the witness or his diagnosis; rather, they were meant to underscore the court's objective—determining the significance of medical diagnosis for legal fact-finding. Most judges do not appear to have conceived of their role as gatekeepers shielding the jury from unwarranted and unsubstantiated medical ideas. Instead, they sometimes appear to have gone out of their way to clarify expert testimony so the jury could better use it when considering the defendant's mental state. If a medical witness spoke of "brain congestion that would deprive him of consciousness," the judge observed simply, "like a man in a sleep?"[40]

Judges could also go out of their way to intercede on a prisoner's behalf, asking a question that could neutralize medical testimony denying the prisoner's derangement. In 1865, Francis Moretti was placed on trial for intent to commit murder. The prosecuting attorney asked the attending surgeon to comment on the defendant's state of mind. He answered, "I saw nothing that would lead me to believe he was insane while he was in the hospital." When the arresting police officer reported that the prisoner had responded to the charge of attempted murder with "How could I when I lost my senses?" the jury queried the medical man, "Do you think the prisoner was in any way insane during the time he was in the hospital?" His reply of "No, I should say not" prompted the judge to ask, "Supposing a man had been out of his senses and then committed such a deed, would the loss of blood and the care taken of him in the hospital have the effect of bringing him to his sober senses?"[41] The physician agreed, and the defendant who moments before appeared certain to be convicted was acquitted on the grounds of insanity—grounds that the medical witnesses had denied.

Not all defendants expressed gratitude to the judge for interceding on their behalf. On trial for the willful murder of his son, William Humphreys listened along with the jury as Dr. Dyer, the medical officer of Brixton, concluded that Humphreys had indeed been insane owing to enduring hallucinations and delusions. On cross-examination, Dr. Dyer maintained that "it is probably due to heredity, but it has been very difficult to get any history out of him." There also seemed to be some difficulty regarding cause of death; the judge informed the jury to determine "whether the wound inflicted was the cause of the meningitis which had led to the death of the deceased."[42] Theophilus Hyslop, a physician called for the defense, affirmed the prison medical officer's finding of insanity and also cast doubt on the infant's cause of death. The prisoner was subsequently found not guilty of willful murder, but the prosecutor informed the court that there remained two additional charges, wounding with either intent to murder or to do grievous bodily harm. When the defense attorney said the prisoner would plead guilty to unlawfully wounding, the judge responded that "he would not like to take a verdict of guilty of unlawful wounding," whereupon the defense attorney relayed the prisoner's desire to plead guilty of wounding to do grievous bodily harm. Rather than bringing the trial to a halt, the guilty plea seems to have energized the prosecutor, who recalled Dr. Dyer "so that the jury could find Humphreys insane at the time he committed the act." Dyer again repeated his inference of insanity, adding that the prisoner did not know the nature and quality of his act. Following the judge's direction—and adhering to the defendant's plea—"the jury returned a verdict of Guilty of wounding with intent to do grievous bodily harm, but at the time he committed the act he was insane, so that he was not responsible for what he did." The enhanced verdict brought a protest from the prisoner: "he had given his counsel the charge and . . . he wanted the jury to say whether he was guilty or not." Instead, Mr. Humphreys found himself "detained until His Majesty's pleasure be known."[43]

That it was the prosecutor and not the defense attorney who called Dr. Dyer back to the witness stand and that it was the judge who directed the jury to the amorphous verdict resonates strongly with Martin Wiener's questioning of the assumed fractious relations between medicine and law. Having been characterized as very dangerous to himself and others, Humphreys's attacks were deemed to be "periodical, [they] may appear at any moment," and the defendant's long-term incarceration was thought appropriate by medical and legal practitioners.[44] Now that he had avoided a death sentence, the defendant pleaded guilty to a lesser offense that might well have garnered a prison sentence; given current sentencing practices, this might have been anywhere from a few months to a few years. The prosecutor's immediate decision to recall Dr. Dyer and the judge's (typically) prescriptive direction attests to the objectives of public safety that medicine and law shared. That the prisoner was left with a guilty plea the court would *not* accept is also part of the history of the evolving symmetry between the interests of legal and medical practitioners.

The spontaneous and unexpected query from the bench is further evidence that judges were not automatically opposed to either the insanity plea or the new medical specialist in mental derangement. A review of the questions asked of the mad-doctor cum alienist by Old Bailey judges reveals that the latter exercised their influence by keeping the jury's attention focused on the essentials of guilt-fastening: the prisoner's knowledge of what it was he thought he was doing and what he would likely have believed about the outcome of his act. Before homicidal mania and its accompanying states of homicidal tendency—masked epilepsy and epileptic mania—had grown to prominence in the courtroom in the latter years of the Victorian era, juries had already confronted the specter of impulsive crime accompanied by more or less "clear-headed" states of functioning.

Judges had been quick to dismiss the jury entertaining any notion of *insane* mens rea when it was framed in language suggesting moral insanity and irresistible impulse.[45] But when involuntary, violent action was attributed to puerperal mania, judges were far more accepting of the proffered mental state, although they still pressed medical witnesses on the behavioral implications of the diagnosis. "Would she know the result of what she was doing?" served to keep the jury's focus on the behavioral consequences of puerperal mania; the diagnosis itself did not end the inquiry into the defendant's mental state. Medical witnesses usually responded that even when the accused women had been conscious of the nature of their acts, they were unable to intrude upon them; thus these witnesses challenged the court to consider criteria for articulating responsibility framed restrictively in cognitive terms.[46] Clearly, one could be aware that one's actions were calculated to take away a life and still be powerless to stop the assault. "It is a medical fact that the desire to kill may go off as suddenly as it comes on . . . on the nearest and dearest . . . the sight of the object is enough."[47]

The free-floating, autonomous "desire to kill"—even when accompanied by a consciousness of what one was up to—provided a critical bridge between puerperal mania and the later diagnosis of homicidal mania. Where they differed was in the area of delusion. While fatal assaults laid at the doorstep of reproductive upheaval rarely invoked delusion, almost half of all medical testimony that invoked homicidal mania drew a connection between maniacal outburst and profoundly aberrant beliefs regarding the events surrounding the crime. Accordingly, judicial questioning of medical witnesses revisited the law's traditional concerns with delusion. Was the defendant able to make the necessary connection between knowing the nature of the act and appreciating *why* it was wrong? Could the medical witness speak with confidence that moral wrong and legal wrong had become separated in the defendant's mind?

The question of delusion's "reach" also touched upon another perennial question. Was it possible that the cognitive error was circumscribed, topographically discrete in the mind, leaving the afflicted to function coherently— able to buy a weapon, secure bullets, and secrete himself away from the public gaze in order to effect his purpose? Medical men proffering this newest variant of impulsive criminality continued to stress the capacity of those afflicted to act with purpose, even as they remained unaccountable for their actions: "I do not think that the making of arrangements for the disposition of property is inconsistent with . . . a person suffering from homicidal mania."[48]

More difficult to negotiate in testimony, however, was the eclipse of the moral faculties, the inability to recognize the mala in se character of one's act. Judges who probed this critical question pushed medical men to the limits of their claims to possess unique knowledge of madness and their willingness to defend such professional understanding in court: "Do you say you are of opinion from what you saw of him at the time that he would be incapable of knowing that it was wrong to kill a man?" The medical witness replied simply, "It is next to impossible that any individual can speak of a person as incapable of knowing that killing another is wrong." One suspects that it was because of this predictable question by the judge that the late-nineteenth-century alienist stressed the inability of a person—even one who knew the difference between right and wrong—to exert his own will when suffering homicidal mania.[49]

As discussed earlier, a popular judicial response to testimony veering into the fraught territory of uncontrollable or irresistible impulse was to interrupt the medical witness to ask, "Has she any delusion at all?" This question strongly implied that the preceding testimony might all be very interesting but that there was really only one question for the jury to consider: What did the prisoner understand regarding what he or she was actually doing at the time of the crime? A parallel judicial effort could sometimes be employed when the court was confronted with a diagnosis of homicidal mania. In 1902, Dr. Daniel Whithill spoke of an "unreflective . . . uncontrollable [insanity]— the impulse is so strong that though a person knows it to be wrong he cannot control it." The medical man concluded with reference to the common law's own formula: "There are cases where a person knows the difference between right and wrong but has no power, from mental defect—you get at the fact of whether it is mental defect by delusions."[50]

The Division of Labor in the Late Victorian Courtroom

Even as late as the mid-1700s, "decisive steps had yet to be taken in the Anglo-American law of evidence."[51] Once the defense attorney arrived at the Old Bailey in a form recognizable to modern eyes—that is, as a full advocate for the accused, not only as a questioner of witnesses—criminal evidence and courtroom procedure became proper subjects for courtroom debate. Courtroom narratives from the Old Bailey suggest an observable refinement in the role of the judge as unofficial counsel for the defense and chief examiner of witnesses. No longer critical to the "discovery" effort, his role now became one of arbitrating between the competing claims of the prosecuting and defense attorneys. Could a delusional mental patient serve as the Crown's star witness to identify the offender?[52] Could a medical witness give an opinion on the mental state of a defendant without ever having met him? Could witnesses refuse to answer questions phrased in a form they rejected? Far from having minimized or constrained the reach of judicial discretion, nineteenth-century parliamentary reforms introducing a new division of courtroom labor only shifted the occasions for discretionary decision making.

The institution of the defense attorney may have ushered in greater scrutiny of trial procedure and courtroom evidence, but the Old Bailey was in the retail, not the wholesale, business. Each objection and every contested motion to alter trial procedure required an on-the-spot decision. The judge had hardly been marginalized by the arrival of the defense attorney and an increasingly combative counsel for the Crown. He exercised his influence on varied questions, certainly, but ones that were just as pivotal to the construction of evidence confronting the jury as in the days when he had been examiner-in-chief.

In many ways, the judge's tendentious comments to the jury were also a continuation of eighteenth-century habits. "Then you will acquit to be sure gentleman," heard in the pre–defense attorney era, revealed the extent of judicial authority that is usually put under the benign heading of a "directed verdict." A full contest of wills between defense and prosecuting attorneys seems to have brought an end to the undiluted directed verdict, but there is clear evidence in the *OBSP* throughout the nineteenth century that the precise wording of verdicts continued judicial efforts to shape the outcome of the jury's finding. Some judges refused to accept an ambiguous finding, while others intervened to remind jurors of the practical implications of their verdict. Most often, one sees a measured effort to bring jury verdicts in line with the law's intent, at least to the extent that the judge interpreted this intent.

Judges ceded territory slowly in the matter of commenting on evidence. When a defense attorney relied upon a family history of insanity to support the contention that the defendant was mentally defective, and the judge announced that he "would take the evidence, but could not see that it was of slightest value," no wink to the jury was needed.[53] Similarly, when a defense attorney asked a prosecution witness whether he had heard from anybody that the defendant attempted to injure himself and that he was mad at the time he did that, the judge did not wait for the response to interject, "That is scarcely satisfactory evidence. Certainly it would not be evidence in any Civil Court," presumably because it constituted hearsay.[54] Witnesses were sufficiently knowledgeable of the term *hearsay* to employ it often in their testimony: "I believe [the defendant's brother] committed suicide, but I only know if from hearsay—no doubt there is considerable insanity in the family."[55] Attorneys objected to a witness's statement as hearsay evidence, which the judge likewise "declined to admit."[56] Finally, medical witnesses also questioned how much reports of inexplicable behavior should inform their own opinions. Police surgeon Andrew Kennedy explained how he reached the decision to certify a lunatic: "If I was told that the prisoner, in addition to chopping up his furniture, had previously broken up asphalt, cut a watch chain to pieces, and hammered a watch out of shape on different occasions . . . it would have made me very suspicious to the state of his mind, but unless I saw it, I should not be justified in certifying him insane—one does not certify on hearsay evidence."[57] When judges refused to admit hearsay testimony, they were exercising their discretion in a well-understood and seemingly well-accepted area. Attorneys could object to the testimony, but only the judge could admit or reject, a critical gate-keeping function judges seemed only too willing to exercise.

Although decisions made with regard to evidence and the appropriateness of any particular verdict suggest the importance the bench attached to its authority, it was in the receipt of expert testimony offered in insanity trials that judges' professional sensibilities and courtroom sovereignty were most engaged. One sees throughout the late Victorian era evidence of the law's efforts to shape not just insanity but, as Martin Wiener has pointed out, defense claims based on drunkenness and provocation in an effort to engineer ever more stringent levels of individual prudence and a rigorous standard of impulse inhibition.[58] In their treatment of medical witnesses proffering various species of insanity, judges revealed an intriguing proclivity to take umbrage at some forms of insanity but not others. Victorian preoccupations with impulse control and mastery over emotions reached their sharpest expression in judicial reactions to moral insanity and other diagnoses of "clear-thinking" insanity in which the failure to master emotions was ascribed to disease rather than character. Comments from the bench regarding this particular variant of insanity could be contemptuous and insulting. Homicidal mania, which retained many of the features of "irresistible impulse" (a condition that judges had jettisoned from consideration when presented as the disease in and of itself), precipitated no such reaction. One assumes that the elision of homicidal mania with delusion and epilepsy, and its association with the imagery of puerperal mania insulated it from vituperative judicial comment.

Finally, a review of the Old Bailey trial narratives highlights the role of the judge in setting not just the tone but also the terms of the debate between medicine and law in the years that witnessed expanding grounds for inferring insanity. Certainly, there was variation in judicial temperament; a judge might make a vigorous attempt to insert himself into the proceedings, or he might be more reticent: "I shall leave it entirely to the counsel who defend the prisoner." But there was no variation in the self-styled authority that judges continued to exercise, whatever the alteration in courtroom roles witnessed in evidentiary and procedural reform. Judicial prerogative was not a matter of parliamentary action or a strategy animating counsel for the Crown or the defense. Preserving the independence of jury decision making may have been their preferred means of justification, but the judiciary reserved for itself the administration of justice: nothing would reach the jurors' ears but through the judge.

On the Origins of Diagnosis

If any man wishes to know the exact high-water mark of contemporary progress in science . . . he should not go to the meetings of societies, or listen to
lectures and papers. He must attend an action in the Law Court . . . [there] . . .
masters of other orders of knowledge, not as they are in the habit of doling it
out in instruction to their pupils, [are] struck out in the course of a fierce conflict of wits which leaves no mercy for the vanquished.

Writing in 1885, William Odling, Waynflete Professor of Chemistry at Oxford
and a frequent witness himself in the law courts, thus extolled the educative
function of courtroom testimony. Odling singled out law reports particularly
for the insight they offered London readers into the knowledge claims made
by scientific communities.[1] Though the quoted passage refers to conflicts
regarding assertions of knowledge in natural philosophy and applied mechanics, it captures beautifully the experiences of medical witnesses offering
diagnoses of madness in 1885 or, indeed, in any year beginning in 1760. It was
the unusual insanity trial that did *not* engage issues of science, the "orders of
knowledge," the conflict in cross-examination, the quality of mercy, and, if
ending in conviction, a vanquished insanity plea. As the form of the criminal
trial evolved from "the Accused Speaks" to the full-blown adversarial contest
between prosecuting and defense attorneys, the knowledge claims by medical
witness were thrown into sharp relief. Their assertion that they possessed
unique insight and thus a privileged role in this new, combative criminal trial
began with naming a diagnosis.

The effort to defend the diagnosis began in the mid-1760s, when John
Monro was asked to account for features of Earl Ferrers's criminality as
"symptoms of lunacy." Specialists in mental medicine had become familiar
with pointed questioning about madness when they presented papers at professional gatherings, where fierce conflict and heated debate were not un-

known, for all the gentlemanly tone of the after-dinner discussion. But the assertion of scientific knowledge—to progress claimed in deciphering the mind of the mad—took on a qualitatively different texture when ventured in the law courts. The stakes were altogether of a different moment, and it was not only the defendant who feared being vanquished or who hoped for judicial mercy. The new specialist in mental medicine soon discovered that he was treated as a witness: his claim to knowledge was scrutinized no less closely than the lay witness's assertion of fact. In this forum, the doctor's assertion of privileged opinion could either rise to professional arrival or could result in his denigration as a partisan or worse; "Experts on Madness! Mad-doctors!" a judge could respond contemptuously. The courtroom drama was drama indeed.

The scope of such Old Bailey theatrics often hinged on the medical man's diagnosis. He could, of course, avoid naming any specific form of derangement and say simply, "I have looked upon him as a man insane," a statement commonly heard in the late eighteenth and early nineteenth centuries. The generic reference to insanity, insensibility, delirium, or "being out of his wits" eventually gave way to the invocation of delusion, beginning with its introduction in *Hadfield* and gathering increased popularity in medical testimony up to *McNaughtan* and beyond. Over the course of the Victorian era, delusion was followed by a plethora of medical diagnoses implicating not only cognitive defect—or *even* cognitive defect—but also the passions and the will either separately or in combination with each other. By the turn of the twentieth century, homicidal mania (with a crime in its name) distinguished itself by its frequency of mention and by the legal concern with ascribing culpability, which it engaged more directly than any other diagnosis that had been employed in court.

Where did this diagnosis come from? Indeed, how are we to make sense of the historical process that deposited the alienist in the courtroom in the first place, along with the content of his testimony? In reviewing contemporary medical texts, Roger Smith identifies the clear importance given to physiognomy and expression, observed while interviewing the patient.[2] As in any medical observation, assessing pulse, breathing, and the state of the bowels was part of the diagnostic process. Additionally, medical men cited evidence of cognitive or emotional disorder (delusion, character change) and the absence of motive.[3] But how were disparate character and behavioral elements—physiological and psychological—sifted, sorted, and fashioned into diagnoses that changed noticeably over time? In his comprehensive analysis of the history and sociology of the professions, Andrew Abbott has advanced a framework for parsing the myriad forces at work in historical change, identifying "determinants," "structure," and "intention" as the contingent elements shaping the "tangled net of events" we know as history.[4] To account for the courtroom introduction of medico-legal diagnoses that began with John Monro's testimony in 1760 and continued up to the early decades of the twentieth century, I enlist Abbott's three elements to examine the historical emergence and trajectory of forensic psychiatric evidence at the Old Bailey, 1760–1913.

Determinants

Biological, social, psychological—indeed, even astrological—causes have all been put forward in Western attempts to explain the etiology and course of madness. Following Thomas Willis's seventeenth-century anatomy of the brain and his coining of the new term *neurologie,* subsequent anatomists continued his focus on the brain stem, the nerves and fibers, and the localization of nervous disorders in the brain. Willis's work on epilepsy was especially pioneering; before him, epileptic seizures were discussed in terms of animal spirits, if not demonic possession. From Willis to Thomas Sydenham—who was convinced that diseases could be categorized as a botanist brings order to plant diversity—one finds a continuity in brain research and the focus on the nerves and the extremes in stimulation as the origin of nervous diseases. Also focusing on nerves, William Cullen coined the term *neurosis,* which in time lost much of its mooring in nervous fibers. Perhaps this was not unexpected: Cullen maintained that elements of human functioning, such as the passions or the will, were not reducible to organic components.

This separation of elements of consciousness from physiology would remain a point of contention between neurologists and medical psychologists right through the nineteenth century. Again, the focus would be on epilepsy, isolated by Willis as a brain disorder. Willis's nineteenth-century laboratory heirs William B. Carpenter and Charles Laycock illuminated reflex systems that were both automatic and unconscious. In Laycock's words, "many will consider it dangerous to concede that apparently pure mental acts are only the results of vital machinery excited into action by physical agencies."[5] Although epilepsy would soon prove to be a professional battleground engaging neurologists and medical psychologists as enemy combatants, a good many belonged to both camps. Early asylums like West Riding Lunatic Asylum had been planned specifically to incorporate neurological research on former patients and were placed far from population centers in order to ensure tranquil surroundings. The failure to discover any culpable lesion, however, and the distance from medical schools and hospitals eventually doomed the asylum as a promising laboratory for neurological research. Whatever partnership might have been effected by putting medical psychologists and neurologists in close proximity with each other eventually dissolved. A contentious argument in mid-nineteenth-century science over who "owned" epilepsy was evidence of the budding professional rivalry. If epileptic seizures and convulsions were a disorder of nervous fibers and motor reflexes and thus functioned at the level of an organism's conservation of life, why were psychological elements part of the story at all?

Medical psychologists who were loath to relinquish Cullen's idea of the retention of the immaterial elements of the mind, as well as voices within and outside of medicine that warned of godless materialism, were not about to characterize the will and the emotions as epiphenomena of nerve synapses. The sway of philosophical and psychological determinants in nineteenth-century conceptions of the mind-body relation could be just as persuasive, as was Charles Bell's research highlighting reflex systems operating automatically and unconsciously. Conceptions of the mind that influenced nineteenth-century medicine therefore included the intellect, the passions (soon to be called *emotions*), and the will. One sees in James Cowles Prichard's term *moral insanity* and in Philippe Pinel's *manie sans délire* a breaking away from a restrictively intellectualist notion of derangement in order to include species of madness that engaged other mental components. Even those medical men who abjured Prichard's neologism and the more exotic Parisian diagnostic imports were not about to relinquish the centrality—and the existence—of a will to conceptions of human behavior. If self-control and self-mastery were *not* part of an individual's resources, what was the objective of treatment? What was its goal, if not to stimulate the cultivation of proper habits of thought and behavior, the better to resist untoward impulses?

Other determinants affecting conceptions of deranged behavior included the cultural and the social. Homicidal mania, among other diagnoses, emerged amid disturbing notions of degeneracy and failed heredity. Thus, the epileptic, the criminal, and the mad were lumped together as a "type." It was perhaps not the first time biology had been invoked to account for social deviance, but it certainly was the most persuasive, given the stature of the era's scientists. Elite medical opinion that had abjured the blasphemous organicism of Franz Joseph Gall and Johann Gaspar Spurzheim at the beginning of the century warmed quickly to the new biology of deviance, if only because the medical practitioner's failure to intervene successfully could be conveniently explained away by the "tyranny of [physical] organization," in Henry Maudsley's memorable words. The role of social factors in the spread of these ideas was also on view. The early popularizers of phrenology had been radical, decidedly non-elite among medical practitioners. They saw in phrenology the promise of science to address and ameliorate forms of criminal and social deviance, and not coincidentally, a role for themselves as practitioners in a new medicine of public health. To have recognized phrenology with scientific acceptance would have been to open the ranks of an established medical hierarchy to brash upstarts, and that was clearly a bridge too far for members of the royal corporations of physicians and surgeons. But with the imprimatur of Darwin and Huxley, discussion among the upper ranks of the newly announced medical profession could turn to *classes* of deviants—the vulnerability to epilepsy now revealed in epileptic character.[6] In this context, homicidal mania almost seems overdetermined given the anxiety inherent in a culture haunted by fears of degeneration.

Clearly, one finds no shortage of determinants informing the creation of this enigmatic diagnosis and, indeed, the testimony proffered by the entire cohort of early forensic psychiatrists. Nor is there a shortage of Maudsley quotes, each asserting with apodictic conviction that insanity was a physical disease. Affirming this concept at every opportunity was not only the key to remaining part of the medico-scientific fraternity, it was essential if the medical man's voice was to be distinctive among all witnesses.[7] But the consideration of physical, psychological, and social causes of derangement is only one aspect of the formation of forensic diagnosis and testimony. As Abbott contends, only in a positivist frame would "determinate cause flood downhill to an inevitable present, as if the rocks of structure did not channel events, nor the dams of intentions divert them."[8] What then greeted the determinants in their descent down to homicidal mania?

Structure

Beginning with the Vagrancy Act in 1744 that swept the wandering deranged into confinement, and continuing with a series of parliamentary decisions installing medical men as supervisors in institutional care, the state served as patron of medicine in general and mental medicine in particular. The population of institutionalized madmen was augmented with the passage of the Criminal Lunacy Act of 1800, which deposited acquitted defendants first in prisons and eventually in a hospital of criminal lunacy in 1863. In the eighteenth century, the state's active involvement in asylum management translated into medicine's successful attempt to wrest asylum supervision from socially minded religious and legal authorities. The effort to establish medicine as the rightful caretaker of the mad was no doubt furthered by Parliament's granting medical men exclusive supervisory control of the public madhouse. As a result of these governmental initiatives, public asylums were fast becoming the point of origin for careers in mental medicine.[9]

Sustained experience with patients gained in asylums served to ground practitioners' claims to expertise in the courtroom, another structured setting that influenced how conceptions of the mind were phrased. Many medical men who eventually entered the law courts had first been employed in prisons, inspecting sanitary conditions, attending to recurring health problems, and treating possible injuries suffered as a result of the crime (or during apprehension). In time, these surgeons would provide further service, having receiving orders: "Mind you see that prisoner, it is very likely we shall want your evidence." The state's interest in the mental soundness of prisoners would take a more definitive turn in the 1860s and 1870s, as the Home Office increasingly turned to its own medical advisors in questions of case preparation and disposition. By 1878, routine medical examination of all prisoners was carried out, which Roger Chadwick contends led to an increase in insanity verdicts (an idea borne out by data discussed in chapter 1) and a similar increase in commitments to Broadmoor.[10] The apparently close working relationship between medicine and government may be one of the reasons for the relative lack of enmity between judges and medical witnesses at the Old Bailey.

By far, the most powerful structural element in the evolution of medical psychology, and particularly diagnosis, would take place at London's central criminal court. It was in the cut and thrust of examination and cross-examination that medical psychology would come into its own.[11] A courtroom niche for the witness in medical psychology had been secured centuries earlier, as common law courts found reason to subpoena persons possessing unusual skills or familiarity with forms of abstract knowledge far beyond the ken of the ordinary jury member. Grammarians, ship builders, businessmen experienced in contractual wording and, of course, physicians were regular participants in civil and criminal hearings. At moments of evidentiary ambiguity, masters of "orders of knowledge"—in Odling's words—were brought forth to comment on facts the judge thought needed clarification and context.

The essence of professional knowledge is the application of specialized learning or unique experience from the general category to the specific case. Professions develop, in Abbott's words, an "internal vocabulary" that distills the universe of observation to classification and useful categories. In medicine, diagnosis is the clearest symbol of a mastery of perception and understanding; what appears mysterious and confounding to the "uninitiated," as the nonmedical observer was labeled in court, is part of a knowable world of debility.[12] In the words of an early nineteenth-century mad-doctor, the skill he represented was one of "piercing sanity's smokescreen." Assertions that one possesses such knowledge can be made in the pages of a professional journal or clinical text; medical witnesses, however, ventured beyond the groves of academe and professional meetings to assert their claim to privileged insight in the law courts. The state provided the forum, the form, and the opportunity for them to acquire a public acknowledgement of expertise (although they also risked being publicly dismissed as having a bloated sense of self-importance). The professional stakes in the courtroom were high indeed.

It has often been maintained that psychiatry began when the state endorsed claims that medical practitioners were the natural and appropriate caretakers of the mad, enabling asylum superintendents to create a formal association and a journal, the early trappings of a profession. I believe that equally, if not more, important was the opportunity to proffer innovative diagnoses in the courtroom; in the process, the law would shape these diagnoses to serve its own purposes. The emergence of homicidal mania in the late nineteenth century appears to be the logical result of the law's incessant demand for precision in medical testimony. Earlier in the century, delusion had found ready acceptance because of the law's unyielding insistence that madness be a matter of cognitive derangement. A person fatefully confused about the nature of his or her action could not choose to commit crime, to act with the "will to harm" articulated by Henri de Bracton in the thirteenth century. But legal opinion that elevated delusion as "the law's insanity" may have gotten more than it bargained for. As early as *Hadfield*, the result of delusion was not just confusion: self-control was annihilated by the overwhelming power of delusory fear or haunting belief to propel the person to act. Medical testimony sometimes graphically included this loss of self-control, but most often it spoke to the fateful error in belief. The court understandably wanted the medical witness to answer decisively. But even if he could comment on issues of cognitive awareness, the medical man was chary of answering the ultimate question: Could the defendant have *chosen* to do otherwise? Was he beyond the resources of self-control?

The alienist's hesitancy to enter into the realm of inevitable consequence was understandable. For all their grounding in reflex theory and physical organization, medical men experienced in treating the mad or observing them in confinement understood that the form deranged behavior took was not the natural result of any organic process. The same diseased nerves that might lead to violence would explain suicide *or* homicide: a violent reflex has no necessary target. For this reason, medical witnesses often spoke of suicidal and homicidal tendencies in mania and in melancholia in the latter decades of the nineteenth century. They could not and would not specify the direction the violent impulse might take, which was precisely the question the court was asking. Mid-nineteenth-century juridical opinion contemptuously had rejected forms of insanity that seemed to remove control from the defendant (moral insanity, lesion of the will, irresistible impulse), sneering that such thinking would excuse the crime *by* the crime. And yet, when faced with the identical features in homicidal mania, the court was passive at least, and solicitous at most. The frequency of homicidal mania's appearance in medical testimony and the absence of a fractious reception suggests a fit with the law's interests reminiscent of delusion's acceptance in common-law jurisprudence earlier in the century. Whether the impetus for innovative diagnoses emerged from the law's interests or the medical witness's conceptual imagination is open to debate, although the two might easily have worked in concert.

Intention

Identifying the interests of medical men in the public and private "lunacy trade" has undergone considerable revision since the history of madness became a growth industry for sociologists and historians of medicine, law, and psychiatry, beginning in the 1960s. Before the experiences of mental patients and their classifiers stimulated a host of radically new academic perspectives, the history of medical participation in the definition and treatment of madness was commonly written at the level of triumphalism—the story of courageous, benevolent men striking carceral chains from the corporeal body and "mind-forg'd manacles" from the mind. These traditionally "in-house" medical biographies were followed by a decidedly less charitable view, replacing selfless devotion to healing with the devices and desires of a rising cohort of middle-class professionals eager to secure a social and financial niche in the consumer-driven world of health care and the state-driven world of seques-tering the mad.

There can be little doubt that specialists in medical psychology were ambi-tious men, dedicated to building careers for themselves, not unlike the cohort of defense attorneys who found their testimony so valuable. Indeed, the ex-amination of witnesses in the *OBSP* often reads as an exemplar of symbiosis: the attorney reads from Alfred Swaine Taylor's medical jurisprudence text, and the medical witnesses utter an often abbreviated assent. Prosecuting attorneys also found a use for medical witnesses, although, like defense attor-neys, prosecutors could never be quite sure what would emerge from court-room examination. But does professional self-interest necessarily translate into intentional thought and a specialist's judgment? This seems a conceptual bridge difficult to reconstruct, and it remains today a daunting challenge for the historian of psychiatry. Certainly, interest and intentional thought can be related, even intertwined. Mens rea, for example, is a matter of intention, not motive. Knowing the latter may clarify the former if established in court; an obvious motive clearly speaks to intention and renders the violence more purposeful than accidental. Is this also true in matters of professional inter-est? Does a vested interest in claiming a professional voice necessarily inform the creation of medical diagnoses?

One way to broach this issue is to consider how structure might influ-ence medical thinking in choosing the subject to decipher. In establishing the asylum as a medical institution, in forming a population of incarcerated felons acquitted by reason of insanity, and, finally, in creating a hospital for the criminally insane, the state had fashioned the structural setting that ena-bled sustained interaction between incarcerated patients and medical super-visors. Medical thinking, like all thinking, is an *intentional* act: the theorists whose work resulted in a qualitative change in descriptive psychopathology were, in the words of historian G. E. Berrios, "men with families, politi-cal interests, fears and ambitions . . . many of their choices determined by non-cognitive factors." We can also consider them as "rational beings who, when faced with real patients exercised as current psychiatrists would like to be thought of as doing, a modicum of descriptive freedom and objectivity."[13] They were doubtless curious, and they were men of their time; their services were called upon by the state, especially in a courtroom that sought a diag-nosis that enabled the law to pull back, justifiably, from criminal sanction in cases of manifest madness. In court and in the asylum, medical men found their work laid out for them. Presented with defendants who were often as bewildered by the crime as was the medical observer, diagnoses emerged that sometimes rested on intellectual derangement and other times a convulsion of ideas. Both tributaries ended in homicide. The availability of populations of incarcerated offenders for intellectually curious medical men seems to have been the optimal condition for refinements in diagnosis.

One parliamentary initiative is particularly revealing. The 1828 Madhouse Act reinforced the supervisory role of medical personnel in asylums. As a condition for gaining their exclusive franchise, medical men were presented with "the medico-legal obligation of documenting changes in their charges."[14] This requirement mandated repeated interaction with their *charges*, affording a longitudinal view on mental derangement. As Berrios comments, repeated interaction between the incarcerated and the classifier yielded a shifting focus from the patient's overt behavior to the "contents of consciousness."[15] One is reminded of the place of asylum supervision in Pinel's avowal that daily supervision of his patients and the resulting conversations had led to his break with centuries of Lockean-inspired notions of insanity as a defect of cognition alone.[16]

There is finally the structural innovation in criminal justice administration that placed surgeons in London's police divisions. Together with prison and jail doctors, these decidedly nonelite medical practitioners dominated the ranks of expert witnesses who appeared at the Old Bailey. Neither celebrated authors nor renowned lecturers, they were instead in the employ of the state, and if known for anything, it was their claim to exposing counterfeited madness. When not unmasking a defendant who "rather overacts his part," they could declare a prisoner perfectly in his intellects. Among these practitioners, however, one factor distinguished their testimony: they had met the accused shortly after the crime. In offenses purportedly animated by an impulse or a crime-specific mania, the accused's calm demeanor became critical to a diagnosis. One need only glance through the early editions of the *Principles and Practice of Medical Jurisprudence* to discover how strategically important the particulars of a crime could be in the forming of a diagnosis. Alfred Swaine Taylor drew his definitive examples of homicidal mania and impulsively driven child murder directly from the Old Bailey; medical witnesses, in turn, cited his volume in their testimony. A police division surgeon advised a jury in 1911, "I agree with this statement in Taylor's [*Principles and Practice*] under the heading of 'Impulsive Insanity': 'Occasionally the act of murder is perpetrated with great deliberation and apparently with all the marks of sanity. [T]he chief evidence of mental disorder is the act itself. Of the existence of insanity in the common or legal acceptation of the term be-fore or after perpetration of the crime there may either be no evidence what-ever or it may be so slight as not to amount to proof. Sudden restoration to reason is not infrequent in such cases of homicidal mania.' "[17] This was a sud-den, instantaneous return to reason, not a restoration to coherence perceived by a medical visitor to the defendant's cell days or weeks after the crime. When jail doctors commented on the defendant's calm in prison awaiting trial, defense attorneys (and judges) were quick to ask whether confinement would be likely to induce relative calm. The witness most often agreed. But a sudden calm—a preternatural calm—following a murderous assault was mystifying to the jury, and only a medical man who saw the accused imme-diately after the crime could describe its features. This inexplicable demeanor just following the crime added significance to the police surgeon's concluding statement: "I do not think that such a person could possess the consciousness of a clear motive for doing the act or a clear recollection of afterwards being actuated by that motive."

The crime's brutality and its suddenness invited speculation about forces beyond consciousness that could propel the unknowing person into un-provoked, fatal attack. One might ascribe intentional empire building to an asylum superintendent or a university lecturer venturing into imaginative diagnostic categories, but it is frankly difficult to so characterize the impres-sions of a divisional police surgeon with no obvious interest in professional mobility. Again, a structural innovation had been accompanied by an inno-vation in medical theorizing. One need not adopt a hagiographic stance that enlightened medical men were *reading* madness in the mind of the mad. Rather, sustained interaction with, and exposure to, a population of offenders might conceivably spark curiosity and the ambition to identify something that had not been heretofore recognized. That this should lead to innovations in diagnosis should not come as a surprise.

A final word about the changes one observes in medico-legal thinking regarding mental impairment and speculation about its precluding a will to harm. Jurists also recorded shifting ideas about volition and unrestrainable impulses, revealing a foundational change among some of London's leading legal minds regarding culpability and noncognitive species of madness. Law and the burgeoning field of medical psychology were always going to be on a collision course in at least one respect; the law required (only) one of two findings: guilt or innocence. Psychiatric testimony, on the other hand, was all about degrees; shadings of impairment did not conform to the law's binary categories of sanity or insanity, guilt or innocence, for that matter. Medical witnesses in the mid-1800s who refused to answer the "right/wrong" question, substituting instead varieties of volitional impairment, met clear resistance not only from judges at the Old Bailey but from the most noted jurist of his day, James Fitzjames Stephen. In a paper to the Judicial Society in 1855, Stephen acknowledged the medico-philosophical opinion supporting the existence of irresistible impulses, but he was quick to point out an inconvenient truth: "There may have been many instances of irresistible impulse of this kind, although I fear there is a disposition to confound them with *unresisted* impulses" (my emphasis).[18] Stephen was concerned with the act itself: Was it willful? Was it chosen? His intention was to shift the focus away from the naming of a disease and back to the offense itself. One is reminded of Thomas Erskine, who, after introducing delusion to the criminal court, insisted that mere presence of delusion would not suffice: a direct, logical connection between the crime and the delusion must be demonstrated.

Later in the century, however, Stephen declared the *McNaughtan Rules* too narrow to encompass the possible states of mental derangement germane to an acquittal. If "prevented either by defective mental power or by any disease affecting his mind from controlling his own conduct," Stephen wrote, it ought to be the Law of England that "the accused's act is not a crime." Stephen's odyssey from resisting the courtroom introduction of irresistible impulse to accepting a form of mental disease that could preclude self-control in itself did not find favor among his brethren on the bench, although none of them penned texts as authoritative as his. The evolution in his thinking is intriguing. Was it the result of his experience listening to medical witnesses in trials when he was presiding at court, or his reading of Henry Maudsley, whose much emphasized "tyranny of [physical] organization" left the possibility of human choice very much in its wake? Or was it perhaps an interest in justice that prompted his change of mind that intellectual derangement had cast insanity too narrowly? Nigel Walker suggests that just such a consideration held sway among medical witnesses—perhaps unconsciously: "The more esoteric the name of the disorder, the more incapacitating it sounds. The psychiatrist is therefore tempted—one might almost say invited—to slap an impressive label on the accused in order to ensure that he arrives at what seems to the psychiatrist to be the right destination." Although deciphering Stephen's own reasons for rethinking his earlier rejection of impulsive insanity is certainly challenging, that it changed and did so in concert with medical ideas reminds the historian again of the collaborative effort the courtroom represented. The proffering of an "impressive label," in Walker's words, served many interests. The court continued the fiction that one was either guilty or not guilty, the witness found the appropriate vehicle to arrive at "the right destination," and the defense lawyer secured an acquittal.[19]

So far from *imposing* medical ideas on an unsuspecting court, therefore, medical opinion was elicited, shaped, prompted, and, yes, sometimes censured. Specialist witnesses in mental medicine emerged along with activist courtroom attorneys, sharing interests in social order and, one likes to think, in social justice as well. The Home Office regularly employed medical advisors, and the Solicitor of the Treasury, acting as public prosecutor, routinely elicited the opinion of private physicians and surgeons when a capital offense was on the docket. In most respects, their participation and perhaps even their testimony were overdetermined. No matter where one looked, specialists in mental medicine were active in questions of criminal culpability and *just* disposition. There is only one problem with an analysis restricted to medical witnesses, judges, and attorneys. None of them made the ultimate decision regarding how the testimony was to be weighed or, indeed, whether it was to be listened to at all.

Another Kind of Knowledge

The history of forensic psychiatry necessarily employs medical texts and journals, legal commentary, lurid newspaper accounts, and, as in the present study, courtroom testimony of specialist witnesses in the public theater that was the Victorian insanity trial. The standard cast of characters includes the judge endeavoring to retain his authority over the proceedings, the emerging voice of the prosecuting and defense attorneys honing their skills at cross-examination, and the medical witnesses asserting their possession of abstract knowledge, revealed most conspicuously in a diagnosis. There remains an additional courtroom member whose voice is captured only with the verdict, which, for reasons given earlier, is a maddeningly ambiguous fact for the historian to interpret. An acquittal need have little to do with the medical witness; the reasons for a conviction may be similarly opaque. Seen over time, rates of acquittal when graphed with rates of medical participation offer the anomalous finding that in the late nineteenth century, a spike in medical participation was accompanied by a corresponding decline in acquittals. If the two had risen together, one would still be hard pressed to argue that the testimony of a medical man was associated with enhanced chances for an acquittal. The opposite inference—that increasing medical expert testimony in insanity trials *led to* a drop in acquittal—can also not be sustained. Still, one cannot help wondering if there might be a threshold rate of participation beyond which a jury responded with suspicion. Though tempting—especially for the historian of forensic psychiatry—these questions cannot be answered, even with a thousand cases.

When one examines verdicts in the aggregate, there is ample reason to suspect that there was more than one type of knowledge at issue in an insanity trial. It was indeed the unfortunate lot of the medical specialist claiming possession of special knowledge to be judged by community members who felt no less competent to claim *common* knowledge of the behavioral and conversational signs that betrayed the accused's tenuous hold on social reality. There is certainly no evidence in the Old Bailey cases that juries voluntarily relinquished what they believed they knew about madness in the face of experts' claims to special knowledge. Juries revealed a confidence in their own judgment in a number of ways.

Most dramatically, jurors could simply ignore the expert's testimony. When a jury heard a prison medical officer testify that a prisoner had "been perfectly rational throughout and showed no signs of insanity at all," and the members returned with a verdict of guilty of the act but not responsible for the crime, it seems they were pitting their common knowledge—say, the prisoner's history of asylum commitments—against the specialist's expertise, finding the latter unpersuasive. Juries were capable of ignoring multiple medical witnesses, each denying the prisoner's insanity, only to find the prisoner guilty but insane. In these cases, the defendant was usually just too pathetic, and the offense—often child murder— inexplicable except by severe mental derangement. Again, the crime, the verdict, and the punishment were driven by the law's insistence on a binary finding: guilt or innocence. Even with medical testimony asserting coherence, the jury was left with its own common cultural consciousness. No sane parent takes a hammer to his children's heads, and no medical witness was going to convince the jury otherwise. By insisting on either/or verdicts, with insanity the only other option, the law compelled juries to draw on their own understanding of emotional impulse, casting the medical testimony to the side. They could on occasion advise the judge that the medical witness's testimony would be superfluous. In 1869, after a defense attorney informed the court of a specialist witness who could speak to the family's history of insanity, "the jury expressed its unanimous opinion that . . . the prisoner was in such a mental condition as to be incapable of distinguishing right from wrong."[20]

The inclination to acquit on the grounds of insanity when no medical testimony was offered—and indeed when a plea had not even been entered—resulted in a test of wills between judge and jury. In 1897, a jury responded to the prisoner's statement, "I did that but I do not know why I did it," by finding the defendant "Guilty, but not responsible for his actions at the time." The judge, however, "declined to take this verdict, no evidence to insanity having been called."[21] The jury relented and convicted the prisoner. Not all juries were so deferential to the courtroom division of labor; some chose to substitute their judgment for the grand jury's charge. If they could not acquit by reason of insanity even when the plea had not been entered, they could at least correct the grand jury's mistake regarding the proper indictment. In a move that resembled the trial jury down-valuing the value of stolen goods so as to preclude a death penalty, juries might decide to down-value the indictment charge from murder to manslaughter or refuse to commit a pathetic defendant to incarceration by finding him or her simply not guilty. In one case of a woman accused of throwing her infant daughter into the Thames, the not-guilty verdict followed lengthy testimony by medical witnesses who agreed that the mother's depression was due to prolonged nursing. Considering "that the occurrence might have been accidental," the jury acquitted her of the felony indictment and also of the remaining charges of assaulting her other child and attempting to drown herself.

Finally, juries could choose to voice their own verdicts, as in the case of the mother who cut off her infant daughter's hand in a state of epileptic vertigo. Given the alternatives of guilty, not guilty, and not guilty on the grounds of insanity, the jury announced "not guilty on the grounds of unconsciousness," confounding the prosecutor and the judge, who had to write to the Home Office in search of a disposition. Some juries were more expansive, explaining their reasoning but framing it in their own language: "We find that the prisoner inflicted the injuries at a time when, owing to physical agony, she was not responsible for her actions. We recommend the prisoner to mercy, and think that had [her employer] taken a greater interest in her, the crime would not probably have been committed." The *OBSP* records: "To be kept in custody until such time as His Majesty's pleasure be known."[22] Since the disposition was identical to "Guilty of the Act but Not Responsible at the Time" (the wording of an insanity verdict after 1883), the practical significance of substituting their own wording for the formulaic verdict seems hardly worth the effort, and yet the insistence on their own phrasing allows a lens into the jury's weighing of the evidence. There could be no question that Lydia Green fatally stabbed her newborn daughter with a pair of scissors. A private physician called to the scene of the crime spoke to the mother, reported that she had been "quite sensible," and drew on his experience with women directly after delivery, when "the patient would be quite conscious." But on the critical question of whether Green knew right from wrong at the moment of the assault, the physician responded, "Possibly a woman might struggle in a mad sort of way with scissors [presumably to cut the umbilical cord herself] without knowing what she was doing—it is difficult to measure what is knowledge and what is not knowledge."[23]

The jury's anomalously worded verdict ascribing the killing to a frenzy produced by physical pain rather than an impulse attendant to postpartum melancholia suggests that the witness's words fell on receptive ears. They could not be sure what the mother knew about right from wrong or the nature of what she was doing, but they could imagine the torment that self-delivery and panic over cutting the umbilical cord would induce. They did not find the mother to have been unconscious at the time, nor were they willing to ascribe the act to puerperal melancholia, a not infrequent finding. Instead, they invoked physical agony as the precipitating condition; it was common knowledge that women in this state were capable of great violence to their infants and occasionally to their spouses. What the medical witnesses supplied was a likely scenario in which the murder weapon began as an innocuous pair of scissors on hand to cut the cord. As for describing a demented mental condition, the medical testimony was apparently less persuasive.

It is, of course, hazardous to read too much significance into a series of verdicts or into the hundreds of verdicts that constitute this study. After my earlier caveats about the lack of transparency in jury findings, it is perhaps peculiar to dwell on this one trial. However, it is not the verdict that I find arresting here; rather, it is the concluding phrase of the medical witness: "it is difficult to measure what is knowledge and what is not knowledge." Even in trials that turned on physical evidence, the jury's acknowledgement of a knowledge base supporting the grounds for expert opinion was far from secure. Expert witnesses often disagreed, to the irritation of judges and to the consternation of other medical men who feared their disputes in court would render their claims to expert knowledge risible. It can only be a matter of speculation whether courtroom disagreements among experts compromised the knowledge claims of experts. To a society that put great store in scientific opinion and the promise that medicine held the key to ameliorating a host of medical ailments, the spectacle may have been disconcerting, but it was probably not delegitimating. Disagreements at the Old Bailey centered mostly on the implications of a diagnosis instead of on whether the defendant was disturbed. Jurors may well have interpreted this as the law's business, not medicine's. In any event, there were few public spats in the courtroom, although, by definition, rebuttal witnesses contradicted previous testimony. Again, as members of their society, jurors would have been disposed to listen to the expertise that men of science had to impart regarding the interpretation of the facts of a case, especially when the defendant's behavior had been so singular.

But listening attentively to credentialed specialists is not the same thing as tugging one's forelock. In refusing to follow the experts' opinions even when no disagreement was heard in court, in finding insanity when no medical witness advised them of the signs of manifest derangement, or in down-valuing an indictment without any prompting from the judge, jurors revealed a degree of independence that belied the law's anxiety that expert opinion would substitute for a normative conception of right and wrong, particularly when given evidence of manifest madness in the form of an incapacitating diagnosis. This is not to argue that Victorian medical men had little influence on the jury's reasoning and subsequent verdict, although it is devilishly hard to imagine how this could be determined. Better, I think, to consider when and in what matters of juror belief expert knowledge elided with common knowledge. A century and a half of trial narratives reveal that stubbornly independent jurors took a healthy dose of folk knowledge into their deliberations.

Psychiatry, and particularly forensic psychiatry, is the most culturally informed of medical specialties. The concerns that guided criminal insanity trials from 1760 to 1913 resonated deeply with growing anxiety about the capacity to control one's own behavior. Does the ability to distinguish right from wrong necessarily constrain unruly impulses? Does heredity doom the less-than-evolved to deviance and their society to face ever growing forms of deviance? What resources can be drawn upon when emotion threatens to propel an individual into a violent, uncharacteristic act? As the focus of medical testimony in insanity trials shifted from delusion to states of suspended consciousness to the specter of uncontrollable homicidal impulses, one begins to see the insanity trial as a revealing lens into the preoccupations and anxieties haunting the larger culture.

That hereditarian taint, evolutionary regression, and degeneracy framed medical testimony can hardly come as a surprise. What other medical specialty addresses deviant behavior employing the full range of biological, psychological, and social determinants? The question for the historian of forensic psychiatry is not whether medical testimony made a difference to the verdict but rather what does the increasing presence of mad-doctors in court—dramatizing through their diagnoses the cultural anxieties that gave this medical specialty its birth—tell us about how a disease of the mind assumed the lead role in the most well attended of London's theaters—the central criminal court?

In many ways, it was the diagnosis that was on trial. Esoteric terminology that failed to elide with folk knowledge would not have fallen easily on the jurors' ears. By the latter decades of the nineteenth and the early years of the twentieth century, medical witnesses had found a way to account for the inexplicable and to present their opinion as rooted in experience-based knowledge. Crime was at the center of homicidal mania, both in name and in origin. Folk knowledge, professional experience, and an accommodating— indeed, inviting—new division of courtroom labor set the conditions for the entrance of a new expert witness armed with a new diagnosis. Its fate, like the defendant's, would be sealed "in the fierce conflict of wits that le[ft] no mercy for the vanquished."[24]

Introduction · Disease and Diagnosis

1. The term *psychiatry* is not part of the English medical world until the late nineteenth century. Its use may appear anachronistic but is meant to signal the origins and trajectory of a medical specialty that emerged gradually, both in print and in court. *Medical psychology* is the historically accurate term although authors and witnesses rarely referred to themselves as belonging to a particular subset of the medical field. *Forensic psychiatry* is the accepted term today. For the sake of capturing the evolution of the specialty, I decided to use it in this book, although *medical psychology* is sometimes employed to convey how contemporary medical men conceived of their efforts to integrate mind and body in their thinking and their craft.

2. The *Old Bailey Sessions Papers* (*OBSP*) were first employed by Nigel Walker in *Crime and Insanity in England*, vol. 1, *The Historical Part* (Edinburgh, 1968), to examine Old Bailey trials quantitatively. The *Papers'* historical and legal worth was brought to light in two seminal articles by legal historian John Langbein: "The Criminal Trial Before the Lawyers," *University of Chicago Law Review* 45 (Winter 1978): 263–316, and "Shaping the Eighteenth-Century Criminal Trial: A View from the Ryder Sources," *University of Chicago Law Review* 50 (Winter 1983): 1–136. Comments on their historical value may also be found in J. M. Beattie, *Crime and the Courts in England, 1660–1800* (Oxford, 1986). For the most recent appraisal of the *OBSP*, see Peter King, *Crime, Justice, and Discretion in England, 1740–1820* (Oxford, 2000), 221.

Chapter One · Nasty, Brutish, and Short

For the title of this chapter, I am indebted to Stephan Landsman, who discovered F. C. Cockburn's description of criminal trials in Tudor and Stuart England as "Nasty, brutish, and essentially short." Quoted in "The Rise of the Contentious Spirit: Adversary Procedure in Eighteenth-Century England," *Cornell Law Review* 75 (1990): 497–605.

1. James Fitzjames Stephen, *A History of the Criminal Law of England*, vol. 1 (London, 1883), 424.

2. John H. Langbein, *The Origins of Adversary Criminal Trial* (Oxford, 2010): 48–66.

3. This was a group of twelve common-law judges, constituting a court for the Crown that deliberated technical questions of law or procedure—they did not hear individual cases. See, e.g., James Oldham, "Informal Law-Making in England by the Twelve Judges in the Late Eighteenth and Early Nineteenth Centuries," *Law and History Review* 29 (February 2001): 181–220.

4. The Whigs, newly prominent in Parliament, sought to ensure that persons accused of treason would be permitted counsel and overturned the ban on attorneys. Their recent experience as the victims of arbitrary political persecution had led to a reappraisal of the defendant as his or her own "best advocate."

5. Langbein, *The Origins*, 148–66.

6. As individual judges took the initiative to extend provisions for legal representation from treason defendants to those indicted in ordinary felonies, other judges followed suit, apparently

concluding that fairness required like actions. The historical emergence of defense counsel in common law courts is treated in a number of excellent works: David Cairns, *Advocacy and the Making of the Adversarial Criminal Trial, 1800–1865* (Oxford, 1998); J. M. Beattie, "Scales of Justice: Defense Counsel and the English Criminal Trial in the Eighteenth and Nineteenth Centuries," *Law and History Review* 9 (1991): 221–67; and Langbein, *The Origins,* esp. 253–343. By the end of the eighteenth century, one in three felony defendants at the Old Bailey were represented by defense counsel; see J. M. Beattie, "Scales of Justice," esp. 236–44.

7. "A Witness swears but to what he hath heard or seen, generally or more largely, to what hath fallen under his senses. But a jury man swears to what he can infer and conclude from the testimony of such witnesses," Bushell's Case (1671), quoted in Learned Hand, "Historical and Practical Considerations Regarding Expert Testimony," *Harvard Law Review* 15 (1901). See also James Bradley Thayer, *A Preliminary Treatise on Evidence at the Common Law* (Boston, 1893), esp. 194–97. John Henry Wigmore also underscored the role of the senses in witness testimony: "the witness must speak as a knower not a guesser. He must see an action take place, not merely believe it took place." *Evidence in Trial at Common Law,* vol. 7 (Boston, 1985), 2.

8. John Locke, *An Essay Concerning Human Understanding* (1690), ed. John Yolton (London, 1961). According to Locke, knowledge consisted of sensory inputs that internal, mental operations eventually conjoined into ideas, conceptions, and associated thought chains. His theories of insanity remained influential among medical authors and practitioners who conceived of madness not as an overthrow of reason but as inherent in the reasoning process itself: "having joined together some ideas very wrongly . . . [the mad] mistake them for truths . . . [as though] incoherent ideas have been cemented together so powerfully as to remain united" (209–10).

9. Geoffrey Gilbert, *The Law of Evidence* (London, 1791), 6.

10. M. Pothier, *A Treatise on the Law of Obligations, or Contracts,* trans. William David Evans, vol. 2 (Philadelphia, 1853), 199.

11. John Henry Wigmore, "The History of the Hearsay Rule," *Harvard Law Review* 7 (May 1904): 437–58.

12. This seems to have been honored more in the breach than in the practice. Printed works of medical jurisprudence often made their way into testimony at the Old Bailey, especially when quoted by their authors during testimony.

13. For an analysis of the philosophical thought guiding the evolving courtroom conception of the appropriate standards of proof, see Barbara J. Shapiro, "To a Moral Certainty: Theories of Knowledge and Anglo-American Juries, 1600–1850," *Hastings Law Journal* 38 (1986): 153–93, and "The Concept 'Fact': Legal Origins and Cultural Diffusion," *Albion* 26 (Summer 1994): 227–52.

14. On occasion, persons believed to possess unique knowledge could serve together on special juries, called in civil as well as criminal cases. The trial of Mary Ann Hunt, *OBSP,* 1846–47, case 1797, 10th sess., 656–82, provides the example of a Jury of Matrons, assembled to inquire whether the defendant, convicted of murder, was indeed "quick with child" as she had alleged when sentenced to death. The delay in execution served Hunt well; she was transported to the penal colony at Port Arthur, Tasmania. Ongoing study of convicts sent to Australia has revealed records that show Hunt served her sentence, married, and returned to England. A record of her case disposition can be found in "Particulars of Mary Ann Hunt. Recommended for Conditional Pardon," PRO 45/9316/15682 (August 25, 1847). The Jury of Matrons could also be installed for determining the pregnancy status of a widow whose recently deceased husband left heirs wanting to establish likely paternity of the expected child. The specific means used to determine pregnancy remains a key secret kept by successive Juries of Matrons. Not a recent innovation, the practice of empaneling "wise women" dates to the Roman Republic. James C. Oldham credits Henri de Bracton (1220) with the first mention of this special jury; its first appearance in a criminal case in England appears to be in 1387. The Jury of Matrons was officially replaced by registered medical practitioners in 1879. See Oldham's "On Pleading the Belly: A

History of the Jury of Matrons," *Criminal Justice History* 6 (1985): 1–64. The public reaction to the confidence placed in the Jury of Matrons could be hostile. See, e.g., "The Jury of Matrons Revived," *London Medical Gazette, or Journal of Practical Medicine*, n.s., 5 (1847): 597–98, 681, 861; and *Felix Farley's Bristol Journal*, October 9, PRO, HO 45/9316/15682.

15. In *Laws of Men and Laws of Nature: The History of Scientific Expert Testimony in England and America* (Cambridge, 2004), Tal Golan explores the various ways that persons thought to possess unique knowledge were brought in to advise the court. Golan dates the first recorded use of medical men in London, "called to advise the court on the medical value of the flesh of wolves," to 1299 (p. 20). For his discussion of experts in the courtroom, see, esp., 18–22.

16. Katherine D. Watson, "Medical and Chemical Expertise in English Trials for Criminal Poisoning, 1750–1914," *Medical History* 50 (2006): 373–90.

17. The variety of backgrounds leading to the appearance of alienists in court is discussed in chapter 4.

18. For a discussion of successive Parliaments resorting to passing ever-more capital statutes, see Leon Radzinowicz, *A History of the English Criminal Law and Its Administration from 1750*, vol. 1, *The Movement for Reform* (London, 1948), esp. 3–49.

19. The jury's effort to navigate around Parliament's capital sentencing statutes is examined in Thomas Andrew Green, *Verdict According to Conscience: Perspectives on the English Trial, 1200–1800* (Chicago, 1985), esp. 378–83. The profusion of outright jury acquittals is also examined in Peter King, *Crime, Justice, and Discretion in England, 1740–1820* (Oxford, 2000), esp. 238–46, and J. M. Beattie, *Crime and the Courts in England, 1660–1800* (Oxford, 1986).

20. The judge's motivation in requesting a pardon was the focus of a heated debate, now several decades old but still capable of generating sparks, depending on one's assumptions about the larger ideological fame in which criminal justice pursued its objectives. See Radzinowicz, "The Prerogative of Mercy," in *History*, esp. 107–37; Douglas Hay, Peter Linebaugh, and E. P. Thompson, eds., *Albion's Fatal Tree: Crime and Society in Eighteenth-Century England* (New York, 1975), 17–63, and John Langbein, "Albion's Fatal Flaws," *Past and Present* 98 (1983): 96–120. To argue the defensible grounds of judicial discretion, Langbein draws upon data in an article by Peter J. King, "Decision-Makers and Decision-Making in the English Criminal Law, 1750–1800," *Historical Journal* 27 (1984): 25–58.

21. Character witnesses were most critical in insanity trials animated by a violent assault and almost always called upon in cases of child murder. Juries were told of a kind, caring, and devoted mother who loved without pause those most near and dear to her right up to the moment she killed them. Spouses were similarly depicted as habitually affectionate, but for the slaying. Such character witnesses did not focus on honesty or integrity—terms we might associate with moral bearing—but on the distant, indeed, the *foreign* nature of the act, given the person the witness knew. Traits such as moral uprightness or integrity were mentioned in trials of theft when necessity was given as the animating factor. "Character-based criminal responsibility" is discussed in Arlie Loughnan, *Manifest Madness: Mental Incapacity in Criminal Law* (Oxford, 2012), esp. 49–57, and Nicola Lacey, "Responsibility and Modernity in Criminal Law," *Journal of Political Philosophy* 9 (2001): 249–76. Character and crime are also explored in Dana Rabin, *Identity, Crime, and Legal Responsibility in Eighteenth-Century England* (New York, 2004).

22. The easy traffic among religion, astrology, and medicine can be seen in the work of Richard Napier, a seventeenth-century clergyman and physician, whose story is told in Michael MacDonald, *Mystical Bedlam: Madness, Anxiety, and Healing in Seventeenth-Century England* (Cambridge, 1981). The endurance of folk beliefs connecting madness and the heavens can be heard in judges' comments in eighteenth-century insanity trials. After a physician testified about the signs and symptoms of the defendant's manifest madness, a judge would ask, "Did you happen to notice if there was a full moon that night?"

23. Nigel D. Walker, *Crime and Insanity in England*, vol. 1, *The Historical Part* (Edinburgh, 1968). The actual name of the asylum was Bethlehem Hospital; it was most often referred to in this period as Bethlem and, on occasion, simply as Bedlam. Although Monro was the first of the mad-doctors to testify, the first recorded acquittal on the grounds of "unsound mind" was in 1505.

24. Matthew Hale's *The History of the Pleas of the Crown* (London, 1736) distinguished between total and partial insanity—partial in degree or fluctuating between dementia and lucidity. Only total insanity, according to the jurist, carried exculpatory significance. Since lunacy was by nature a labile condition, courts were advised to consider only a total, permanent want of reason as a state of being sufficiently debilitating to warrant an acquittal on the grounds of insanity. That said, how jurists wrote and how juries decided varied. In court, delirium, insensibility, and melancholia were not characterized as partial derangement; juries most likely came to their conclusions based on the perceived nature of the defendant (his character), the crime itself, and the likelihood that some force other than purpose or intent was responsible for the outrage. With few exceptions—the Ferrers trial being one of them—Old Bailey juries were not constrained by formal legal opinion, although judges were sometimes explicit and sometimes prescriptive in their instructions. For a discussion of Hale and examples of eighteenth-century judicial instructions, see Joel Peter Eigen, *Witnessing Insanity, Madness and Mad-Doctors in the English Court* (New Haven, 1995), 36–39, 44–52.

25. For a discussion of the enduring presence of this type of scoundrel in the Victorian era, see Heather Shore, *Artful Dodgers: Youth and Crime in Early Nineteenth-Century London* (London, 1999).

26. See Eigen, *Witnessing Insanity*, 40–41.

27. For the purposes of the first two figures, the cases have been divided into personal and property offenses. Personal offenses include kidnapping, rape, assault, and murder. Property offenses include stealing/theft, burglary, embezzlement, forgery, counterfeiting (and "coining"), and breaking and entering. There are 994 total trials in this study; the first two figures contain 985 trials because nine offenses did not fit these binary categories. Thus, trials for bigamy, "inciting to mutiny," treason, and "being at large" (having returned to England before a term of transportation had expired) are not included in the rates offered in figures 1.1 and 1.2, although they are included in figure 1.3 since this last is not separated by type of offense. The research on eighteenth- and nineteenth-century crime is vast. For a comprehensive review, see J. J. Tobias, *Crime and Industrial Society in the Nineteenth Century* (London, 1967); David Philips, *Crime and Authority in Victorian England: The Black Country, 1835–1860* (London, 1977); J. S. Cockburn, ed., *Crime in England, 1550–1800* (Princeton, 1977); Clive Emsley, *Crime and Society in England, 1750–1900* (London, 1987); and John Brewer and John Styles, eds., *An Ungovernable People: The English and Their Law in the Seventeenth and Eighteenth Centuries* (New Brunswick, 1980).

28. Data from the first third of this study (1760–1843) can also be found in Eigen, *Witnessing Insanity*, see esp. 18–28. The years have been grouped slightly differently to present the Old Bailey cases in periods reflecting roughly similar trial numbers. The year 1843 appears twice because the data in the earlier book ended with the McNaughtan trial; material found in Joel Peter Eigen, *Unconscious Crime: Mental Absence and Criminal Responsibility in London* (Baltimore, 2003), took place after *McNaughtan*, beginning in 1843.

29. For a comprehensive analysis of the changing dynamics in personal crimes of violence, see Lawrence Stone, "Interpersonal Violence in English Society, 1300–1980," *Past and Present* 101 (1983): 22–33.

30. Attorneys were known to encourage their clients to change their plea from insanity to guilty in property crimes; the former plea ensured indeterminate confinement in Broadmoor, the latter a fixed term of several months in prison.

31. *Criminal Lunatics Act of 1800* ("for the safe custody of insane persons charged with offenses"), 40 Geo. 3, c. 94, 21, 22.

32. George Rudé, *Criminal and Victim: Crime and Society in Early Nineteenth-Century England* (Oxford, 1985): 50–64.

33. Martin J. Wiener, *Men of Blood: Violence, Manliness, and Criminal Justice in Victorian England* (Cambridge, 2004).

34. Quoted in Rabin, *Identity, Crime,* 7.

35. The ambiguity of exactly what a verdict conveys about any one jury's thinking is also discussed in Eigen, *Witnessing Insanity,* 23–24.

36. The change in the insanity verdicts, from not guilty to a somewhat qualified guilty, is explored in Joel Peter Eigen, "'An Inducement to Morbid Minds': Politics and Madness in the Victorian Courtroom," in Markus Dubber and Lindsay Farmer, eds., *Modern Histories of Crime and Punishment* (Stanford, 2007), 66–87.

37. The finding of "unfit to plead" and its relation generally to substantive criminal law is most recently discussed in Loughnan, *Manifest Madness,* esp. 67–88. See also Walker, *Crime and Insanity,* 219–41.

38. The term *delusion* became prominent in medical testimony: it distinguished lay from expert testimony and was the term of preference for medical witnesses throughout the years leading up to *McNaughtan* and all the way into the twentieth century. For a discussion of the role of delusion in the early years of medical testimony, see Joel Peter Eigen, "Delusion in the Courtroom: The Role of Partial Insanity in Early Forensic Testimony," *Medical History* 35 (1991): 25–49.

39. These were years of "manifest madness," according to Loughnan. The phrase "madness was spectacularly on view" can be found in Roy Porter, *Mind-Forg'd Manacles: A History of Madness in England from the Restoration to the Regency* (London, 1987), 35.

40. Indeed, the most frequently appearing medical witness up to *McNaughtan* was Gilbert McMurdo, surgeon to Newgate Gaol. He usually denied the defendant's mental derangement when called to the dock.

41. Roger Chadwick, *Bureaucratic Mercy: The Home Office and the Treatment of Capital Cases in Victorian Britain* (New York, 1992), 232–73.

42. Ibid., 237–43.

Chapter Two · Delusion and Its Discontents

1. The Hadfield trial is most comprehensively discussed in Richard Moran, "The Origin of Insanity as a Special Verdict: The Trial for Treason of James Hadfield (1800)," *Law and Society Review* 19 (1985): 487–519. Nigel Walker concludes that the "Dr. Creighton" mentioned in the trial narratives was Alexander Crichton, author of *Inquiry into the Nature and Origin of Mental Derangement* (London, 1798). "Creighton" testified that he visited Hadfield in detention, and in language that would become familiar to the court in subsequent medical testimony, he said, "[I]t requires that the thoughts which have relation to his madness should be awakened in his mind, in order to make him act unreasonably" (Nigel Walker, *Crime and Insanity in England,* vol. 1., *The Historical Part* (Edinburgh, 1968), 76. Further commentary may be found in Jacques M. Quen, "James Hadfield and Medical Jurisprudence of Insanity," *New York State Journal of Medicine* 69 (1969): 1221–26, and Joel Peter Eigen, *Witnessing Insanity: Madness and Mad-Doctors in the English Court* (New Haven, 1995), 48–52.

2. Nigel Walker maintains that de Bracton's thirteenth-century pronouncement may or may not have been the prevailing thought among jurists of his day. It may only have been de Bracton's opinion, cautioning historians of law not to seize upon this as a ruling sentiment. Walker, *Crime and Insanity,* 26. A consideration of *intention* in common-law doctrines of responsibility may be found in Eigen, *Witnessing Insanity,* 35–39.

3. Matthew Hale, *The History of the Pleas of the Crown* (London, 1736), esp. 30–37.

4. Stanley Jackson, *Melancholia and Depression: From Hippocratic Times to Modern Times* (New Haven, 1986).

5. The association of delusion with shadows on the mind would find expression in other Old Bailey trials as well. For an overview of humoral theory and other organic bases of madness since antiquity, see Jackson, *Melancholia and Depression*.

6. William J. Battie, *A Treatise on Madness* (London, 1758), 5–6.

7. Thomas Arnold, *Observations on the Nature, Kinds, Causes, and Prevention of Insanity* (London, 1806), 47–52.

8. John Johnstone, *Medical Jurisprudence of Madness* (Birmingham, 1800), 23.

9. George Edward Male, *Elements of Juridical or Forensic Medicine: For the Use of Medical Men, Coroners and Barristers* (London, 1818), 202.

10. Knowledge, for Locke, was a matter of sensory inputs that mental operations eventually conjoined into ideas, conceptions, and associated thought chains. Madness was not the overthrow of reason but inherent in the reasoning process itself: a matter of "incoherent ideas" being cemented together so powerfully as to remain united. Whether this fateful error in cognition went by the name of "deluded imagination," "notional insanity," or the "erroneous association of ideas on particular subjects," madness according to the *school* of "associationism" implicated the knowing faculties; the passions and the will were not key to its notion of mental derangement. To observe the connection between Locke's ideas and one of the earliest "schools" of medical psychology, see David Hartley, *Observations on Man, His Frame, His Duty, and His Expectations* (London, 1749).

11. Philippe Pinel is largely credited with this first major change in descriptive psychopathology. His ideas are comprehensively sketched out in *A Treatise on Insanity*, trans. D. D. Davis (Sheffield, 1806). Pinel maintained that his neologism, *manie sans délire*, grew out of his work as physician superintendent of the Bicêtre and the Salpêtrière. Only the opportunity for repeated and sustained conversations with the mad, he maintained, rather than a familiarity with "inherited medical systems," afforded the medical man insight into the mind of the deranged. For an analysis of the *clinical* component of his medical diagnosis, see Dora B. Weiner, "Mind and Body in the Clinic: Philippe Pinel, Alexander Crichton, Dominique Esquirol, and the Birth of Psychiatry," in G. S. Rousseau, ed., *The Languages of Psyche: Mind and Body in Enlightenment Thought* (Berkeley, 1990): 331–402.

12. J. E. D. Esquirol, *Mental Maladies: A Treatise on Insanity*, trans. E. K. Hunt (Philadelphia, 1845). Monomania was a version of the partial insanity concept, according to medical historian G. E. Berrios, although as long as the afflicted's mind was turned to the fear or obsessional desire, the derangement was full blown. Short of a total, permanent state of madness, monomania shared with other states of derangement the lingering ambiguity of "total vs. partial" in Matthew Hale's analysis of states of insanity: partial in degree, partial in duration. Similar to persons afflicted with delusion, the monomaniac was able to function in many if not most of life's conventional pursuits. When the fatal "string was drawn" as mad-doctor John Haslam memorably phrased the moment when lucid functioning descended into madness, "by some unaccountable association . . . the map of his mind will point out that the smallest rivulet flows into the great stream of his derangement." *Medical Jurisprudence as It Relates to Insanity* (London, 1817), 15–19.

13. For a discussion of "lesion of the will" and other contributions of Étienne-Jean Georget, see his *Examen médicale des procès criminels des nommés Léger, Feldtmann, Lecouffe, Jean-Pierre et Papavoine, dans lesquels l'aliénation mentale a été alléguée comme moyen de défense, suivi de quelques considérations médico-légales sur la liberté morale* (Paris, 1825). Georget's attempt to "medicalize" the insanity defense in Paris is offered in Jan Goldstein, *Console and Classify: The French Psychiatric Profession in the Nineteenth Century* (Cambridge, 1987), 165–78.

14. Prichard's ideas are comprehensively explored in the following texts: *A Review of the*

Doctrine of a Vital Principle as Maintained by Some Writers on Phrenology: With Observations on Physical and Animal Life (London, 1829), A Treatise on Insanity and other Disorders Affecting the Mind (London, 1835), and On the Different Forms of Insanity in Relation to Jurisprudence, Designed for the Use of Persons Concerned in Legal Questions Regarding Unsoundness of Mind (London, 1842). An overview of nineteenth-century Scottish intellectual thought can be found in G. P. Brooks, "The Faculty Psychology of Thomas Reid," Journal of the History of the Behavioral Sciences 12 (1976): 65–77, and Frank M. Albrecht, "A Reappraisal of Faculty Psychology," Journal of the History of the Behavioral Sciences 6 (1970): 36–40.

15. "Moral insanity" and "lesion of the will" had both been mentioned in the defense of Edward Oxford, on trial in 1840 for shooting off two pistols at the queen. It is not clear if the pistols were loaded with anything more than gunpowder, thus "shooting off" is probably the best way to describe the assault. The medical testimony focused not on delusion or another cognitive defect but rather on a "derangement of feelings," of how one ought to feel toward her sovereign majesty. This testimony and Oxford's acquittal created a furor in legal circles—as well as among the police—and one thinks, contributed to the legal outrage at the McNaughtan acquittal three years later. In response, the House of Lords summoned the trial judges to answer a number of questions about the proper focus of medical testimony in order to establish guidelines for judges and juries in future criminal trials that featured a plea of insanity. For a discussion of the Oxford trial, see Richard Moran, "The Punitive Uses of the Insanity Defense: The Trial for Treason of Edward Oxford (1840)," International Journal of Law and Psychiatry 9 (1986): 171–90. See also Walker, Crime and Insanity, 186–87, and Eigen, Witnessing Insanity, 149–52. The Oxford courtroom narrative can be found in OBSP, 1840–41, case 1877, 9th sess., 464–510.

16. OBSP, 1842–43, case 374, 5th sess., 761, 763. The most comprehensive analysis of the McNaughtan trial is offered in Richard Moran, Knowing Right from Wrong: The Insanity Defense of Daniel McNaughtan (New York, 1981). The five questions asked of the judges and their answers are given in McNaughtan Case, 10 Clark and Finnelly 203–14.

17. See, e.g., the critical review of moral insanity penned by the editors of the British and Foreign Medical Review (July 1840).

18. OBSP, 1843–44, case 2396, 12th sess., 797–80.

19. See Goldstein, Console and Classify, and Joel P. Eigen, "A Mania for Diagnosis: Unraveling the Aims of Nineteenth-Century French Psychiatry," History of the Human Sciences 2 (1989): 241–51.

20. Goldstein, Console and Classify, 189–96.

21. OBSP, 1897–98, case 396, 8th sess., 739.

22. OBSP, 1833, case 1304, 7th sess., 728–36.

23. The two standard sources for la folie ciculaire (or la folie à double forme) are J. P. Falret, "De la folie circulaire ou forme de maladie mentale caractérisée par l'alternative régulière de la manie et de la mélancholie," Bulletin de l'Académie National de Médecine 19 (1854): 382–415, and J. Baillarger, "De la folie à double forme," Annales Médicales Psychologiques 12 (1854): 369–91.

24. OBSP, 1843–44, case 2396, 12th sess., 801–3.

25. OBSP, 1847–48, case 948, 5th sess., 865.

26. OBSP, 1893–94, case 380, 6th sess., 497.

27. Raptus melancholicus is found infrequently in the scientific and medical literature, although it does appear in forensic cases. It was used most often to account for sudden and unexpected suicide attempts.

28. As Shelley Day points out, "Temporary derangement was not a reason for a pardon, much less a defense that would lead to an acquittal" ("Puerperal Insanity: The Historical Sociology of a Disease" [DPhil, Cambridge University, 1985], 80). See also George K. Behlmer, "Deadly Motherhood; Infanticide and Medical Opinion in Mid-Victorian England," Journal of the History of Medicine and Allied Sciences 34 (1979): 403–26; Mark Jackson, "Suspicious

Infant Deaths, the Statute of 1624, and Medical Evidence at Coroners' Inquests," in Michael Clark and Catherine Crawford, eds., *Legal Medicine in History* (Cambridge, 1994): 64–86; and Hillary Marland, "'Destined to a Perfect Recovery': The Confinement of Puerperal Insanity in the Nineteenth Century," in Joseph Melling and Bill Forsythe, eds., *Insanity, Institutions, and Society, 1800–1914: A Social History of Madness in Comparative Perspective* (London, 1999): 137–56. The indulgence just before execution was the last in a series of "filtering processes" that had been in operation to the moment of sentencing. Few women faced a capital sentence for killing their children, although it was not unheard of in the present study. Roger Smith, *Trial by Medicine: Insanity and Responsibility in Victorian Trials* (Edinburgh, 1981), esp. 146–68.

29. *OBSP*, 1902–3, case 766, 11th sess., 1142.

30. *OBSP*, 1904–5, case 708, 11th sess., 1547–48.

31. Rat poisoning figured in a particularly gruesome killing in 1862. After mixing the lethal powder in her children's dinner, the defendant laid them out carefully on their bed, picked up a razor, and slashed their throats. It was the "morbid dwelling on the deed"—the prisoner's careful arrangement of the bodies—that revealed to the two medical witnesses a "strange state of mind," which they attributed to her suffering melancholy. *OBSP*, 1861–62, case 745, 9th sess., 300–315.

32. The medical witness's mention of an "instinct of self preservation" is an intriguing adumbration of Freud's discussion of the melancholia and aggression in "Mourning and Melancholia" (1917).

33. Haslam, *Medical Jurisprudence*, 15–19.

34. Delusion also rose to critical legal significance in civil trials. Sir John Nicoll elevated its legal standing in 1851: "The true criterion, the true test, of the absence or presence of insanity, I take to be the absence or presence of what, used in a certain sense of it, is comprisable in a single term—namely, delusion" (*Dew v. Clark and Clark* (1826), 3 Addams' Ecclesiastical Reports 91).

35. Joel Peter Eigen, *Unconscious Crime: Mental Absence and Criminal Responsibility in the Victorian Court* (Baltimore, 2003), 129–44.

36. *OBSP*, 1875–76, case 413, 11th sess., 496–97.

37. John Locke, *An Essay* (Oxford, 1894), book 2, chap. 27, 447.

38. *OBSP*, 1854–55, case 464, 6th sess., 658; Thomas Mayo, *Medical Testimony and Evidence in Cases of Lunacy* (London, 1854).

39. Henry Maudsley, *Responsibility in Mental Disease* (New York, 1875), 186.

40. Ibid., 246–47.

41. Ibid., 194.

42. James Cowles Prichard, the creator of the term *moral insanity* joined other medical men convinced of a separate derangement of the feelings in bristling at the "settled doctrine of English Courts that there can be no insanity without delusion"; see Prichard, *On the Different Forms*, 16.

Chapter Three · When Practitioners Become Professionals

1. *OBSP*, 1789, case 494, 5th sess., 605–6. The de Castros were part of a notable cohort of Jewish physicians who had emigrated from Spain. For more information on the brothers, Dr. Hart Meyers (also Jewish, from New York), and the community of Sephardic medical men in London, see Richard Barnett, "Dr. Jacob de Castro Sarmento and the Sephardim in Medical Practice in Eighteenth-Century London," *Transactions of the Jewish Historical Society of England* 27 (1982): 84–114.

2. *OBSP*, 1889–90, case 457, 8th sess., 807–8.

3. Although an asylum physician was indeed the first medical witness, by far the most frequent expert witness in the late 1700s and early 1800s were jail and prison surgeons. Given the Crown's practice of engaging prison medical men to visit defendants thought to be contemplat-

ing raising mental derangement as a defense, it would be easy to argue that privately retained medical men became a feature of courtroom practice as a reaction to the state's ongoing policy.

4. For a discussion of the role that neighborly conversation with and casual observation of the accused's behavior played in the layperson's testimony, see Joel Peter Eigen, *Witnessing Insanity: Madness and Mad-Doctors in the English Court* (New Haven, 1993), 82–106.

5. Christopher Lawrence, *Medicine in the Making of Modern Britain, 1700–1920* (London, 1994), 55–57. See also Janet Oppenheim, *Shattered Nerves: Doctors, Patients, and Depression in Victorian England* (Oxford, 1991).

6. W. F. Bynum, *Science and the Practice of Medicine in the Nineteenth Century* (Cambridge, 1994), 11.

7. In addition to Bynum, excellent material on the medical backgrounds of the wide array of practitioners in eighteenth- and nineteenth-century England can be found in Lawrence, *Medicine in the Making*.

8. See, e.g., Thomas Willis, *The London Practice of Physick: Or the Whole Practical Part of Physick Contained in the Works of Dr. Willis. Faithfully made English and Printed together for the Public Good* (London, 1689); Charles Bell, *The Anatomy of the Human Body, containing the Anatomy of the Bones, Muscles, Joints, Heart, and Arteries by John Bell, and that of the Brain and the Nerves, The Organs of the Senses, and the Viscera*, vol. 2 (London, 1811); Charles Symonds, *The Circle of Willis: The Harvaeian Oration, Delivered at the Royal College of Physicians, Oct 18 1954* (London, 1954); and Alexander Shaw, *Narrative of the Discoveries of Sir Charles Bell on the Nervous System* (London, 1839). Janet Oppenheim's *Shattered Nerves* provides a comprehensive overview of the contributions of Willis and Bell.

9. Above all, it was the broad humanistic training—a thorough immersion in the classics and particularly the ideas of the ancients—that Oxbridge stressed, not laboratory science. Laboratory science did not gain a foothold in the elite universities until the early twentieth century.

10. Bynum, *Science and the Practice*, 47–55.

11. Ibid., 48–49.

12. Ibid., 179.

13. The centrality of science to the practice of medicine, or at least to the claims that medical men made as the rightful caretakers of disease, stemmed from the place of naturalism in the assertion of expert knowledge. Treating madness scientifically was a natural extension of this embrace of the material world as the basis for knowing.

14. According to Christopher Lawrence, Victorian society increasingly turned to experts who claimed authority on the basis of scientific knowledge (*Medicine in the Making*, 53). For the centrality of authoritative knowledge in the assertion of professional voice, see Andrew Abbott, *The System of Professions: An Essay on the Expert Division of Labor* (Chicago, 1988).

15. Bynum, *Science and the Practice*, 118.

16. Anyone could call himself a doctor (see a mesmerist's claim to "grow an eye" that begins the next chapter). An array of "healers" was always on hand to entice the ailing Londoner away from the credentialed practitioner.

17. Lawrence, *Medicine in the Making*, 18–19.

18. Ibid., 12–15; Bynum, *Science and the Practice*, 5, 12.

19. Lawrence, *Medicine in the Making*, 12–15; Bynum, *Science and the Practice*, 49.

20. Lawrence, *Medicine in the Making*, 22.

21. Established in 1796, the York Retreat offered a qualitatively different approach to addressing the needs of the insane. The literature on moral treatment and the retreat is vast. An excellent source for examining this Quaker-inspired, innovative approach to treating the mad can be found in Anne Digby, *Madness, Morality and Medicine: A Study of the York Retreat, 1796–1914* (Cambridge, 1985).

22. For the most comprehensive treatment of the activity of private madhouses, see William

Ll. Parry-Jones, *The Trade in Lunacy: A Study of Private Madhouses in England in the Eighteenth and Nineteenth Centuries* (London, 1972).

23. See, e.g., the career of John Haslam, apothecary to Bethlem, in Andrew Scull, Charlotte MacKenzie, and Nicholas Hervey, *Masters of Bedlam: The Transformation of the Mad-Doctoring Trade* (Princeton, 1996): 10–47.

24. The law's role in creating a population of incarcerated mad vagrants began in 1744 with the Vagrancy Act. The authority to institutionalize the mad was effectively transferred to the criminal courts with the Criminal Lunatics Act of 1800 calling for the detention of all those found under the special verdict of not guilty by reason of insanity.

25. The active interest taken by the solicitor to the Treasury developed out of an informal practice that employed surgeons in Newgate Gaol as courtroom witnesses early in the nineteenth century. The Treasury also called upon the most eminent of London's mad-doctors to visit prisoners awaiting trial to assess the state of their intellects. Chapter 5 provides information on the professional backgrounds of these witnesses.

26. John Conolly, physician to Hanwell Asylum, was particularly likely to cite his institutional affiliation and also the number of patients under his care. See, e.g., *OBSP*, 1840, case 1877, 9th sess., 505–8; 1846–47, case 2310, 12th sess., 1144; 1849–50, case 1300, 9th sess., 387; 1850–51, case 1502, 9th sess., 368–69.

27. Bynum, *Science and the Practice*, 195.

28. Conolly was lampooned in the popular press for his suspected mercenary motives, which were the subject of a contemporary best seller, *Hard Cash*, by Charles Reade (London, 1864). Reade depicted Conolly as "blinded by self interest . . . likely to find insanity wherever he looked." The asylum physician's colorful career is the subject of Andrew Scull's "A Victorian Alienist: John Conolly, FRCP, DCL (1794–1866)," in W. F. Bynum, Roy Porter, and Michael Shepherd, eds., *The Anatomy of Madness: Essays in the History of Psychiatry*, vol. 1, *People and Ideas* (London, 1985), 103–50.

29. Neurological approaches to mental diseases can be found in Willis, *The London Practice*, 488–96, and William Cullen, *Nosology; or, a Systematic Arrangement of Diseases* (Edinburgh, 1800), esp. 49–154.

30. Michael Anthony Finn, "The West Riding Lunatic Asylum and the Making of the Modern Brain Sciences in the Nineteenth Century" (PhD diss., University of Leeds, 2012); Oppenheim, *Shattered Nerves*, 71, 78.

31. Whether Victorian alienists sought a role in the maintenance of social order by encouraging patients to develop habits of discipline and self-control or whether this attitude was created by elite social opinion is not clear. It is clear, however, that medical men specializing in madness were central to the effort to help shore up the (perceived) weak will, rampant among certain sectors of the London populace; see Oppenheim, *Shattered Nerves*, 52.

32. Roger Smith, *Trial by Medicine: Insanity and Responsibility in Victorian Trials* (Edinburgh, 1981).

33. Charles Mercier, *Criminal Responsibility* (Oxford, 1905).

34. Oppenheim, *Shattered Nerves*, 46. See also Smith, *Trial by Medicine*.

35. Henry J. Maudsley, quoted in Scull, MacKenzie, and Hervey, *Masters of Bedlam*.

36. Oppenheim, *Shattered Nerves*, 43, 55–76.

37. Even phreno-mesmerists had to accept a role for the will, characterized in their writing, as an "organizing property" effecting coherence among so many disparate organs. For a comprehensive study of phrenology, see Roger Cooter, *The Cultural Meaning of Popular Science* (Cambridge, 1985), and "Phrenology and British Alienists, ca. 1825–45," in Andrew Scull, ed., *Madhouses, Mad-Doctors, and Madmen: The Social History of Psychiatry in the Victorian Era* (Philadelphia, 1981), 58–104.

38. Degeneration and evolutionary theory are discussed in the context of homicidal mania in chapter 6.

39. This issue would drive a wedge between psychiatrists and neurologists regarding which scientific specialty was the rightful caretaker of epilepsy. Thomas Willis's work on the pathology and neurophysiology of the brain maintained that epilepsy was a matter of nerve deterioration in the brain rather than in the convulsed organ. There is thus a consistent focus on nerves and epilepsy, continuing up to William Carpenter and Charles Laycock's nineteenth-century identification of "ideo-motor reflexes," framing epilepsy as a neurological rather than a psychiatric disorder.

40. Andrew Scull, *Museums of Madness: Social Organization of Insanity* (London, 1979).

41. The strategic place of asylum supervision in the careers of the major nineteenth-century mad-doctors (John Haslam, John Conolly, W. A. F. Browne, Samuel Gaskell, John Charles Bucknill, and the ever voluble Henry Maudsley is offered in Scull, MacKenzie, and Hervey, *Masters of Bedlam*.

42. William Cullen, *Nosology*, 1:15.

43. For a comprehensive history of melancholia, depression, and a host of other mental afflictions, see Stanley W. Jackson, *Melancholia and Depression: From Hippocratic Times to Modern Times* (New Haven, 1986).

44. By the nineteenth century, medical thinking conceptualized illness by situating people in relation to one another, measuring their deviation from supposed normality. Lawrence, *Medicine in the Making*, 45. Of course, there have been efforts since antiquity to identify and describe separate species of mental disease, which is the subject of Jackson's *Melancholia and Depression*.

45. "Descriptive Psychiatry and Psychiatric Nosology During the Nineteenth Century," in Edwin R. Wallace IV and John Gach, eds., *History of Psychiatry and Medical Psychology* (New York, 2008), 353–80.

46. The career of Alfred Swaine Taylor is instructive here. He held an early chair in medical jurisprudence and eventually authored the nineteenth century's definitive text on forensic medicine, with more than one hundred pages devoted to insanity. Taylor's forensic work is reviewed in Tal Golan, *Laws of Men and Laws of Nature: The History of Scientific Expert Testimony in England and America* (Cambridge, 2004). Katherine Watson also discusses Taylor's forensic contributions in *Poisoned Lives: English Poisoners and Their Victims* (London, 2006).

47. *OBSP*, 1894–95, case 518, 9th sess., 757.

48. This was also explored in an earlier publication, Joel Peter Eigen, *Witnessing Insanity: Madness and Mad-Doctors in the English Court* (New Haven, 1993). Comparisons with the original display (table 5.1, p. 122) are easier to make for the beginning of the current table than with later years because the groupings have been constructed to accommodate the entire survey of cases, from 1760 to 1913. The reason for the uneven number of years covered in the groupings is that I thought it better to have comparable numbers of *cases* (except for the last two sections, where the numbers increased so qualitatively). I wanted to have the percentage distributions within each time period reflect the patterns within each period rather than to equalize the number of years, with each section covering the same number of years.

49. *OBSP*, April 1910, p. 691.

Chapter Four · The Diagnosis in the Dock

1. *OBSP*, September 1908, 725–32. (By 1908, the *OBSP* editors began to delete the case and session numbers for individual trials. The month and year, however, are sufficient to identify the appropriate volume, and page numbers are given to simplify location). Although certainly far-fetched, the mesmeric ophthalmologist's capacity to draw willing clients reminds us that

doctors were not uncontested healers in nineteenth-century London. See Christopher Lawrence, *Medicine in the Making of Modern Britain* (London, 1994), 37. For the long tradition of medical quackery in Britain in the *long* eighteenth century and earlier, see Roy Porter, *Health for Sale: Quackery in England, 1660–1850* (Manchester, 1989), and *Quacks, Fakers, and Charlatans in Medicine* (London, 2003).

2. Knowledge is the critical element here; the essence of a profession is the possession of "abstract knowledge" (Thomas Mayo, *Medical Testimony and Evidence in Cases of Lunacy* [London, 1854]) and specialized skills gained through a particular course of study or unique work experience. Andrew Abbott, *The System of Professions: An Essay on the Division of Expert Labor* (Chicago, 1988).

3. Expert testimony could also cast ambiguity on seemingly obvious lay observations. John Haslam's dismissive attitude toward the unqualified observations of the madman's neighbor is discussed below.

4. *OBSP*, 1813, case 11, 1st sess., 14.

5. John Charles Bucknill and Daniel Hack Tuke, *A Manual of Psychological Medicine: Containing the History, Nosology, Description, Statistics, Diagnosis, Pathology, and Treatment of Insanity* (Philadelphia, 1858).

6. The role of delusion's recondite character as the defining element distinguishing medical from lay testimony is explained in Joel Peter Eigen, "Delusion in the Courtroom: The Role of Partial Insanity in Early Forensic Testimony," *Medical History* 35 (1991): 25–119.

7. John Haslam, *Observations on Madness and Melancholy: Including Practical Remarks on Those Diseases; Together with Cases: And an Account of the Morbid Appearances on Dissection* (London, 1809), 45–47. See also his *Medical Jurisprudence as It Relates to Insanity, According to the Law of England* (London, 1817), 15–17.

8. *OBSP*, 1842–43, case 874, 5th sess., 761, 763.

9. J. M. Pagan, *The Medical Jurisprudence of Insanity* (London, 1840), contended that a "disease of the moral faculties may exist when it is impossible to discover any intellectual disorder" (23). His beliefs followed the writings of James Cowles Prichard, cited in chapter 2. Prichard lamented the English courts' insistence on intellectual derangement being central to insanity. Moral insanity's originator complained of the "settled doctrine of English Courts that there can be no insanity without delusion." *On the Different Forms of Insanity in Relation to Jurisprudence, Designed for the Use of Persons Concerned in Legal Questions Regarding Unsoundness of Mind* (London, 1842), 16.

10. See, e.g., *OBSP*, 1849–50, case 1300, 9th sess.; *OBSP*, 1851–52, case 572, 7th sess.; *OBSP*, 1866–67, case 912, 11th sess.

11. *OBSP*, 1850–51, case 1502, 9th sess., 368–69.

12. *OBSP*, 1886–87, case 300, 5th sess., 397.

13. *OBSP*, 1890–91, case 409, 7th sess., 728.

14. *OBSP*, 1856–57, case 318, 4th sess., 459.

15. *OBSP*, 1903–4, case 197, 4th sess., 315.

16. *OBSP*, 1846–47, case 2310, 12th sess., 1144; case 1546, 4th sess., 477.

17. *OBSP*, 1855–56, case 263, 4th sess., 78.

18. *OBSP*, 1856–57, case 649, 7th sess., 138; 1873–74, case 123, 3rd sess., 163; 1875–76, case 254, 5th sess., 448.

19. The first mention of doubled consciousness dates to 1817. Several additional case reports surface by the middle of the century, usually involving servant girls who wake from deep sleep to reveal personalities and temperaments wildly at variance with their traditional functioning; see Samuel L. Mitchill, "A Double Consciousness, or a Duality of Person in the Same Individual: From a Communication of Dr. Mitchill to the Reverend Dr. Nott, President of Union College.

Dated January 16, 1816," in *The Medical Repository of Original Essays and Intelligence Relative to Physic, Surgery, Chemistry, and Natural History, etc.*, n.s., 3 (18th from the beginning) (New York, 1817), 186. A comprehensive survey of the phenomenon of doubled consciousness can be found in Ian Hacking, "Double Consciousness in Britain, 1815–1875," *Dissociation* 4 (1991): 134–46. The resonance with hypnotism and mesmerism was obvious: an "alter" or second state of being apparently lurked somewhere below the conscious surface that would appear prominently in medical writing as *dédoublement de la personnalité*. Although this concept remained foreign to the English courts, it introduced the notion of *vertige* (absence) into the criminal courts as the clinical basis for epileptic vertigo.

20. *OBSP*, 1876–77, case 413, 11th sess., 495–97.

21. *OBSP*, 1876–77, case 246, 4th sess., 458–59.

22. *Times of London*, November 26, 1847, 3a, December 16, 1847, 7f, 8a and b.

23. James Fitzjames Stephen, *A General View of the Criminal Law of England* (London, 1863), 95. Two years later, Stephen's strong assent in the arguments about the potency of impulses is cited in Alfred Swaine Taylor, *The Principles and Practice of Medical Jurisprudence* (London, 1865), 1102.

24. *OBSP*, 1874, case 93, 2nd sess., 166.

25. *OBSP*, 1873, case 185, 8th sess., 154.

26. *OBSP*, 1875–76, case 4, 8th sess., 153.

27. Esquirol's formulation *monomanie* is discussed in chapter 2. For the most comprehensive analysis of the French school of *maladies mentales*, see Jan Goldstein, *Console and Classify: The French Psychiatric Profession in the Nineteenth Century* (Chicago, 1987).

28. *OBSP*, 1904–5, case 708, 11th sess., 1547–48.

29. Freud considered the self-destructive character of mourning (the refusal to take nourishment, to engage at all with the outside world) to be a sign of having lost the "instinct for self preservation"—exactly the words used by the asylum medical officer in court twelve years before the classic essay appeared. Also prefiguring Freud's ideas is the pairing of aggression with melancholia, a condition widely believed to be more depressive than maniacal. See "Mourning and Melancholia," *The Standard Edition of the Complete Psychological Works of Sigmund Freud*, trans. James Strachey (London, 1917), 14:245–58.

30. *OBSP*, 1902–3, case 497, 8th sess., 814.

31. *OBSP*, 1874–75, case 93, 2nd sess., 165.

32. *OBSP*, 1856–57, case 480, 6th sess., 723; 1894–95, case 518, 9th sess., 757.

33. *OBSP*, 1893–94, case 849, 12th sess., 1200–1201.

34. The relation between puerperal mania and homicidal mania is examined in chapter 5. The frightening character of such inexplicable violence and the suspected materialist origins of the mental derangement combined the two diagnoses particularly vividly.

35. Joel P. Eigen, "Prosecuting Criminal Lunacy in Early Modern England: Did Gender Make a Difference?" *International Journal of Law and Psychiatry* 21 (1998): 409–19.

36. Luff was particularly fond of referring to his text. See *OBSP*, 1894–95, case 814, 12th sess., 1118.

37. *OBSP*, 1876–77, case 246, 4th sess., 453–60; *OBSP*, 1892–93, case 859, 12th sess., 1270.

38. *OBSP*, 1887–88, case 349, 5th sess., 630–31.

39. *OBSP*, 1855–56, case 263, 4th sess., 475–79.

40. *OBSP*, 1892–93, case 482, 7th sess., 758.

41. *OBSP*, 1879–80, case 428, 7th sess., 105.

42. *OBSP*, 1894–95, case 257, 5th sess., 410.

43. Bucknill and Tuke, *A Manual*, 316.

44. Although perceptually conspicuous, Bucknill and Tuke warn that "any and all of these

symptoms may be reversed," again underscoring their caution to the diagnostician: "no class of diseases with which man is afflicted are so various in their manifestations as those known under the general term of insanity" (269).

45. Ibid.

46. *OBSP,* 1892–93, case 859, 12th sess., 1270.

47. *OBSP,* 1896–97, case 106, 2nd sess., 189.

48. *OBSP,* 1900–01, case 142, 3rd sess., 200; *OBSP,* 1897–98, case 113, 3rd sess., 187; *OBSP,* 1897–98, case 390, 8th sess., 722.

49. *OBSP,* 1894–95, case 110, 2nd sess., 192; *OBSP,* 1862–63, case 957, 9th sess., 424; *OBSP,* 1869–70, case 76, 1st sess., 88.

50. *OBSP,* 1893–94, case 612, 10th sess., 860.

Chapter Five · The Witness Takes the Stand

1. Table 3.1 (in chap. 3) lists medical witnesses by professional affiliation. Table 5.1 illustrates how defendants and medical men first became acquainted. While 21 percent of surgeons were categorized as "private"—that is, they had no institutional affiliation—13 percent of defendants in this period first met a medical man in a private capacity, either as a neighbor or acquaintance. The first third of these cases, which took place between 1760 and 1843, was examined in an earlier publication, Joel Peter Eigen, *Witnessing Insanity: Madness and Mad-Doctors in the English Court* (New Haven, 1993); see esp. 120–32. In order to equalize the years in terms of number of trials each, the periods for the earlier years have been modified. Comparisons with table 3.1 can be made without difficulty.

2. Christopher Lawrence, *Medicine in the Making of Modern Britain* (London, 1994).

3. Martin Wiener chronicles the reaction to violent assaults, particularly domestic assaults, in *Men of Blood: Violence, Manliness, and Criminal Justice in Victorian England* (Cambridge, 2004). For an enlightening contrast between homicidal men and women, see 123–69.

4. Women's violence almost always targeted children, although husbands were sometimes at risk.

5. Of all the medical men who testified at the Old Bailey before *McNaughtan,* McMurdo made by far the most appearances, testifying in seventeen trials.

6. *OBSP,* 1833, case 815, 4th sess., 393–402.

7. *Prosecution of Offense Acts,* 42 and 43 Vict. c. 22, amended five years later, 47 and 48 Vict. c. 58.

8. Quoted in Daniel Hack Tuke, *A Dictionary of Psychological Medicine* (London, 1884), 1003–4.

9. *OBSP,* 1879–80, case 423, 9th sess., 298.

10. *OBSP,* January 1907, 422.

11. *OBSP,* 1902–3, case 262, 4th sess., 396.

12. The Hadfield case is discussed in chapter 1.

13. Nigel Walker discusses the common law's exception regarding culpability given to youthful offenders and lunatics in *Crime and Insanity in England,* vol. 1, *The Historical Part* (Edinburgh, 1968): 28–29, 40, 174.

14. *OBSP,* 1900–1901, case 628, 11th sess., 788.

15. *OBSP,* 1877–78, case 499, 7th sess., 33; *OBSP,* 1893–94, case 612, 10th sess., 858.

16. Bastian routinely informed the court that he "always examine[d] prisoners in murder trials, and at the House of Detention."

17. *OBSP,* 1901–2, case 842, 10th sess., 801–2.

18. *OBSP,* May 1906, 500.

19. *OBSP,* June 1911, 257.

20. *OBSP,* 1879–80, case 528, 8th sess., 153.

21. *OBSP,* 1897–98, case 113, 3rd sess., 189.

22. Ibid.

23. Ibid.

24. *OBSP,* 1904–5, case 709, 11th sess., 1555–56.

25. *OBSP,* 1893–94, case 380, 6th sess., 498. Other official records kept by infirmary doctors and asylum physicians include dates of transfer from the jail to the workhouse infirmary or previous asylum hospitalization(s).

26. *OBSP,* 1882–83, case 964, 12th sess., 771–73.

27. *OBSP,* 1893–94, case 612, 10th sess., 859.

28. *OBSP,* 1902–3, case 647, 11th sess., 1031.

29. *OBSP,* 1879–80, case 444, 10th sess., 486.

30. *OBSP,* 1889–90, case 688, 11th sess., 1103–4.

31. *OBSP,* 1840, case 1577, 9th sess., 505.

32. *OBSP,* 1904, case 708, 11th sess., 1548.

33. *OBSP,* 1901–2, case 735, 12th sess., 1028.

34. *OBSP,* 1882–83, case 74, 1st sess., 161.

35. *OBSP,* 1800–1801, case 446, 5th sess., 320.

36. Caleb Williams, M.D., *Observations on the Criminal Responsibility of the Insane, Founded upon the Trials of James Hill and William Dove* (London, 1856), cxiii.

37. *OBSP,* 1855–56, case 184, 3rd sess., 301.

38. *OBSP,* 1904–05, case 332, 6th sess., 879.

39. *OBSP,* 1897–98, case 113, 3rd sess., 186.

40. *OBSP,* 1813, case 11, 1st sess., 14.

41. *OBSP,* 1853–54, case 1122, 12th sess., 1365.

42. Ibid., 1366.

43. Ibid., 1366–67.

44. *OBSP,* 1858–59, case 519, 7th sess., 145.

45. Ibid.

46. *OBSP,* December 1906, 217–22.

47. *OBSP,* April 1906, 381.

48. *OBSP,* July 1908, 515.

49. *OBSP,* April 1911, 11–12.

50. Ibid., 10–11.

51. Ibid., 11.

52. Ibid., 12.

53. Ibid., 14.

54. *OBSP,* April 1912, 10–14.

55. John Langbein, *The Origins of Adversary Criminal Trial* (Oxford, 2003), 19–20.

Chapter Six · Homicidal Mania

1. *OBSP,* 1894–95, case 814, 12th sess., 1116.

2. *OBSP,* March 1906, 169.

3. Homicidal monomania had appeared once in medical testimony earlier in the century but was never mentioned again. It was treated as a variation of monomania, which fell into desuetude by the mid-1800s.

4. *OBSP,* 1859–60, case 723, 10th sess., 545.

5. *OBSP,* 1856–57, case 480, 6th sess., 722–23.

6. *OBSP,* 1882–83, case 74, 1st sess., 157; 1897–98, case 113, 3rd sess., 177.

7. A "shadow on the mind" is as old as Aristotle and as current as *McNaughtan*: "I mean that black spot on his mind," referring to the assassin's delusion.

8. *OBSP,* 1871–72, case 650, 10th sess., 311.

9. *OBSP,* 1842–43, case 874, 5th sess., 761.

10. *OBSP,* 1879–80, case 428, 7th sess., 101.

11. *OBSP,* 1871–72, case 630, 10th sess., 311; 1887–88, case 407, 6th sess., 800.

12. *OBSP,* 1895–96, case 504, 9th sess., 43.

13. *OBSP,* 1859–60, case 723, 10th sess., 545.

14. *OBSP,* July 1910, 377.

15. Ibid., 381.

16. The classic work on doubling, or *dédoublement de la personnalité,* was written by French physician Eugène Azam: "La double conscience," *Revue scientifique,* 2nd ser., 8 (1878): 185–86. A comprehensive explanation of his thinking can be found in Azam's *Hypnotisme, double conscience, et alterations de la personnalité* (Paris, 1887).

17. *OBSP,* 1887–88, case 407, 6th sess., 86.

18. *OBSP,* 1901–2, case 349, 6th sess., 531.

19. *OBSP,* 1894–95, case 720, 11th sess., 1017.

20. *OBSP,* 1879–80, case 428, 7th sess., 101–2.

21. *OBSP,* 1896–97, case 106, 2nd sess., 187.

22. *OBSP,* 1871–72, case 117, 3rd sess., 156.

23. *OBSP,* 1866–67, case 884, 11th sess., 533, 537.

24. *OBSP,* October 1911, 684.

25. *OBSP,* 1869–70, case 36, 1st sess., 35–36.

26. Alfred Swaine Taylor, *Principles and Practice of Medical Jurisprudence* (London, 1865), 1101–2.

27. *OBSP,* 1902–3, case 113, 2nd sess., 228–33.

28. *OBSP,* 1861–62, case 745, 9th sess., 300–313.

29. *OBSP,* 1874–75, case 93, 2nd sess., 165–66.

30. *OBSP,* January 1912, 577.

31. For a comprehensive study of the history of medical and cultural thought regarding epilepsy, see Owsei Temkin, *The Falling Sickness: A History of Epilepsy from the Greeks to the Beginnings of Modern Neurology* (Baltimore, 1971).

32. *OBSP,* January 1912, 576.

33. Masked epilepsy or *l'épilepsie larvée* featured a sudden explosion of energy; a ferocious assault committed in plain sight was described as its definitive feature. Dr. Ardin-Deltiél, *L'épilepsie larvée, Le Progrès Medical,* 3rd ser., 52 (December 29, 1900): 495.

34. The indifference to detection is reminiscent of moral insanity. There is also the purposelessness of the fatal action that challenged the law's central tenet of culpability: intentional behavior.

35. Henry Maudsley, *Responsibility in Mental Disease* (London, 1874), 166.

36. Ibid., 334.

37. *OBSP,* 1894–95, case 814, 12th sess., 1119; 1893–94, case 612, 10th sess., 860.

38. *OBSP,* 1891–92, case 225, 3rd sess., 415.

39. *OBSP,* 1893–94, case 612, 10th sess., 860.

40. *OBSP,* 1910–11, May 31st, case 251, 255.

41. *OBSP,* 1893–94, case 612, 10th sess., 860.

42. Ibid.

43. The critical importance Maudsley placed on the "intergenerational transfer of acquired morbid characteristics as the explanation of both insanity and other forms of social pathology" is discussed in Andrew Scull, Charlotte MacKenzie, and Nicholas Hervey in *Masters of Bedlam: The Transformation of the Mad-Doctoring Trade* (Princeton, 1996), esp. 251–55.

44. Henry Maudsley, *Body and Mind* (London, 1873), 76.

45. Daniel Pick, *Faces of Degeneration: A European Disorder, c. 1848–1918* (Cambridge, 1989), 206.

46. Ibid., 206–7.

47. Henry Maudsley, "Homicidal Insanity," *Journal of Mental Science* (October 1863): 329.

48. Henry Maudsley, "Judges, Juries, and Insanity," *Popular Science Monthly* 1 (1872): 441.

49. Ibid., 444.

50. Maudsley, "Homicidal Insanity," 341.

51. Karl Danziger, "Mid-Nineteenth-Century British Psychophysiology: A Neglected Chapter in the History of Psychology," in William R. Woodward and Mitchell G. Ash, eds., *The Problematic Science: Psychology in Nineteenth-Century Thought* (New York, 1982), 119–46.

52. Discussion of the "ideo-motor principle of action" acting directly on motor processes, bypassing the mental processes of reflection and volition, can be found in William B. Carpenter, *The Doctrine of Human Automation: A Lecture* (London, 1875), and Thomas Laycock, "Reflex, Automatic, and Unconscious Cerebration: A History and a Criticism," *Journal of Mental Science* 21 (1876): 477–98. Human movements cast in automatic terms carried obvious implications for discussions of responsibility. Thus, "complex movements could occur without volition or even in opposition to volition when mediated by brain reflexes"; see Roger Smith, *Trial by Medicine: Insanity and Responsibility in Victorian Trials* (Edinburgh, 1981), 46–50. Beyond scientific opinion focusing on the specter of automatic, non-willed behavior, popular culture brimmed with salon hypnotists and music hall mesmerists whose demonstrations of the ideas implanted below the subject's consciousness and capable of animating the most burlesque antics are comprehensively chronicled in Alison Winter, *Mesmerized: Powers of Mind in Victorian Britain* (Chicago, 1998).

53. Maudsley, *Physiology and Pathology*, 310–11.

54. Maudsley, *Responsibility*, 195. Italics in the original.

55. Smith, *Trial by Medicine*, 52–53.

56. Maudsley, *Physiology and Pathology*. As Roger Smith explains, the law's conception of individuals as possessing "mental elements" before movements was "exactly what the new physiological psychology questioned." Mischievous and destructive acts were those of an "automatic machine" incited by sensory impressions (*Trial by Medicine*, 52).

57. Maudsley, "Judges, Juries," 442.

58. What appears to be a revenge killing by a melancholic patient resembles "that which may be aroused in a sane mind . . . to be equally under control by the insane mind. Such is the false conclusion of a subjective psychology . . . for . . . when a positive delusion exists in the mind the rest of the mind is so far affected that uncontrollable impulses spring up without being dictated by the delusion and the impulses which are in relation with the delusion acquire an irresistible force" (Maudsley, "Homicidal Insanity," 338).

59. Maudsley disagreed with Erskine's position: "how mistaken Lord Erskine was, as far as science is concerned, when he laid it down that 'to deliver a lunatic from responsibility to criminal justice, the relation between the crime and the act should be apparent'" ("Homicidal Insanity," 339).

60. Maudsley, *Physiology and Pathology*, 327.

61. Maudsley, *Responsibility*, 230.

62. Ibid., 166.

63. *OBSP*, 1854–55, case 615, 8th sess., 132.

64. *OBSP*, 1871–72, case 117, 3rd sess., 182.

65. Ibid., 151.

66. Ibid., 182.

67. The Watson trial may be read in full in *OBSP*, 1871–72, case 117, 3rd sess., 147–90. Maudsley's extensive testimony covers three pages and starts at p. 182.

68. *OBSP,* 1902–3, case 497, 8th sess., 815.

69. *OBSP,* 1871–72, case 117, 3rd sess., 185–88.

70. *OBSP,* July 1910, 382.

71. Roger Smith, "Defining Murder and Madness: An Introduction to Medicolegal Belief in the Case of Mary Ann Brough," in Robert Alun Jones and Henrika Kuklick, eds., *Knowledge and Society: Studies in the Sociology of Culture Past and Present,* 4 vols. (Greenwich, CT, 1983), 4:173–225, on p. 197.

72. "Baron Rolfe's charge to the Jury in the case of Boy Allnutt, who was tried at the Criminal Court for the Murder of his Grandfather, on the 15th of December, 1847," *Journal of Psychological Medicine and Mental Pathology* (1848): 193–219; *Times of London,* November 26, 1847, 3a, December 16, 1847, 7f, 8a and b.

73. James Fitzjames Stephen, "On the Policy of Maintaining the Limits at Present Imposed by Law on the Criminal Responsibility of Madmen," *Papers Read to the Juridical Society 1855–58* (London, 1855).

74. Nigel D. Walker, *Crime and Insanity in England,* vol. 1, *The Historical Perspective* (Edinburgh, 1968), 26.

75. Pick, *Faces of Degeneration,* 207.

76. Bénédict-Augustin Morel, *Traité des dégénérescences physiques, intellectuelles et morales de l'espèce humaine* (Paris, 1857).

77. Robert Burton, *The Anatomy of Melancholy* (London, 1621).

78. *OBSP,* 1784, case 388, 4th sess., 546.

79. *OBSP,* 1859–60, case 723, 10th sess., 545.

80. Pick, *Faces of Degeneration.*

81. *OBSP,* 1883–84, case 289, 4th sess., 516.

82. *OBSP,* 1904–5, case 521, 9th sess., 1162.

Chapter Seven · The View from the Bench

1. *OBSP,* November 1910–11, 10.

2. Ibid., 12. The issue of rebuttal testimony and the Resolution of the Judges regarding the calling of medical witnesses when none appeared for the defense, or in those trials when no plea of insanity had been introduced (although alluded to by defense witnesses), was given extensive coverage by the publisher of the *OBSP* in a section of the reports that appeared in the second half of the nineteenth century called "Points of Law and Practice." In several such "Points," reference was made to the issue of the permissibility and timing of rebuttal testimony. Judges acknowledged the principle that the Crown could not introduce the topic of the defendant's sanity, then proceeded to ignore it. They routinely granted requests by the Crown to depart from the principle, sometimes grudgingly but always citing the rationale that it was better for the jury to be fully informed of evidence bearing on insanity.

3. *OBSP,* November 1910–11, 12.

4. *OBSP,* 1846–47, case 1797, 10th sess., 681.

5. The House of Lords asked the judges who tried McNaughtan to articulate the appropriate grounds for a determination of insanity. Although legal and medical historians have focused most of their attention on "knowing the nature and quality of the act" and "knowing the difference between right and wrong," the issue that sparked the most courtroom debate concerned the actual grounds for medical testimony: Could medical witnesses base their conclusions on evidence presented in court? In subsequent trials, this question became interpreted broadly to permit rebuttal testimony by medical men brought forward by the prosecution.

6. *OBSP,* 1846–47, case 1797, 10th sess., 681.

7. *OBSP,* September 1909, 580.

8. *OBSP,* November 1910–11, 10.

9. *OBSP,* 1871–72, case 117, 3rd sess., 147–90.

10. *OBSP,* 1876–77, case 246, 4th sess., 456.

11. *OBSP,* 1895–96, case 451, 8th sess., 744. Winslow was also singled out by a trial judge several years later for having offered his opinion of a prisoner's mental state to persons not related to the case; his opinion ended up in a newspaper. Winslow responded, "I am not responsible for what the press put in [the paper]—Five or six people called upon me one day and in the course of the conversation I gave that information." The judge "intimated to the witness that he should be more cautious in the matter of giving information on such occasions." *OBSP,* 1904–5, case 618, 10th sess., 1396.

12. *OBSP,* 1876–77, case 246, 4th sess., 435–60.

13. *OBSP,* November 1910–11, 10.

14. *OBSP,* 1910–11, 5–7.

15. *OBSP,* September 1909–10, 582.

16. *OBSP,* January 1912, 542.

17. "Case of Imprisonment of Edward Bushell for alleged Misconduct as a Juryman," 22 Charles 2 A.D. 1670, *Vaughan's Reports,* 135, *Howell's State Trials,* 6:999.

18. *OBSP,* 1897–98, case 134, 3rd sess., 218.

19. *OBSP,* September 1910, 558. See also *OBSP,* July 1909, 422: "By the direction of his Lordship the Jury returned a verdict of 'Guilty, but insane,' so as not to be responsible in law for his acts at the time of committing the crime."

20. *OBSP,* 1870–71, case 579, 10th sess., 350.

21. *OBSP,* October 1911, 680. Of course, judges were also capable of "leaning against" the prisoner and dismissing medical evidence in the bargain. After several medical witnesses in an 1887 trial testified about a prisoner's delusions, episodes of inexplicable violence, and paroxysms of fury, the judge announced that he "was of opinion that there was no evidence of insanity that he could leave to the jury," resulting in a conviction and a sentence of hard labor in prison (*OBSP,* 1887, case 382, 577–81).

22. *OBSP,* October 1911, 680.

23. Ibid.

24. *OBSP,* 1904–5, case 748, 12th sess., 1596–1605.

25. *OBSP,* May 1910, 251–56.

26. *OBSP,* July 1907, 584.

27. *OBSP,* November 1908, 16.

28. *OBSP,* September 1908–9, 725–32.

29. *OBSP,* 1785–86, case 599, 6th sess., 522–23.

30. *OBSP,* 1801, case 446, 5th sess., 320.

31. *OBSP,* 1876–77, case 246, 4th sess., 459.

32. *OBSP,* 1873–74, case 23, 1st sess., 24.

33. *OBSP,* May 1907, 382.

34. *OBSP,* 1855–56, case 386, 5th sess., 689.

35. *Times of London,* December 16, 1847, 9b. The trial can be found at *OBSP,* 1847–48, case 290, 2nd sess., 280–94.

36. *Times of London,* December 16, 1847, 9b.

37. For all the riches the *OBSP* deliver up to the historian, there is one shortcoming that reminds us that these documents were written not for the benefit of generations of legal students of evolving jurisprudence but to sell newspapers. Although judicial questions and comments are reported in the trial narratives—and, as we have seen already, instructions to the jury might also be included—the *Papers'* editors apparently made the decision to let the reader know whose question the medical witness was answering, without always providing the actual wording of the query. It is usually possible to recreate the question by examining the answer the

witness gives, particularly his first words. But the precise phrasing of the question is often lost to us in the records from the late nineteenth and early twentieth centuries, exactly the period that witnessed the rapid introduction of homicidal mania in courtroom testimony.

38. *OBSP*, 1846–47, case 1797, 10th sess., 677.

39. *OBSP*, 1856–57, case 318, 4th sess., 459.

40. *OBSP*, 1845–46, case 1008, 7th sess., 27.

41. *OBSP*, 1862–63, case 700, 7th sess., 246.

42. *OBSP*, January 1912, 472.

43. Ibid., 473.

44. Wiener perceptively points out that, far from being at odds with each other, practitioners of law and medicine aimed to incapacitate dangerous persons. The judge could do so as well. Wiener cites the case of two men convicted of wife murder who were reprieved on the grounds of insanity and detained at Broadmoor for an indeterminate stay in *Men of Blood: Violence, Manliness, and Criminal Justice in Victorian England* (Cambridge, 2004), 208–9. Roger Chadwick has noted another reason for the infrequency of rancor between medicine and law, except in capital cases where the consequences could be so dire. Incarceration, for the Victorians, was the "therapy of choice . . . both penal and mental health institutions were substantially under the control of the Central Government." *Bureaucratic Mercy: The Home Office and the Treatment of Capital Cases in Victorian Britain* (New York, 1992), 235.

45. "What else does criminality imply but that passion [nurtured by the individual] has got the mastery of reason—that the importunity of temptation is too clamorous to allow the voice of reason to be heard. What is this but the subjugation of reason to vice?" "Baron Rolfe's charge to the Jury in the case of Boy Allnutt, who was tried at the Central Criminal Court for the Murder of his Grandfather, on the 15th of December, 1847," *Journal of Psychological Medicine and Mental Pathology* (1848): 193–219.

46. Defenses framed in terms of puerperal mania date to the seventeenth century, although acquittals were not automatic, even when the jury accepted the debility caused by "reproductive upheaval." See endnote 29, chap. 2.

47. *OBSP*, 1871–72, case 156, 3rd sess., 222.

48. *OBSP*, 1879–80, case 428, 7th sess., 103.

49. *OBSP*, 1869–7, case 36, 1st sess., 35–36.

50. *OBSP*, 1901–2, case 735, 12th sess., 1028.

51. John H. Langbein, "The Historical Foundations of the Law of Evidence, a View from the Ryder Sources," *Columbia Law Review* 96 (1996): 1168–1202.

52. The case of Samuel Hill raised different issues for judicial discretion and elicited a forceful statement on the part of the judiciary that existing digests and precedents would not substitute for the judges' own finding. The case stemmed from a killing in an asylum, allegedly committed by the keeper and witnessed by a delusional patient. Although existing common law precluded admitting the testimony of madmen, the appeals judges dispensed with Buller's *Nisi Prius* and relied on their own authority to determine the competence of the witness. See Joel P. Eigen, *Unconscious Crime: Mental Absence and Criminal Responsibility in the Victorian Court* (Baltimore, 2003), 99–104.

53. *OBSP*, 1904, case 618, 10th sess., 1393.

54. *OBSP*, June 1906, 11.

55. *OBSP*, 1855–56, case 263, 4th sess., 263.

56. *OBSP*, 1864–65, case 218, 4th sess., 299.

57. *OBSP*, 1903, case 558, 902.

58. Martin Wiener, "Judges v. Jurors: Courtroom Tensions in Murder Trials and the Law of Criminal Responsibility in Nineteenth-Century England," *Law and History Review* 17 (1999):

467–506, and "The Sad Story of George Hall: Adultery, Murder, and the Politics of Mercy in Mid-Victorian England," *Social History* 24 (1999): 174–95.

Conclusion · On the Origins of Diagnosis

1. Quoted in Tal Golan, *Laws of Men and Laws of Nature: The History of Scientific Expert Testimony in England and America* (Cambridge, 2004), 130–31.

2. Roger Smith, *Trial by Medicine: Insanity and Responsibility in Victorian Trials* (Edinburgh, 1981), 60–62.

3. Ibid.

4. Andrew Abbott, *The System of Professions: An Essay on the Division of Expert Labor* (Chicago, 1988).

5. Quoted in David Healy, *Mania: A Short History of Bipolar Disorder* (Baltimore, 2008), 35.

6. The Medical Registration Act of 1858 follows one year after the publication of Bénédict-Augustin Morel's thesis on degeneration and precedes by one year the publication of Charles Darwin's *On the Origin of Species*.

7. Physicalism, Smith summarizes insightfully, was "central to claims of medical expertise . . . no alienist believed the mind could be disordered independent of the body, but they were receptive to the importance of psychological disturbance" (*Trial by Medicine*, 40, 43).

8. Abbott, *System*, 319.

9. Andrew Scull examines the asylum as the "breeding grounds" for the emerging professionalism of the mad-doctors in *Museums of Madness: The Social Organization of Insanity in Nineteenth-Century England* (New York, 1979), 43.

10. Roger Chadwick, *Bureaucratic Mercy: The Home Office and the Treatment of Capital Cases in Victorian Britain* (New York, 1992), esp. 236–42.

11. Cross-examination could also lead to dawning self-consciousness as a medical professional. When asked by an attorney whether he answered as a neighbor, an acquaintance, a magistrate, or as a physician, John Birt Davis informed the court, "I answer as a physician," an awareness that may well have taken shape while he was testifying (*OBSP*, 1840, case 1877, 9th sess., 495).

12. The reverse was true as well. Medical men were quick to point out that the nonmedical observer was only too ready to pronounce madness—and its cessation—in the behavior or conversation of the defendant. The expert witness, on the other hand, knew this "return" to be but a lucid interval in a torrent of derangement. Apothecary to Bethlem John Haslam was doubtless the most disparaging of the neighbors' observations and inferences.

13. G. E. Berrios, "Descriptive Psychiatry and Psychiatric Nosology During the Nineteenth Century," in Edwin R. Wallace IV and John Gach, eds., *History of Psychiatry and Medical Psychology* (New York, 2008), 354.

14. Ibid., 355.

15. Ibid., 360.

16. Dora B. Weiner, "Mind and Body in the Clinic: Philippe Pinel, Alexander Crichton, Dominique Esquirol, and the Birth of Psychiatry," in G. S. Rousseau, ed., *The Languages of Psyche: Mind and Body in Enlightenment Thought* (Berkeley, 1990), 331–402.

17. *OBSP*, Oct. 1911, 684.

18. James Fitzjames Stephen, "On the Policy of Maintaining the Limits at Present Imposed by Law on the Criminal Responsibility of Madmen," *Papers Read to the Juridical Society 1855–58* (London, 1855).

19. Walker is particularly dismissive of the sleight-of-hand in wording insanity verdicts. In 1800, for example, the verdict was disguised as an acquittal (not guilty on the grounds of insanity); in 1883, it was disguised as a conviction (guilty of the act but not responsible for the crime).

Walker sums up the impossibility of trying to shoehorn insanity into the law's binary exigencies: "one does not solve a dilemma by shifting from horn to horn" (*Crime and Insanity,* 244).

20. *OBSP,* 1869–70, case 36, 1st sess., 37.

21. *OBSP,* 1897–98, case 134, 3rd sess., 218.

22. *OBSP,* 195–96, case 28, 1st sess., 29.

23. Ibid., 28.

24. Golan, *Laws of Man,* 131.